Porneia

FAMILY, SEXUALITY AND SOCIAL RELATIONS IN PAST TIMES

GENERAL EDITORS

Peter Laslett, Michael Anderson and Keith Wrightson

Western Sexuality: Practice and Precept in Past and Present Times
Edited by Philippe Ariès and André Béjin
Translated by Anthony Forster

The Explanation of Ideology: Family Structures and Social Systems
Emmanuel Todd
Translated by David Garrioch

The Causes of Progress: Culture, Authority and Change
Emmanuel Todd
Translated by Richard Boulind

The English Noble Household, 1250–1600
Kate Mertes

An Ordered Society: Gender and Class in Early Modern England
Susan Dwyer Amussen

Porneia: On Desire and the Body in Antiquity
Aline Rousselle
Translated by Felicia Pheasant

Medieval Prostitution
Jacques Rossiaud
Translated by Lydia G. Cochrane

Porneia: On Desire and the Body in Antiquity
Aline Nousselle
Translated by Felicia Pheasant

FORTHCOMING

Wet Nursing: A History
Valerie Fildes

Illegitimacy and Society in Eighteenth-Century Scotland
Rosalind Mitchison and Leah Leneman

Highley 1550–1880: The Story of a Community
Gwyneth Nair

Mobility and Marriage: The Family and Kinship in Early Modern London
Vivien Brodsky

The Country House Society
Jessica Gerard

The Family and the English Revolution
Christopher Durston

A History of Lesbianism
Julia Penelope

Porneia

On Desire and the Body in Antiquity

Aline Rousselle

Translated by
Felicia Pheasant

BLACKWELL
Cambridge MA & Oxford UK

English translation © Basil Blackwell Ltd, 1988
First published in France as
Porneia, © 1983 Presses Universitaire de France, Paris

First published in English 1988

First published in paperback 1993

Blackwell Publishers
108 Cowley Road, Oxford, OX4 1JF, UK

Basil Blackwell Inc.
238 Main Street
Cambridge, Massachusetts 02142, USA

British Library Cataloguing in Publication Data

A CIP catalogue record for this book is available from the British Library.

Library of Congress Cataloging-in-Publication Data

Rousselle, Aline
  [Porneia. English]
  Porneia: on desire and the body in antiquity/Aline Rousselle;
translated by Felicia Pheasant.
  p. cm.—(Family, sexuality, and social relations in past
times)
  Translation of: Porneia.
  Includes bibliographies and index.
  ISBN 0–631–19208–5: $50.00
  1. Sex customs—Rome—History. 2. Family—Rome—History.
3. Sexual ethics—Rome—History. 4. Fertility, Human—Social
aspects—Rome—History. 5. Chastity. 6. Celibacy—Christianity—
history. I. Title. II. Series.
  [DNLM: 1. History of Medicine, Ancient. 2. Morals—history.
3. Sex behaviour—history. WZ 51 R866p]
HQ13.R6813   1988
306.7′0945′632—dc 19
DNLM/DLC
for Library of Congress   87–31934
                               CIP

Typeset in 10 on 12 pt Garamond
by Cambrian Typesetters, Frimley, Surrey
Printed in the USA

To Jean Méloux

Nulla venit sine te nox mihi nulla dies.

Ovid, *Tristia*, III, III, 18.

Contents

Translator's note

Unless otherwise indicated in the footnotes, translations of texts quoted are my own. Despite the dangers and difficulties of translating quotations which are already a translation of the original, it has sometimes seemed best to convey the version of a text which the author wished to use rather than give an existing English translation which may differ in some respects from the rendering chosen by the author. In addition to those translations quoted in the text and mentioned in the footnotes, for readers' convenience I have listed in the bibliography English translations of other texts referred to by the author.

I should like to thank my husband John for his support and encouragement always, my children Somerset and Francesca for their patience and Jessica Jeavons for her companionable help.

Felicia Pheasant

Abbreviations

Alph.	*Apophthegmata Patrum, series alphabetica*
Amm. Marc.	Ammianus Marcellinus, *History*
AP	Galen, *On the Affected Parts*
BAC	*Bulletin archéologique du Comité des travaux historiques et archéologiques*
Bar.	*HC, Barrenness*
BIFAO	*Bulletin de l'Institut français d'Archéologie orientale du Caire*
CJ	*Corpus Juris Civilis*, II, *Codex Justinianus*
CIL	*Corpus Inscriptionum Latinarum*
CMG	*Corpus Medicorum Graecorum*
Coll.	John Cassian, *Collationes*
CRAI	*Comptes Rendus de l'Académie des Inscriptions et Belles Lettres*
CUF	Collection des Universités de France
D	*Corpus Juris Civilis*, I, *Digesta*
Dis. Wom.	*HC, Diseases of Women*
GCS	Die griechisch-christliche Schriftsteller der ersten Jahrhunderte
Gen.	*HC, Generation*
Gen. An.	Aristotle, *Generation of Animals*
Gyn.	Soranus, *Gynaecology*
HA	Aristotle, *History of Animals*
HC	*Hippocratic Collection*
HM	*Historia Monachorum in Aegypto*
IFAO	Institut français d'Archéologie orientale du Caire
IJ	*Corpus Juris Civilis*, I, *Institutes of Justinian*
Inst.	John Cassian, *De Institutis coenobiorum*
LH	Palladius, *Lausiac History*
LI	Oribasius, *Libri incerti*
Med. Coll.	Oribasius, *Medical Collection*

MEFRA	*Mélanges de l'Ecole française de Rome. Antiquité*
Nat. Ch.	HC, *Nature of the Child*
Nat. Fac.	Galen, *On the Natural Faculties*
Nat. Wom.	Hippocrates, *Nature of Women*
PG	J.-P. Migne, *Patrologiae Cursus Completus, series graeco-latina*
PJ	*Sayings of the Desert Fathers*, Pelagius and John collection
PL	J.-P. Migne, *Patrologiae Cursus Completus, series latina*
RE	A. Pauly, G. Wissowa, *Real-Encyclopädie der klassischen Altertumwissenschaft*, Stuttgart
REL	*Revue des Etudes latines*
RHD	*Revue historique de Droit français et étranger*
RIDA	*Revue internationale des Droits de l'Antiquité*
RSAC	*Recueil de Notices et Mémoires de la Société archéologique de Constantine*
SDHI	*Studia et Documenta Historiae et Juris*
SC	Sources chrétiennes
Superf.	HC, *Superfoetation*
Uses of the Body	Galen, *On the Uses of the Parts of the Body of Man*

Introduction

When Palladius' *Lausiac History* was being translated from Greek into Latin an error crept into one of the episodes of Macarius' life. The Greek text relates that Macarius was weaving a basket and praying when a mosquito bit his leg. He crushed the mosquito angrily with his hand and then to punish himself for this violent outburst in the midst of his meditation he dived naked into a swamp infested with insects and emerged six months later quite unrecognizable. The Latin text read by western monks makes no mention of a mosquito, but says instead that it was a thought of *porneia*, or *fornicatio*, a surge of sexual desire, which drove Macarius into the swamp.

This is not to say that the eastern monks never mentioned desire. On the contrary, it was the bluntness of their writings that prompted this study. They went into the desert to find God, but what they discovered first was their own bodies. Their experiences became a model for Christians in the West as well as in the East, and it was this that suggested to me the idea of tracing the way in which physical beauty, the beauty of both the male and the female body, which was so important to the Greeks, and which they adored in others if they did not possess it themselves, became such an intolerable obstacle to the accomplishment of God's will. This work is not based on ideas about the body or sexuality. Methodius' description of the beauty of the human body, in *The Symposium*, is more inclined to arouse emotion than a wish to study the subject. Our primary concern here is everyday behaviour, although of course it is difficult to separate behaviour from ideas. The doctors and scientists of antiquity, whose writings provide much of the material used in this study, the men who formulated and interpreted Roman law, and the pagan and Christian theologians of the third and fourth centuries were intellectuals who through their works influenced the lives of others.

I should like to express my thanks for the help I received from Drs Colette and Marc Pépin; Françoise Leost, a veterinary surgeon; Nicolas Grimal for information about Pharaonic Egypt; Michel Chalon and Henri Michel who made available to me a number of books which were not in the Montpellier libraries; Jean-Jacques Rassial for his silence and André Burguière for his patience.

What I am attempting to examine is the reverse process, the influence of behaviour on ideas during a period of intense intellectual study when attitudes to the body had a special place in society.

My subject is not love, whether heterosexual or homosexual, and this book is not a history of emotions. My subject is rather the social background to emotional or sexual relations in the last years of antiquity. The texts I have used reveal an acute awareness of and anxiety about the self. But the reader will not find studies of individual cases. We will not be meeting a Roman household or an Egyptian couple, interesting as this would be. But perhaps we will have a clearer and more accurate idea of the lives of couples such as Pliny and Calpurnia, Hadrian and Antinous, Paulinus and Therasia, once we have examined the law that governed their lives and understood the rules which influenced their physical behaviour.

All our information about the men and women of antiquity comes from male sources. The lawyers and doctors were men, or at least all those who left written works were men. Our only direct access to the women of antiquity is through the skeletons and belongings found in tombs. The sculptures and paintings are the work of men. I do not wish to imply that men are not capable of loving or understanding women, but they act as a screen between us and the women about whom we should like to know more. What we lack is not so much factual information about women as firsthand knowledge of their view of the world and their opinions about men. So the little we know from ancient doctors' writings about women's bodies is precious, particularly their reports of the questions women asked and their ideas about their own bodies.

But what the written sources give us is primarily information about the law, ideas about women, their physical nature and the life that men allowed them to lead.

And yet the women of ancient times did write. We possess many letters from men to women because women kept the letters they received, but their own writings have been lost or destroyed. It is thus presumptuous for the historian to speak of love in ancient times: we can only describe the male side of any relationship. We have no account of either the spoken or the written words even of the men who were loved by the great men of the time.

What we may seek to discover from the documents is therefore the general nature of relations between men and women, or between men (we know little about female homosexuality), the conditions in which they became attracted to one another, felt desire for one another and lived together. It was into this society, generally thought of as dissolute and permissive, that Christianity was born and grew, and against this background that it taught that virginity was the ideal state. The message of Christianity was that each individual must come to terms with his or her own body and should not be concerned with anyone else's. The emphasis shifted from the analysis of attraction to the study of desire.

This is why it is so fascinating to gain insight into the relationship the men of the Roman Empire had with their bodies and the anxieties they confided in their doctors when their attempts at continence provoked in them reactions which took them by surprise. Their questions are those of all adolescents, and they are fundamental to the human condition, but here they are asked by adults.

The joy of being moved by the splendour of the world and the beauty of male and female bodies, the beauty of objects, the joy of feeling that one is alive because one is affected by external stimuli, even though they may cause disappointment or pain, gave way to concern that attraction to others distracted the individual from concentrating on himself.

One wonders if the Romans' renunciation of the exaltation of male homosexuality was not the first sign of this change, this anxiety and this concentration on the inner will, for homosexuality in that period represented the attractions of the world, and at the same time the love of something close to oneself, for women were so different, so far removed from men's thoughts and eyes.

Attraction to other people, which brought the individual face to face with his own desire, was not seen by the philosophers as a purely positive impulse. Passion for another's body disturbed, obsessed and obstructed reason and the freedom of the mind. Both pagans and Christians repeatedly used the image of homosexual passion to represent the enslaved mind. This did not reflect a moral judgement, but rather the fact that it was considered important to dissociate the mind from physical desire. The medical writers of the time echoed this view, and the scholars and politicians, like the philosophers before them, agreed that desire should not be allowed to intrude into intellectual or political life.

This had implications for the upbringing of children and adolescents, whose bodies and imaginations must be kept strictly under control. The men of the period emerge from my research as individuals absorbed by the changes which desire of another has brought to their perception of themselves. Perhaps because from their earliest childhood other people had always rejected their kisses and caresses, they seem to have been more anxious about the response with which they would meet than concerned to prolong and repeat such new pleasures.

In the face of the remarkable extent to which virginity gained popularity among the upper classes of the Roman Empire at the end of the fourth century, and setting aside for the moment the fact that the lower classes provided a great number of monks, first in Egypt and then throughout the Roman world, one soon begins to wonder how widespread was the practice of abstinence among the pagan predecessors, sometimes the fathers, of these Roman nobles. But we must consider the link between chastity and solitude. I think one needs to look not at the exceptional behaviour of people like the Vestal Virgins or a few pagan priests, but rather at everyday heterosexual relationships between ordinary people. In other words I believe we have to see this behaviour not as the extension of the practices of a few pagans or Jews to a much wider group, but as one of the consequences of the laws and the heterosexual relationships of the ordinary people of the time.

It is not that we cannot identify in the gospel the roots of this popularity. But the Christian doctrine of spiritual castration, although invented in Jewish society and first preached to the Jews, developed to the point of becoming one of the essential tenets of a religion not within the Jewish context but rather among the Greeks and Romans and among all those peoples of the Mediterranean who had come under first the Greek influence and then the Roman.

It soon becomes clear why it is useful to examine the medical, legal and religious documents side by side. Of what significance was improved care of the newborn child if the mother, her legs apart, still in the position in which she had delivered her child, was forced to remain silent and excluded from the decision as to whether he should be accepted into the family, or left to die or become a slave? What are we to make of the claims that women achieved greater legal rights in Imperial Rome, particularly in relation to their powers to leave an inheritance to their children, if in practice they had no say in whether they themselves were married or divorced? And how do we interpret the statement that debauchery and dissolute behaviour were the rule in Roman times if the law shows us that in the most respectable marriages the wife suffered in lonely silence while the husband ruled over a number of female or male concubines?

From the towns and villages of Egypt, from the rich houses of Asia Minor and Syria, from the highest Roman aristocracy, thousands of men of their own free will made the decision to go off by themselves and attempt to eradicate desire without the aid of any physical emasculation.

Aristotle's pronouncement that women did not produce sperm meant that half of the human race were eunuchs incapable of transmitting life or reproducing except insofar as they provided the environment in which the male's sperm might develop. But in the struggle against desire which was distinct from procreation women became men's equals and were accorded a new dignity.

For women as for men, any contact with another's body, whether pleasurable or not, became a sign of mortality and of loss; any manifestation of desire for another's body, called *porneia*, became a measure of human weakness in the service of God.

1

The Bodies of Men

As we trace the way in which the cult of the healthy body gave way to monastic asceticism we will not be concentrating on the mystical aspect of man's relationship with God. We will concern ourselves solely with the conditions in which continence emerged historically as the favoured state in which to approach God. This is not an essay on morality or religious history, but rather an attempt at a historical study of behaviour, which might prepare the way for a historical account of ideas and their influence, although of course behaviour and ideas are continually influencing one another in this area. Although this study was initially prompted by philosophical and religious texts on the value of virginity, since what we are concerned with is the relationship of the men and women of the Roman Empire with their own bodies, it is first and foremost to the doctors of ancient times that we need to turn for information about these bodies.

My aim is not to assess the accuracy of the ancients' knowledge, either anatomical or physiological, of the male and female bodies. Indeed their errors of interpretation, rather than of observation, tell us more about men in ancient times than do those ancient discoveries which have been confirmed by recent scientific research. The doctors of antiquity set down for us the observations they were able to make. Dissection of the human body was not practised. Galen derived his (mistaken) ideas on the structure of the human womb from dissecting monkeys.[1] Nevertheless everything that could be observed with the naked eye or by means other than dissection by urban physicians who dealt with accidents, armed combat and the injuries sustained at the games in Imperial Rome was noted down by doctors whose numerous works circulated throughout the Mediterranean. Physiology, the study of the internal functions of the body, was based on logic or even analogy rather than observation.

The gradual advance of medical science is charted in a considerable

[1] George Sarton, *Galen of Pergamon*, 1954.

corpus of works attributed to Hippocrates and Galen. Whereas the *Hippocratic Collection* draws on different works from various periods stretching at least from the sixth century BC to the beginning of the Christian era, Galen's work is more specifically his own, dating from the second half of the second century AD. The *Hippocratic Collection* was the basis for all the medical studies of antiquity, even though doctors like Galen disagreed with some of its statements, and it was still being read and used at the end of the fourth century AD when Oribasius,[2] doctor to the Emperor Julian, at the Emperor's request selected and arranged a corpus of quotations known as his *Medical Collection*.

The works of Galen and Oribasius provide the background to a study of the third and fourth centuries, which saw the emergence of chastity as an ideal, and the origin of abstinence as a feature of monastic life. Both men were born in Pergamum. Galen, who died around 200, was the official doctor of the Imperial Court of Rome from 169 to 192 under Marcus Aurelius and Commodus. His was a creative and inquiring spirit. His immense work has not survived intact, for part of it was lost in a fire in Rome. Apart from the manuscripts preserved by Arab doctors, certain passages by Galen were copied by Oribasius in the second half of the fourth century AD. Oribasius was similar to Galen in many respects, but lacked his genius. He was first and foremost a doctor, but also a man of wider ambitions with a particular interest in history. As a young and brilliant doctor he had come to Julian's notice in 355 and the Emperor had taken him into his service. It was for Julian that he produced in Gaul a summary of Galen's works.[3] Julian then asked him to make a collection of the most important writings of the best doctors, and this he did, arranging extracts from various writers in chapters according to subject, without including any comments of his own. Galen had almost completely replaced the *Hippocratic Collection* as the major medical work, and Oribasius used his work, pointing out that it was better because more faithful to Hippocrates.[4] The other doctors quoted by Oribasius, all of whom had written in Greek, had almost all lived in the first, second and third centuries AD, and therefore under Roman domination whether they had practised and written in Rome, like Soranus of Ephesus in the first half of the second century, in Rome and in Egypt, like Rufus of Ephesus around AD 100, or in Pergamum, in Rome and then again in Pergamum, like Galen (130–*c*.200). All were pagan. And Julian himself, for whom Oribasius compiled this work, had turned from the Christianity of his upbringing to paganism. It is to another non-Christian, Ammianus Marcellinus, that we owe the most sensitive

[2] Barry Baldwin, The career of Oribasius, 1975, pp. 85–97.
[3] *Med. Coll.*, I, 1.
[4] Ibid., I. 1.

portrait of this pagan Emperor.[5] Ammianus describes Julian's nights at the time when the Emperor, still officially Christian, was resisting the siege of Sens: he would spend a third of the time resting and the remainder he would devote to political business and prayer to Mercury. But after his account of the pagan prince's death, Ammianus concludes with a long tribute to this remarkable man:

> In the first place, he was so conspicuous for inviolate chastity that after the loss of his wife it is well known that he never gave a thought to love: bearing in mind what we read in Plato, that Sophocles, the tragic poet, when he was asked, at a great age, whether he still had congress with women, said no, adding that he was glad that he had escaped from this passion as from some mad and cruel master. Also, to give greater strength to this principle, Julian often repeated the saying of the lyric poet Bacchylides, whom he delighted to read, who declares that as a skilful painter gives a face beauty, just so chastity gives charm to a life of high aims. This blemish in the mature strength of manhood he avoided with such care, that even his most confidential attendants never (as often happens) accused him even of a suspicion of any lustfulness.
>
> Moreover, this kind of self-restraint was made still greater through his moderation in eating and sleeping, which he strictly observed at home and abroad.[6]

It is difficult to forget Julian's chastity, his ordered lifestyle and asceticism, when reading the texts collected for him by Oribasius, who would have us believe that he was himself responsible for Julian's rise to the throne. Oribasius' son, Eustathius, one of the first Christian physicians, to whom St Basil wrote two letters, was perhaps responsible for his father's return to grace after a period of exile following Julian's death, during which time he came in contact with a number of pagan kings. Oribasius in some ways makes it unnecessary for us to consult all of the medical writers of antiquity individually for he tells us which aspects of their works were considered significant during these two centuries.

The doctors of Imperial times do not simply tell us what ideas and norms various schools of medicine imposed on families of the time; we can also glean some information about contemporary life, not recorded in literature or other textual or artistic sources, from their criticism of certain practices and their descriptions of behaviour which reflect the

---

[5] Ammianus Marcellinus, *History*, books XXIII–XXV.
[6] Ibid., XXV, 4, 2–4, tr. John C. Rolfe, 1935–39.

theories which were taken for granted in the Roman world of the third and fourth centuries. All these doctors were writing for the upper classes, for the rich and leisured women who employed other women to nurse their children, and they gave as an example to their wealthy readers the strong bodies of the women whom poverty forced to work. Perhaps these wealthy women had even more free time than the men described by Galen:

> Those who are able to take a great deal of exercise and sleep as long as they like, and who have chosen a life away from public affairs, may without danger eat sticky foods containing thick humours, particularly if they never experience any feeling of heaviness or tension in the abdomen after eating a lot of such foods. But those who do not take exercise before meals, either because they are old or because they are simply not in the habit of doing so, should keep away from such dishes. Persons who lead a completely sedentary life should not touch foods which contain thick humours, for the greatest obstacle to health is inactivity, and the greatest aid in this respect is moderate exercise.[7]

Thus we see that the ideal of the man living under the Roman Empire was at odds with the ideal of the citizen of ancient or classical Greece. Public service, the service of the Emperor or honorary or remunerative office in local affairs prevented him from taking proper care of his body and even from sleeping enough. Since he was unable to adopt the lifestyle which would have been best for his health, the doctors recommended a regimen which would keep him healthy taking into account the conditions under which he lived. But for the wives and children of such men, who were not forced to ruin their health by long hours of work or worry, the doctors suggested a rather different way of life. The lifestyle of the women and children of the upper classes was, as it were, the ideal of the whole society, though it was not the lifestyle of the popular classes. It was the suggested model and in many respects it is still the one put forward today.

The aspect of ancient life about which we know most is a man's life outside the home. Next comes domestic life, the activities of women and slaves, then the upbringing of children. About the man's life in his own *domus*, in general we know only what the law tells us: it is almost as if Roman men had no family life, although we know that they ate with their wives and children. These men in public life had to avoid an over-abundance of humours, known as the plethora. They did not have time to

---

[7] *Med. Coll.*, III, 1.

go to the baths every day and take exercise. The late nights and the declamations they were called upon to give dried out their bodies, according to the doctors, and they had no time to restore the body's moisture at the baths. (This was the medical theory of the dry and the wet.) The doctors prescribed creams and massages which their patients could apply themselves to stimulate the muscles, but in the final analysis the doctors of the third and fourth centuries AD believed that a life of politics destroyed the balance between dry and wet in the body. In this period political life no longer meant popular assemblies or debates in the *curia*, but the life of servants to the Emperor, which might involve considerable risks depending on the nature of the Emperor. Oribasius collected a number of texts for these busy men, or for the doctors they consulted. We know then that these Romans were not able to take as much exercise or sleep as their doctors would have liked; but the two areas in which they could exercise some control were diet and sexual habits. Moderate exercise was of course recommended: they were warned not to abandon muscular exercise altogether. Oribasius quotes Galen's warning that a sedentary life can lead to cold plethora: 'One should certainly not neglect physical exercise, as do some of those who cultivate the sciences very earnestly.'[8] The foods to be avoided were heavy cereals such as wheat and spelt, pork, lamb, sesame seeds, vaccet onions and dates.[9] It was doubtless for such sedentary people that he recommended blood letting in the spring to prevent the plethora, a practice to which he devoted twenty-two chapters of book VII.

Oribasius covers three aspects of the sexual life of mature men. Let us leave on one side the plasters and ointments used to treat 'paralysis of the virile member' and let us examine the more general advice he gives in the chapters on hygiene and healthy living. All his advice is centred on two subjects: moderation in sexual intercourse and how to prepare for fathering a child. These matters are not dealt with in the *Hippocratic Collection*, which imposes no restrictions on male and female desire, but they do feature in the controversies reported by Soranus and Galen in the second century AD. The emphasis on the essential healthiness of the body, even when it is sick, which we find in the *Hippocratic Collection*, has given way to a normative rather than preventive approach in medicine. We find rules for living coupled with threats of physical deterioration – and it is the doctors who draw up the rules. According to Galen: 'If a healthy man is in the hands of a doctor versed in the art of conserving health, he will be a happy man provided he is placed in the doctor's care from birth.'[10] And the following advertisment for the

---

[8] Ibid., VI, 11.
[9] Ibid., III, 5.
[10] *LI*, 11, from Galen.

medical profession comes from Athenaeus: 'There is almost no moment of the day or night when we do not need medical help: whether we are walking, sitting, putting on ointments, taking a bath, eating or drinking, sleeping or waking, whatever we are doing during the course of our life and in the midst of our various occupations, we need advice to enable us to lead our lives healthily and safely.'[11]

Oribasius borrows from Diocles, who practised in the fourth and third centuries BC, a model daily routine with slight seasonal variations.[12] The *Medical Collection* also gives advice as to how to preserve one's health even when this model routine cannot be followed. One should get up shortly before sunrise, when the numbness of sleep has passed. One should rub one's neck and move one's bowels, and then anoint oneself with oil, gently exercising all the joints. Next one should attend to the face, teeth and hair. 'After the morning toilet . . . those who are obliged to devote themselves to some occupation, or who choose to do so, should begin their work.' Those who are at leisure to do as they please should take a walk of about 2 km in winter, 1 km in summer. Then they should sit down and attend to their private affairs 'until it is time to turn to the care of the body', either at the gymnasium or at the baths[13] where they rub their bodies with oil. Then comes a light luncheon and a sleep in the shade. Then back to one's private business, a walk and a rest. One should then return to the gymnasium to exercise and take a cold bath. One should not take one's evening meal until one is sure one has completely digested one's lunch, as a rule shortly before sunset.

In between the three periods devoted to toilet and exercise there seems to have been little time left in the morning or after the siesta for work. Moreover it was considered better to devote the morning to a walk than to work. The classical Greek ideal of looking after the body through physical exercise was ever present. Oribasius's sixth book explains the benefits to the body of these different periods of the day, the importance of rest and sleep and the physical benefits of mental activity such as conversation or declamation. He explains in detail physical exercises and massage, and the benefits of walking and riding in a carriage, and to end a healthy day he advocates moderate sexual intercourse. The book owes most of its ideas to Galen and to Antyllus, a doctor of the second century AD.[14] Galen lists exercises which increase resistance to illness. Antyllus used exercise, including swimming and horse riding, to cure patients who

---

[11] Ibid., 21.
[12] Ibid., 22.
[13] Could Diocles, in the third century BC, have referred to the alternatives of baths and the gymnasium, or is this an addition dating from the Imperial period?
[14] M. Wellmann, s.v. Antyllos, in *RE*, vol, 2, col. 2644.

were ill, although he did indicate some cases where exercise would not be appropriate.

Oribasius devotes one chapter to declamation. In this area all the doctors are indebted to Galen's writings on the voice, quoted by Oribasius.[15] Galen notes the working of the intercostal muscles and the role of respiration. Antyllus says that if a man is tired he can substitute an exercise in declamation for his morning walk or work, once he has moved his bowels, undergone gentle massage and washed his face. The chapter on techniques of declamation in the ancient world is quite remarkable.[16] Ideally one should declaim epic verse from memory, but if this is not possible it should be iambic verse, or elegiac or lyric poetry. Epic verse is, however, the best for one's health. One should practise vocal exercises, moving from low notes to high notes and extending one's range. Low notes, which open up the neck, let more air into the lungs and so Antyllus advises his readers not to practise high notes, even if they like their sound. The aim is to develop a strong voice and keep it strong for a long time. To this end Antyllus discusses the art of breathing, which is the technical basis of singing. He considers exercise of the voice to be superior to other kinds of exercise which 'strain the body and thicken it . . . The body is refined by the training of the voice, and can then easily be moulded to any purpose, whereas other types of exercise make it hard and insensitive; this is why most athletes are more stupid than the average person. Thus preference should be given to vocal exercise.' Antyllus goes so far as to say that those who do not know any verse by heart and have to read it, sometimes with difficulty, eliminate through abundant perspiration what those who are better trained eliminate by means of breathing. Thus the second century Roman doctor gives those in public life a healthy prognosis providing they do their daily exercises in declamation. This is doubtless what Fronto had in mind when he advised Marcus Aurelius instead of perfecting his speech to take care of his figure so that he would not run out of breath in front of the Senate.[17]

Declamation, whose anatomical and physiological benefits Antyllus reveals, was already familiar to everyone through education. H.-I. Marrou[18] does not consider this physical aspect of the teaching of literature. In his fine book on education in ancient times, Marrou looks at physical and intellectual education separately, as the fact that they were carried on in two different places, gymnasium and school, might well lead one to do. Of course we know that music was taught at school, but we have failed to see how far the ancients considered it as a physical activity,

[15] *LI*, 44.
[16] *Med. Coll.*, VI, 9.
[17] P. Monceaux, *Etude sur la littérature latine d'Afrique. Les païens*, 1894, p. 218.
[18] H.-I. Marrou, *Histoire de l'éducation dans l'Antiquité*, 1965.

exercise for the ear and the breathing, and how far the learning of poetry
was a physical process involving breathing and attention to voice quality
– all aspects which we have come to ignore. A spoken text – and in
antiquity texts were always spoken – is a form of conscious physical
expression.

Just as at school pupils were made to do breathing and singing exercises
before they tackled a text, in the gymnasium they would produce sounds
as they worked on their breathing, which, as Galen expressly says, was a
form of vocal training. Holding one's breath, as pupils were taught to do
at the gymnasium, exercised the muscles of the abdomen and the chest.[19]
So the controlled breathing needed for epic poetry in fact involved
abdominal exercise.

Thus Galen's question: 'Is health care a matter for the instructor at the
gymnasium or for the doctor?' is partly resolved. Those who could
devote themselves to the care of their bodies were looked after by the
instructor at the gymnasium; those who gave speeches were taking
suitable exercise; it was the writers, the scholars, who most neglected
physical exercise because it was not part of their daily activity.

Oribasius' sixth book, which, after four chapters on rest, sleep and
waking, concentrates on exercise and massage, ends with two chapters on
sexual relations. Chapter 37 draws on Galen, and chapter 38 reproduces a
chapter by Rufus of Ephesus, a doctor who was a contemporary of
Soranus and slightly before Galen, and whose work is mainly known
through fragments quoted by Oribasius, Aetius, Paul of Aegina and
Rhazes. Both texts quoted argue in favour of moderate sexual intercourse
and are therefore at odds with Epicurus, whose view that sexual
intercourse was harmful had been adopted by the medical writers of the
first century AD, as Soranus tells us. Rufus ventures to state that 'coitus is
in truth not wholly bad in all respects'.

Oribasius faithfully reports the ancient debates on the harmfulness of
sex. Galen had hinted that he disagreed with Epicurus' view that sexual
intercourse was always harmful. But Epicurus was speaking as a
philosopher. The question entered the province of the doctors when it
began to be more widely discussed and when doctors were able to
influence the sexual lives of their patients or when their patients asked for
their advice. At the end of the first century, there were two opposing
schools of thought on the matter. Soranus makes it clear that both agreed
that sexual abstinence was the ideal.[20] But doctors disagreed about its
harmfulness to the body. Some considered that abstinence was worse
than a moderate amount of sexual activity.

---

[19] *Med. Coll.*, VI, 13, Galen.
[20] *Gyn.*, I, 30–31.

In his book on gynaecology Soranus states: 'All excretion of seed is harmful in females as in males', and 'intercourse is harmful in itself'.[21] He means of course that ejaculation is dangerous for the man, although in his general discussion he does recognize the dangers of pregnancy which a woman risks if she engages in sexual intercourse. But it is clear that the dangers facing the woman are nothing compared with those facing the man.

From the twenty-three chapters contained in Galen's two books on sperm, and the chapters on sperm found in his other books, Oribasius produced one short chapter, grouping together various disparate comments. We know that the Collection is incomplete, particularly book XXII,[22] but Oribasius is unlikely to have to have included any other passages because chapter two already contains short quotations from seventeen chapters taken from five books by Galen.

Oribasius' account of Galen's views reveals a grasp of anatomy which was distorted by preconceived physiological notions. As breath was the most obvious characteristic of life, male sperm which transmitted life must transmit breath, and therefore must contain air. Despite the great emphasis they placed on observation, ancient anatomists could not free themselves from this wholly intellectual concept of the circulation of air in the body, and they believed that the purest air was carried in ever richer blood towards the testicles which passed it on in sperm. Anatomical studies confirmed this picture: the aorta and the trachea, at first confused because doctors had correctly observed their similar consistencies, gave rise to the theory that the heart had a respiratory function and the lungs a function related to the blood.[23] When the heart's role in the circulation of the blood was discovered, the ancients decided that the blood must carry air to the spinal cord. It was the spinal cord which took this air-rich blood towards the testicles. From the vessels situated on the spinal column a spermatic artery and vein ran down alongside the convolutions of the epididymis. This vessel led to the neck of the bladder and the penis. Galen stated that in the course of its journey through these vessels and their convolutions, the blood gradually became white and finally became sperm when it reached the testicles.

As the body's air supply was never interrupted as long as the individual went on breathing, it seemed that there was no reason to worry that loss

[21] Ibid., I, 30–33, tr. Owsei Temkin, 1956.

[22] C. Daremberg's introduction to vol. III of the Collection Médicale.

[23] M.-P. Duminil, La description des vaisseaux dans les chapitres 11–19 du Traité de la Nature des os, 1980, pp. 135–48.

On the pneumatic school, see F. Ruesche, Blut, Leben, Seele, 1930, and on the importance of breath in philosophical and religious doctrines, G. Verbeke, L'évolution de la doctrine du pneuma du stoïcisme à saint Augustin, Etude philosophique, 1945.

of sperm would result in loss of *pneuma*. (Certainly Hippocrates was not concerned about this.) It must have been observation that gave rise to concern,[24] for no philosophical debate would have led the physicians to carry out medical research into the matter. What the doctors observed was the tiredness caused by sexual activity: Oribasius' two chapters on sexual relations stress this tiredness.[25] In this context Rufus recommends heterosexual activity, noting that male homosexual activity is more violent and therefore more tiring. The chapter on sperm gives the scientific explanation, taken again from Galen, for the advice given in the two chapters on sexual relations.[26] Galen considers the effect of castration on the male body and writes:

> The testicles are even more important than the heart, since, besides the heat and strength they give to animals, they are responsible for the continuance of the species, for they impart to the whole body a power similar to the sensory and motor power which the brain communicates to the nerves, and to the pulsatory power that the heart communicates to the arteries, and this power causes the male's vigour and virility . . . When, as a result of continual sexual excess, all the sperm has been lost, the testicles draw seminal liquid from the veins immediately above them. These veins contain only a small quantity of this condensed liquid; so when they are suddenly deprived of it by the testicles, which are stronger than they are, they in turn drain the veins above them and so on. This draining process does not stop until it has involved every part of the body, so if it is constantly repeated and if all the vessels and all the parts of the body are forced to give up their supplies until the strongest part is finally satisfied, the result will be that all the parts of the animal (or the living creature) are drained not just of seminal fluid but also of their vital spirit for this is taken from the arteries along with the seminal

[24] As soon as one begins to work on medical texts one sees that notions which others consider fanciful are in fact the result of observation. M. D. Grmek, La légende et la réalité de la nocivité des fèves, 1980, p. 108: 'The fact that great importance was attached to magic does not mean that magic could not make use of objective empirical knowledge. In short, "superstition" is not necessarily "false", just as "science" is not always "correct".' Empirical discoveries are sometimes lost in the process of scientific rationalization. For example, D. Gourévitch has shown that the knowledge that raw liver was effective in treating day blindness (nyctalopia) was forgotten amid discussions of which animal's liver was the most suitable, Le dossier philologique du nyctalope, 1980, pp. 167–88. In gynaecology, Greek women knew that garlic had antiseptic properties, but this knowledge was set aside by the medical theory that garlic had repellent properties and could be used to make the stomach or the womb reject its contents; A. Rousselle, Observation féminine et idéologie masculine; le corps de la femme d'après les médecins grecs, 1980, pp. 1089–115.

[25] *Med. Coll.*, VI, 37 and 38.

[26] Ibid., XXII, 2.

fluid. It is hardly surprising, therefore, that those who lead a debauched life become weak, since the purest part of both substances is removed from their body. As well as this, pleasure itself can dissolve vital tension to such an extent that people have died from an excess of pleasure. We should therefore not be surprised if those who indulge moderately in the pleasures of love become weak.

This vivid picture of the draining away of the vital spirit was reflected in the worries expressed by the men who consulted their doctors and in the theory that the doctors developed in response. So, when Rufus of Ephesus warned against the serious consequences of 'the retention of sperm during the act itself', what he was condemning was not a practice inspired by the desire to avoid conception, even though it may have been used for this reason, but a practice intended to limit the loss of vital spirit.[27] Here as elsewhere, the practices and methods used have complex and interwoven historical and social significance. It was with the same aim of conserving the vital spirit that Apollonius advised scarification rather than bleeding wherever possible, for blood, which like sperm carried *pneuma*, should not be wasted.[28]

It was extremely important to avoid wasting the vital spirit through unnecessary loss of sperm or blood, since it was out of this vital spirit that the brain formed the more elaborate psychic *pneuma* or 'animal spirit'.[29]

What worried the doctors' aristocratic clientele then was not desire, but fatigue. Oribasius does not repeat Galen's example of Diogenes satisfying himself because the prostitute he sent for urgently took too long to arrive. Masturbation for relief is not dealt with in the *Medical Collection*, or for that matter in Soranus' *Gynaecology*. Nor are the problems caused by abstinence, to which we shall return. Clearly, these medical texts do not reflect the behaviour of all men in the Roman Empire in the second, third and fourth centuries. The theories and advice we have been discussing were designed for a very specific group of men.

For his sixth book Oribasius borrows from Antyllus' fourth book, entitled *How the individual can look after his health*, his chapters on going to bed, rest, abstinence, sleep, late nights, conversation, declamation, walking, racing, passive movement, riding, playing with a hoop, swimming, wrestling, simulated combat, gesticulation, jumping, ball games, corycus (a kind of sand bag used by athletes), weight-lifting and armed combat. The list shows clearly that the whole range of everyday activities was considered as contributing to the well-being of the body. This book, like

[27] Ibid., VI, 38.
[28] Ibid., VII, 19.
[29] *LI*, 41, Galen, and *Med. Coll.*, XXIV, 13, Galen.

Soranus' *Gynaecology*,[30] is written for the (male) head of the family. Oribasius' first two books deal with food, and are based essentially on Galen, though they contain some material from Athenaeus, Rufus, Mnesitheus of Athens, Xenocrates and Philotimus. Book III, which discusses the diets recommended for different types and seasonal changes in diet, suggests that the first two books be used in planning the family's meals. The reader is expected to make practical use of Oribasius' work. First he must identify his type or temperament. In book III, 1, the reader who engages in politics learns that as he does not have time to exercise his body, he must avoid thick foods. Book III, 5 lists these foods. Book I (chapters 4, 5, 28 and 53) gives details of the flours and vegetable substances to avoid, and book II, 8 explains that pork, which this reader must not eat, is the richest, most nourishing meat. What he must avoid is not food which we know today to be high in calories, but food which the ancient doctors considered very rich and difficult to digest. Since he is not able to take exercise in the morning or the evening, the busy man can not eliminate through physical activity the food eaten at one meal before it is time to eat the next, as ancient doctors recommended. Examination of his own body by means of tests which include checking the urine, makes this clear.[31]

There is no one chapter which deals at length with sexual behaviour, but all the elements of advice on this subject are given in the sections dealing with the properties of the various foods and diet: drying and relieving foods are anaphrodisiac, while moist foods help the production of sperm. In amongst the chapters on conception, childbirth and bringing up children, there are four chapters on sex from the point of view of the man's health – the woman's health is not considered. These chapters cover preparing to father a child,[32] sexual relations,[33] and excess of unhealthy sperm.[34] Besides these, there are also two chapters on sexual intercourse to conclude the book which deals with daily care of the body and physical exercise.[35]

A few paragraphs are devoted to the treatment of impotence. Rufus discusses two cases of sexual impotence, that of a Corinthian who was unable to ejaculate, whom he cured by means of a moistening diet, and that of a twenty-two-year-old Milesian who could not ejaculate during sexual intercourse although he frequently ejaculated in his sleep. This patient was cured by horse riding and castor syrup. To treat what was

[30] On the readers for whom Soranus' *Gynaecology* was written, see the introduction to Temkin's translation, pp. XXXVII–XXXVIII.
[31] *Med. Coll.*, VI, 12.
[32] *LI*, 7, from Athenaeus.
[33] Ibid., 8 and 9, from Galen and Rufus.
[34] Ibid., 10.
[35] *Med. Coll.*, VI, 37 and 38, from Galen and Rufus.

politely called 'paralysis of the virile member' some physicians used mustard poultices[36] or even suppositories made from cornflower, pitch and wax,[37] or suppositories made from Judea bitumen or even from resin mixed with opopanax or hyssop. This of course is remedial medicine and not health care, as indeed are the chapters on surgery in book L (1–8), which deal with phimosis, adhesion of the foreskin and non-religious circumcision, in other words the kinds of minor operation which are necessary in all eras and all places. There are also two chapters on subjects more specific to the particular period and the society – infibulation and reconstruction of the foreskin.

Infibulation involved piercing two holes in the end of the foreskin in the part under the glans, and allowing them to form scar tissue so that they did not close up. A metal ring or brooch was then inserted into the holes.[38] Chapter 2, taken from Antyllus, and therefore Roman in period, explains the procedure for reconstructing a foreskin which has been shorted 'as a result of some accident'. This is medical confirmation of a practice which had given rise to one of the scandals which prompted the Maccabaean wars: 'They built a sports-stadium in the gentile style in Jerusalem. They removed their marks of circumcision and repudiated the holy covenant. They intermarried with Gentiles, and abandoned themselves to evil ways.'[39] Finally, one chapter, of which Oribasius' manuscript gives only the title and the source, is reproduced by Paul of Aegina, in his abridged version of the *Medical Collection*. It is a chapter by Heliodorus on castration.

All this, however, concerns specific cases. What we are really concerned with is the social model of the time, a lifestyle suitable for all and yet adapted to suit the individual. Once it had been made clear that sexual relations were undesirable and that they were tiring 'for the chest, the lungs, the head and the nerves',[40] consideration had to be given to those men who had not chosen abstinence: the doctor was called upon to restore a body exhausted by sex, or to advise how to avoid exhaustion. The first advice was to choose the right time: neither at night while the body was digesting, nor in the morning on an empty stomach. Intercourse might take place before a meal or a bath because both of these activities combatted tiredness. But then the patient would not have time to take the exercise which should precede his bath. The doctor advised that the best time was at bedtime, after a moderate meal.[41] It was not a

---

[36] Antyllus, Oribasius, *Med. Coll.*, X, 13.
[37] *Med. Coll.*, VIII, 39, Rufus.
[38] Jüthner, s.v. Infibulatio, in *RE*, vol. IX, 2, col. 2545.
[39] I Maccabees 1, 14–15, New English Bible with Apocrypha, 1970.
[40] *LI*, 8, Galen.
[41] Ibid., 8, Galen.

bad idea to take some exercise before sexual intercourse.[42] Rufus
suggested a good walk, a race, or horse riding.[43] Afterwards the patient
should have a dry massage followed by a rubdown with oil. The doctors
in fact devoted more space to the health of those men who did engage in
sexual activities than to those whose problem was that they were unable
to do so.

The diet drawn up for patients who made love, and which would be
improved if the patient wished to produce a child,[44] was not intended as a
recipe for good love-making. It was above all a diet designed to
counteract the recognized harmfulness of sexual activity:

> Those who engage in sexual relations, and particularly those who do
> so without restraint, must take greater care of themselves than
> others, so that by ensuring that their bodies are in the best possible
> condition they may suffer less from the harmful effects of sexual
> activity; to this end they must go for walks, have gentle massage and
> hot baths if that is their custom, and take pure food which is
> nourishing and yet light, and an ample supply of suitably diluted
> drinks; they must have sufficient sleep and avoid the tiredness that
> comes from anger, pain, joy, excessively weakening activities, steam
> baths, sweating, vomiting, drunkenness, heavy work, becoming too
> hot or too cold.[45]

This way of life must be observed even more strictly if the patient had
decided to produce an heir. The semen produced before a meal or a bath
was not adequate in such cases. What was required was semen
strengthened by a suitable meal. The man should abstain from sexual
intercourse for a few days, to intensify desire and increase the supply of
semen. He must be careful about what he ate and avoid foods which
caused constipation, which were pungent, acid or bitter; he must avoid
activities which caused worry or grief, and even avoid excitement and
extreme pleasure. Galen's short chapter on substances which help the
production of sperm and those which inhibit it enabled the reader to
adjust his diet according to the requirements of his sexual activities.[46] Of
all foods, the one which best prepared the body for love-making was the
chick-pea,[47] and more generally, all nourishing and flatulent foods

[42] *Med. Coll.*, VI, 37, Galen.
[43] Ibid., VI, 38.
[44] *LI*, 7, Athenaeus, and 8, Galen.
[45] *Med. Coll.*, VI, 38, Rufus.
[46] Ibid., XIV, 66.
[47] Ibid., I, 18.

(literally which produce air): vaccet onions, chick-peas, broad beans, octopus, pine kernels, scincos, and orchis (whose name in Greek means testicle), flax seeds and rocket. Starchy foods were to be eaten boiled or roasted. Flatulent foods were important because 'sperm is produced from good food . . . and at the same time contains gas.' As sperm was thought to carry *pneuma* it was logical to consider it as a mixture of '*pneuma* and a foaming liquid'.[48] When this life-giving breath is sucked into the womb, it 'quickly evaporates if it does not find a suitable environment', so no one sees this foam for the gas escapes as soon as it is in contact with the air. Interestingly, although the *Hippocratic Collection* also says that sperm is a kind of foam and transmits breath, its advice is the opposite. In the first place it devotes most attention to the woman, and only to those difficult cases where there is some doubt about her fertility. In such cases the man is required to avoid all flatulent foods, especially broad beans and peas.[49]

It is quite clear from Oribasius' extracts that in order to produce a child the most important thing is to prepare the man so that he produces good quality sperm. The aim, moreover, is not so much to increase desire by the use of aphrodisiac foods such as chick-peas, rocket or onions, as to obtain thick and copious sperm.

Galen is finally forced to write that 'one cannot absolutely forbid people to indulge in intercourse'[50] and Rufus of Ephesus in the same period argues in favour of sexual activity,[51] stating that heterosexual relations tire a man less than homosexual relations: 'It is not absolutely harmful in all respects' to make love. Indeed sexual relations can be used to cure delirium, epilepsy, headaches, anorexia and nocturnal sperm emission.

Nevertheless medical opinion at the time favoured those who abstained. Galen says that one should not suddenly become continent, especially in one's youth. Indeed continence was called *encrateia*, and known as sperm retention. If certain precautions were not taken, it could make an individual sluggish and lazy, irritable and depressed. The doctors were ready with advice on reducing desire and the supply of sperm by means of a diet designed to cool and dry the body.[52] Dietary abstinence, we are told, reduces the body's moisture.[53] But cooling foods – lettuce, courgettes or marrows, blackberries, melon and cucumber – enable one to retain sperm without destroying it. There was of course one radical solution to the problem and that was castration: 'This would be the

[48] Ibid., XXII, 2, Galen.
[49] *Dis. Wom.*, I, 75.
[50] *LI*, 8.
[51] *Med. Coll.*, VI, 38.
[52] Ibid., XIV, 66.
[53] Ibid., VI, 3.

answer for those who wished to abstain from sexual contact', says Galen, 'if vigour and virility were not removed along with the testicles.'[54]

We will not deal here with the actual effects of these regimens on sexual activity, although we will return to this later. Let us simply note at this stage that the question was raised in all seriousness and doctors were expected to answer it. It was even thought to be a fact that chaste men were taller and stronger than those who did not remain continent.[55] The number of men who wished to lead a life of continence was so great that research was devoted to them, books were written for them, and those who were unable to abstain completely from sexual activity had to be reassured. Self-imposed restraint in sexual relations had thus become quite a common feature of the society. This is doubtless one of the factors, on the male side, responsible for the fall in the number of births among the upper classes of the Roman Empire. It is clear, however, from the laws of Augustus, which remained in force until the fourth century, that although there may have been a shortage of legitimate heirs, born within true marriage, this did not mean that there was an absence of sexual activity outside marriage. M.-Th. Fontanille believes that medicaments designed to bring about abortion and which often caused permanent sterility were responsible for the decline in the number of births.[56] But Galen makes it clear that many Roman men went as far as possible in the sexual act, but stopped before ejaculating.[57]

This is why it was so important to choose the right day for the conception of an heir. The *pneuma* which the man went to such lengths to retain, by adopting a strict lifestyle and constantly watching his diet, was to be used for one fertile sexual act, which would take place in the evening, just after the woman's menstrual period. The woman should then cross her legs to keep in this precious semen, and, according to Soranus, should spend several days in bed if she wanted to be certain of conceiving.[58] For this reason, says Soranus,

> Since women usually are married for the sake of children and
> succession, and not for mere enjoyment, and since it is utterly
> absurd to make enquiries about the excellence of their lineage and
> the abundance of their means but to leave unexamined whether they

---

[54] Ibid., XXII, 2.

[55] *Gyn.*, I, 30.

[56] M.-Th. Fontanille, *Avortement et contraception dans la médecine gréco-romaine*, 1977.

[57] On the Catholic controversy surrounding *amplexus reservatus* in the twentieth century, J.-T. Noonan, *Contraception. A History of its Treatment by the Catholic Theologians and Canonists*, 1966, where the issue is, of course, birth control and not the preservation of the vital spirit: the same practice but with a different aim.

[58] *Gyn.*, I, 36 and 46.

can conceive or not, and whether they are fit for childbearing or not, it is only right for us to give an account of the matter in question.[59]

The *Hippocratic Collection* does deal with the problems of sterile women. It devotes a whole book to them, and the chapters on women's illnesses constantly echo the concerns of those who are unable to conceive or who are unable to carry their pregnancies to term. The women of the fifth and fourth centuries BC had themselves compared their bodies, considering external and internal details, in order to find out what caused sterility and miscarriage. The medical books reveal the anxiety felt by women unable to conceive. But what began as medical observation aimed at helping women becomes in Soranus' hands a description of the type of woman to avoid, or, looked at another way, a study of the general and genital anatomy of the fertile woman, the future mother.

These anatomical studies were of course drawn up for men. Soranus describes how, once the decision to marry had been taken, the midwife would visit the fiancée to examine her on behalf of the future husband. She examined first the general appearance of the girl, who might not even have reached the age of puberty. Diocles thought that fertile women had broad hips, freckled skin and were solid, even masculine. Soranus preferred women who, without being too weak, were not quite so strong or masculine. The girl's colouring was considered important: if she blushed suddenly or if her skin grew dark, that meant that she burned with such strong desire that she would destroy a man's seed. But a girl who showed neither joy nor sadness would not do either. After this general examination the midwife would then go on to examine the girl's genitals. Some doctors recommended tests using vaginal suppositories or vaginal fumigation. All agreed, from the writers of the *Hippocratic Collection* on, that good internal communication between the respiratory tracts and the uterus was essential for fertility.[60] So if the smell of substances placed in the vagina reached the woman's mouth it was thought that she would be a good bearer of children. Soranus advised against carrying out this test, and thought it was sufficient to examine the vagina in order to establish whether the uterus and cervix were straight. The vagina should be neither too dry nor too moist, and the uterus neither too loose nor too tight. The midwife then enquired about the regularity and nature of the girl's periods, if she had reached puberty, and her digestion and her moods: a passionate woman's pregnancies would be constantly at risk.

[59] Ibid., I, 34, tr. Temkin.
[60] The book on *Barrenness* refers to the use of fumigations to discover whether the odour of the products used in a vaginal fumigation reached the patient's mouth.

The doctor, then, helped men to take possession of the female body. In more general terms, he assisted the domination of the male, the *dominus*, over the bodies which were in his power. In arriving at this conclusion as to the role of the doctor, the position and significance of particular sections of Oribasius' material are relevant. Daremberg grouped together under the title *Libri Incerti* a number of chapters which undoubtedly formed part of Oribasius' *Medical Collection* and were included as such in a fourteenth-century collection.[61] Dietz, who had classified them, thought in 1832 that they belonged to books XXI and XXII of the *Medical Collection*, which we know to be incomplete. Daremberg, on the basis of the outline of the *Collection* which Oribasius gives in his dedication to Julian, attempted to slot these chapters into various sections of the *Collection*. But they do, in fact, seem to be logically arranged as they stand. All that survives of book XXII is eight chapters, which is very little, all dealing with sperm, gestation, the foetus and abnormalities. The books discovered by Dietz deal with the woman's age at the time of marriage, advice for the pregnant woman, conception, and the upbringing of children up to the age of twenty-one. This is followed by chapters taken from Galen on general appearance, the external physical signs of a good or a bad constitution, but with no specific mention of women or children. Daremberg felt that these chapters belonged to Oribasius' second section, which deals with the nature and anatomy of men, whereas everything that deals with women and children, he felt, belonged to the third section on health care. Of course other sections mention constitution, but not from the rather negative standpoint of looking for the signs of a poor constitution, which recalls Soranus' attempt to pin down the outward signs of female sterility. The signs are as follows. Small heads and small eyes are always bad signs, but not all large heads are good: the eyes and also the proportions of the head have to be right. Exaggerated development of the forehead or the back of the head is an unfavourable sign, especially if the convex shape is caused by protuberance or excessive smallness one way or the other. A developed back of the head is better than a rounded forehead, unless the neck is strong. Examination of the palate can serve to corroborate this unfavourable prognosis, for 'those whose head is ill proportioned' have a very concave palate and often markedly projecting jaws. All of this indicates that the individual will have head aches and inflammations. If we regard this material as separate from the advice on family life and bringing up children, we might interpret it as a system by means of which doctors could classify patients by type. Chapters 35 and 36 explain how to tell the difference between trembling caused by illness and that caused by fear of a powerful person,

[61] Daremberg, Introduction to vol. III of the *Coll. Med.*, p. II–IV.

and how to recognize the signs of fear, anger and anxiety. Now clearly all these signs are relevant to the head of the household who has to choose slaves and delegate various responsibilities, although this is not specifically stated. Moreover, a poor constitution does not imply a bad character, but simply that the individual is likely to succumb easily to ill health. The dividing line is, however, very narrow, and the chapters on the care of the new-born show the importance attached to the shape of the skull and the jaw, which the nurse is required to mould after each of the three daily baths prescribed for babies.[62] In this way, the *pater familias* does all he can to ensure that his child has a good head.

Medicine in the service of man is clearly more specifically medicine in the service of a particular man, a rich man taken up with his own business and that of the state. Can a doctor tell a man so dependent on his career that his health and his physical beauty are at risk? There were certainly those who abandoned the cult of the body for philosophy, and they perhaps justify Marrou's fine writings in praise of the thinkers of antiquity, but alongside these, how many more gave up the proper care of the body for a political career, and economic and social success, the rigours of which were quite different from those of the intellectual life.[63]

[62] *LI*, 17, Galen, and 20, Rufus.
[63] Marrou, *Histoire de l'éducation*, p. 86.

2

The Bodies of Women

None of Oribasius' chapters on preserving good health deals with women. The healthy daily routine, massages and exercises he describes in various chapters are intended for men, though of course comments about types of foods, drying and moistening diets, and warming or cooling diets are as relevant to women as they are to men. For a detailed consideration of women's health we must turn to the *Hippocractic Collection*, which does contain books on women's ailments, all considered in relation to the uterus.[1] As the women of classical Greece themselves noticed, symptoms of pneumonia, stomach pains, paralysis, and stiff joints in women can sometimes indicate a genital disorder. For example, genital tuberculosis which has deteriorated into tuberculosis of the bones may have the appearance of pneumonia;[2] a contracted hip and pains in the thighs may be produced by a fibromatose uterus;[3] and painful points in the neck, the fore-arm and the lower back[4] may accompany the often fatal spontaneous abortion of an extra-uterine pregnancy. Symptoms which might call for bandaging or muscular exercises in a man might very well necessitate treatment of the genital organs in a woman. All this the ancients saw very clearly, and they took the view that all symptoms in a woman must be considered in relation to the genital area.

The women of the time made the most detailed observations of their own bodies. Some acquired more expertise than the rest and became, as it were, specialists in their neighbourhood, their village or their household. We have no special name for these women: they were midwives who treated the whole range of women's illnesses.[5] The ancient doctors whose

[1] Rousselle, *Observation féminine et idéologie masculine*, pp. 1085–115.

[2] *Nat. Wom.*, 38; *Dis. Wom.*, 129.

[3] *Nat. Wom.*, 47; *Dis. Wom.*, 4, 38, 131.

[4] A. Laffont, *Manuel de gynécologie*, 1952, p. 452–3; it is best to use text books which were written a while ago at a time when general practitioners devoted considerable attention to the observation of clinical signs.

[5] On the *feminae medicae*, see Paola Manuli, Fisiologia e patologia del femminile negli scritti ippocratici dell'antica ginecologia greca, 1980, n. 1, p. 396.

writings have come down to us owe their knowledge about women's ailments to these women, but in the hands of the doctors the knowledge acquired by these midwives lost much of its observational basis. For example, it was not until the twentieth century that the clinical description of the abortion of a tubal pregnancy was re-established.

But before we can accuse the ancient doctors of failing to pay sufficient attention to women, an accusation which is frequently levelled at them, we must consider how difficult it was for them to gain access to women's bodies.[6] Dissection was not practised, which is why they extrapolated from the results of their observations of female animals. Hence Galen's view that women had a double womb,[7] which was accepted by all the anatomists of antiquity, and Aristotle's observation of female animals on heat and their secretions,[8] which did not have much influence except insofar as it was reflected in his fantastic theories about female physiology, which he arrived at by means of reason rather than observation. If they had little knowledge of female corpses, they had even less of living female bodies. Whereas their surgical treatment of gladiators and soldiers had made them familiar with the male body, they had no experience of difficult deliveries or fatal miscarriages from which to learn about the female body, for women called on other women to help them and rejected men on such occasions. In the whole of the *Hippocratic Collection* we find only two examples of a doctor carrying out a vaginal examination.[9] The numerous details given in the books of the *Hippocratic Collection* on the *Nature of Women, Barrenness*, and *Diseases of Women* were given to the doctors by midwives or by female patients themselves. Even the midwife would only carry out an examination in cases where the patient could not examine herself, for example to tell whether the walls of the uterus were too smooth[10] (because it was thought that they needed to be rough in order to retain male sperm).

In general, women examined themselves when they were in good health, and were thus able to discover polyps or callosities[11] which they

[6] M.-Th. Fontanille, *Avortement et contraception*, p. 7; Paola Manuli, Fisiologia e patologia, pp. 395–7, shows how difficult it was for doctors to examine women. The training of doctors in medical theory in fact resulted in women knowing less about their bodies than they had in previous eras.

[7] Galen, *De Uteri Dissectione*, ed. Kühn, vol. 2, pp. 887–908; Sarton, *Galen of Pergamon*, p. 49; this was probably Galen's first book of anatomy. According to Temkin, *Soranus' Gynaecology*, p. 7, n. 7, it is not clear whether Soranus is speaking of animal or human dissection. See L. E. Edelstein, The development of Greek anatomy, 1935, pp. 235–48; but dissection was certainly carried out: Soranus, *Gyn.*, I, 8 and 17.

[8] *HA*, 572 *a* and *b*.

[9] L. Bourgey, *Observation et expérience chez les médecins de la collection hippocratique*, 1953, p. 177, n. 6, finds only two examples of vaginal examination carried out by doctors.

[10] *Dis. Wom.*, 21.

[11] *Dis. Wom.*, 40.

would have cauterized. If they consulted a midwife they would examine themselves in order to be able to answer her questions so that she could prescribe treatment.[12] Such problems as displacement, retroversion or anteversion of the uterus and induration, gaping or occlusion of the cervix would have been discovered during the course of routine examinations by the women themselves. Women's knowledge was thus firmly based on observation, and this is what the doctors who wrote the *Hippocratic Collection* reproduced for the benefit of other male doctors. They show us doctors hiding behind a curtain during a delivery, questioning the midwife and ready to intervene in cases where the patient was in real danger.[13] On the whole they were scarcely more knowledgeable than the layman. Diocles of Carystus (*c.*340–260 BC) thought that all women had their menstrual periods at the same time, following the cycles of the moon, and so did Empedocles.[14] Lycus, who is quoted at the end of Oribasius' book XXIV, after giving a description of the female genital organs, taken from Soranus, states that the vagina needs to be extremely deep so that it can catch the sperm ejaculated by the penis.[15]

Male doctors, then, who had no knowledge of female anatomy or physiology, but fantasies only, used logical reasoning to construct a male science of the female body, incorporating all the facts gathered patiently over the years by women who had built up an empirical science which had never been written down but had grown through oral tradition.

Greek and Roman women were not willing to be examined by men[16] and Soranus said he was writing essentially for midwives who were able to have access to female patients. Women's bodies were shrouded in such secrecy that Galen learned more from dissecting female monkeys, insofar as their organs were the same as human ones, than all the men of ancient times learned through their sexual contacts with their own wives.

On the basis of the observations they made during dissection the doctors arrived at a description of the female genital apparatus: they stated that it was identical to the male apparatus except that it lacked the convolutions of the epididymis and was situated in the abdomen on a level with the bladder. The vocabulary used to describe the internal reproductive organs, with the exception of the uterus and the cervix, was exactly that used for the male organs: the ovaries were testicles and the Fallopian tubes, which they described perfectly, were a vas deferens. They even spoke of female sperm. Only the uterus and the external genital area were given new names, doubtless by women. But the male

---

[12] Rousselle, Observation féminine, pp. 1095–6.
[13] *Nat. Fac.*, III, 3; *Gyn.*, IV, 7 and 9.
[14] *Gyn.*, I, 21.
[15] *Med. Coll.*, XXIV, 33 and 30.
[16] *Dis. Wom.*, 1, 62.

doctors explained that 'the internal genital organs surround the neck of the womb just as, in men, the foreskin grows around the glans.'[17]

The doctors were quite clear about the reproductive function of the male: what they wanted to know about was the woman's role in producing a child. Their investigations of female genital anatomy were aimed at clarifying the question of female sperm. They wanted to know whether women played a twofold role in producing a baby, contributing the placenta and also sperm, a type of refined and frothy blood which carried *pneuma* as did the sperm contributed by the father.

It is fascinating to see how they arrived at conclusions on the basis of scientific observation.

Despite its accessibility, they knew very little about the vagina. Soranus thought that only dissection would convince the Roman doctors that in a virgin the vagina was not normally sealed by a membrane stretching between the neck of the womb and the hymen. How, he asked, could the menstrual blood pass through the vagina of a virgin without causing the acute pain which was produced by defloration?[18] He pointed out that Greek girls, who were not married until they had reached puberty, had their first periods without pain or tearing. The Romans refused to yield to this argument. In their society girls might be married at twelve, sometimes even younger, and were immediately deflowered, some of them becoming pregnant before they had had a menstrual period. The Romans were thus able to mistake for a universal anatomical feature what is in fact a rare malformation. In this way anatomical knowledge was influenced by social customs. For the Greek doctors too the vagina remained the most mysterious area of the female genitalia.

On the basis of their physical sensations, the Greek women described by the *Hippocratic Collection* came to conclusions about their own physical processes which men could verify through their heterosexual experiences. They observed feelings of desire, and secretions which they saw as being related to desire and also to pleasure, and they considered these identical in timing and nature to male sensations and emissions. Women were sure that they ejaculated and they told men so, stating that they could not conceive without reaching orgasm. So the doctors described both male and female sperm and spoke of women as well as men having emissions during their sleep, linked to erotic dreams. Women considered that it was an excellent sign of fertility if they frequently experienced nocturnal emissions.[19] 'If the seed which comes from both parents remains in the womb of the woman, it is first of all thoroughly

---

[17] *Med. Coll.*, XXIV, 32.
[18] *Gyn.*, I, 17.
[19] *Bar.*, III.

mixed together – for the woman of course does not remain still.'[20] Female desire and orgasm, which were considered necessary for conception, are referred to in all writings on the subject. Conception and pregnancy were thought of as the remedy for all female ailments, for a pregnant woman was a healthy woman, whose body was functioning normally, and as soon as medical treatment was over 'when desires surface after the menstrual period a wife should go to her husband's bed'. Medical theory found an explanation for women's emission of sperm, which applied equally to men: the heat of desire and the movements of the body in love-making shook the blood and made it foam, slightly less in women than in men, but necessarily in both.

These beliefs held by women, which the writers of the *Hippocratic Collection* were prepared to accept, were developed by an anonymous doctor whose work is included in Aristotle's *Historia Animalium*. His work is later than Aristotle's own writings, but the ideas it develops were known to Aristotle because he argues against them. The doctor reports the theories held by women and must have received his accounts of the sensations they experienced from women themselves. They told him that they distinguished between two sorts of secretions, in the same way as men: 'A type of local sudation, comparable to the flow of saliva which often occurs in the mouth, particularly in the presence of food',[21] and sperm itself, ejaculated at the moment of female orgasm. The sperm emitted at orgasm was essential for conception, so the man and the woman must:

> progress at the same speed . . . If the woman does produce her share of sperm and contribute to the generation of a child, it is evident that both partners must work together. So if the man proceeds too fast and if the woman has difficulty in keeping up with him (for women are slower than men in many spheres), this can prevent conception. This is why a man and woman who have no children may produce children with other partners whose pace in intercourse suits their own. So if the woman is perfectly prepared and has the right thoughts at the height of her excitement, and if for his part the man is preoccupied and remains cold, then the two will be in harmony with one another.[22]

Of course women explained their need for sexual satisfation as being related to reproduction, and did not speak of the need for satisfaction for its own sake.

[20] *Nat. Ch.*, XII, 1, tr. I. M. Lonie, in *Hippocratic Writings*, ed. G. E. R. Lloyd, 1978.
[21] *Bar.*, III, in *HA*, X.
[22] *Bar.*, V.

Nevertheless, medical theory took note of women's descriptions of their sensations and their certainty about contributing their own sperm to the conception of a child, and directed couples towards sexual practices which ensured that each partner found pleasure in the other's body.

Anatomical and physiological theories were based then on women's descriptions of their sensations:

> This is how nature has designed the route followed by sperm in women. They have a canal which corresponds to the male sexual organ, but in their case it is contained within the body. They draw sperm into this canal through a small orifice situated next to the place from which their urine flows. This is why this part of the body is not the same at the height of sexual excitement as before this state is reached. Sperm passes from this canal into the uterus.[23]

It was *pneuma* which was drawn in through this canal, and clearly it is the clitoris which was held to be its orifice. The *pneuma* reached the woman's spermatic secretions, which came down through the neck of the womb and were then drawn back up into the uterus together with the male sperm to bring about conception.

Female desire is scarcely mentioned in Aristotle's writing. He did observe female animals on heat, but stated that, apart from mares, women were the only females which 'allowed coitus' during pregnancy, because there was no risk of super-fecundation. Aristotle discovered, or at least he was the first to state, that women could conceive even if they did not reach orgasm[24] and that indeed women did not achieve orgasm very often. He referred to 'the pleasure that some women sometimes experience'. Aristotle did not deny that women secreted during sexual intercourse: 'This fluid, however, is not seminal; it is peculiar to the part from which it comes in each several individual.'[25] Aristotle also observed that the place where women felt pleasure, namely the clitoris, was not the place from which their sperm was said to flow, namely the cervix,[26] and he stated that nature could not have created female sperm which would be emitted by the uterus only to be 'sucked back into it, for nature does nothing superfluous'.

Advances in observation thus set science back a long way, demolishing women's claims that they produced sperm – the truth of which was only re-established when ovulation was discovered – and at the same time destroyed the traditional basis of reciprocal pleasure in heterosexual love-

---

[23] Ibid., V, in *HA*, *X*, 637 *a*.
[24] *Gen. An.*, 739 *a*; 727 *b*.
[25] Ibid., 727 *b*, tr. A.L. Peck, 1943, and 738 *b*.
[26] Ibid., 728 *a*.

making. 'Women believe that it is necessary for the sperm from both the male and female partner to be emitted at the same time.'[27]

New theories on anatomy and physiology could now be built upon these observations. Aristotle, who was not a doctor but a naturalist and logician, drew a parallel between women's blood (and the milk into which it changed after childbirth) and male sperm: 'The female is, as it were, a sterile male'[28] and 'the female is, as it were, a castrated male; the menses are a type of impure sperm.' A woman was impotent, nothing more than a recipient: 'the female, in fact, is female on account of inability of a sort, viz., it lacks the power to concoct semen'.[29] This radical position of Aristotle's, which continued to be discussed by philosophers, was the most famous in the whole history of the development of ancient theories on the woman's role in conception. As well as their personal sexual relationships, doctors had access to women in ways that philosophers did not, but despite this, the doctors did not dispute the accuracy of Aristotle's observations or the logic of his reasoning.

Three and a half centuries after Aristotle, the works of Soranus and even Galen show the confusion caused by his observations. And yet no one, except perhaps Rufus of Ephesus, actually put his theories into practice. Rufus justified his advice to abstain from sexual intercourse if one had elephantiasis on the grounds that women and eunuchs – in other words those who did not produce sperm, according to Aristotle's theory – rarely suffered from this dreadful illness.[30] But even in Aristotle's time, Herophilus and Diocles knew of the Fallopian tubes. Herophilus described them as semi-circular and Diocles called them horns.[31] Galen stated that female sperm was produced by these tubes and ejaculated into the womb.[32] He said that this sperm excited the woman, making her ready for love, and opened the cervix so that the uterus could take in male sperm. He did not confuse female sperm with 'a liquid produced by the glands . . . (which) runs out of the vagina at the moment when the woman reaches the height of pleasure in intercourse'.

Doctors from Herophilus to Diocles and Galen, then, had almost all the information they needed to accept the existence of a female equivalent of sperm and had established a picture of female anatomy which was almost correct. Soranus, considered as the greatest gynaecologist of

---

[27] *Bar.*, V.

[28] *Gen. An.*, 1, 20.

[29] Ibid., 728 *a*, tr. Peck; 763 *b* – 765 *b*. P. Demont, *Remarques sur le sens de* τρεφω, 1978, pp. 358–84, explains that the process is not one of coction, but that the sperm coagulates or sets in the same way as milk.

[30] *Med. Coll.*, XLV, 28.

[31] Ibid., XXIV, 29, Galen.

[32] Ibid., XXII, 2.

antiquity, because his short book on gynaecology has survived, practising in Rome half a century before Galen, could not, however, accept this description. Oribasius, who was unable to choose between the two alternative anatomical schools, reproduced Soranus' text[33] alongside Galen's description. Soranus gives the positions and size of the uterus and quite accurately describes the external genitalia and the other parts of the female reproductive system, mentioning the clitoris but saying nothing about it. The testicles (ovaries) are described as connected to the uterus,

> slightly flattened, rounded and a little broadened at the base. The seminal duct runs from the uterus through each didymus and extending along the sides of the uterus as far as the bladder, is implanted in its neck. Therefore the female seed seems not to be drawn upon in generation since it is excreted externally.[34]

Was it the description of a canal which collects *pneuma* above the urinary meatus, given by the anonymous doctor whose work was included in Aristotle's, which led Soranus to link the female spermatic canal to the elimination of urine? Was he influenced by the fact that women differ from men in that their urinary and genital channels are separate? The question raised by Aristotle as to the existence of female sperm and its role in reproduction was still influencing doctors' views on the subject. Galen, who like the writers of the *Hippocratic Collection* considered that women did produce sperm, did not go so far as to claim that it was the exact equivalent of male sperm: it was imperfect and less refined than that produced by men.[35] But it was a kind of sperm and it did carry *pneuma*. For Aristotle, women produced neither *pneuma* nor sperm, and it has been said that the idea that a woman could pass on *pneuma* to her child, even though she did not produce sperm to help create him, was a moral victory for stoicism.[36] The medical tradition of which Galen was a part held quite different views: it recognized female sexual desire and also the fact that women produced sperm which, when mixed with male sperm, created a child. Oribasius quotes Galen's passage on sperm in which he states that the menses have both a dynamic and a material force.[37] Nevertheless only male sperm 'built arteries, veins, nerves, bones and

---

[33] Ibid., XXIV, 31–2, *Gyn.*, I, 6–18.
[34] *Gyn.*, tr. Temkin.
[35] Galen, *Uses of the Body*, XIV, 10–11.
[36] M. Spanneut, *Le stoïcisme des Pères de l'Eglise de Clément de Rome à Clément d'Alexandrie*, 1957, p. 178.
[37] *Med. Coll.*, XXII, 2.

membranes, not with blood but with its own substance', that is to say sperm built the noble white parts.

On this and other points Soranus belonged to the Aristotelian tradition which held that women conceived without feeling anything. In its chapters on sterile women the *Hippocratic Collection* had listed the steps to be taken to ensure conception. Soranus disputed all this, and Galen echoes the debate. It was women themselves who first felt that they had to retain male sperm in order to conceive. This is the logical inversion of the advice to expel male sperm immediately after intercourse in order to prevent conception.[38] So when the women described in the *Hippocratic Collection* did want to become pregnant, they remained lying down with their legs crossed.[39] They discussed the length of time male sperm remained in their bodies, and concluded that it could be retained for up to seven days. The debate in learned circles concerned the need to retain male sperm, which was essential to conception, over a long period by remaining in bed. Galen begins his first chapter on sperm[40] with this debate on the absolute necessity of retaining sperm and even ensuring that it is drawn in by the uterus which can thus be said to show two opposite tendencies, the first at conception when it pulls in sperm, and the second at the end of labour when it pushes out the child. This suggests that there may have been two schools of thought on this subject.

Women were no longer mistresses of their own bodies, relying on their own observations and the interpretation of these observations by a few specialists who were women. The questions we have been discussing were now considered in the light of what amounted to a male policy towards women, a gynaeconomy, which required the contribution of the doctors to make it more effective, and which in this case consisted of legally sanctioned domination by fathers and husbands, indeed by men in general, over women's bodies.

First there was the question of the girl's age on marriage, which depended on her father and the wishes of the man who sought to marry her. In Rome the marriage contract was not between the father and the future husband, as it was in Athens and throughout Greece generally.[41] In Rome the contract was between the two spouses and the consent of both partners was indispensable.[42] Even in Greek law, over the centuries the woman began to appear in Hellenistic Egyptian contracts alongside her

---

[38] *Gen.*, V, 1.
[39] *Nat. Wom.*, 11.
[40] Galen, *De Semine*, ed. Kühn, vol. IV, p. 592 et seq.
[41] C. Vatin, *Recherches sur le mariage et la condition de la femme mariée à l'époque hellénistique*, 1970, Introduction.
[42] Jean Gaudemet, 'Justum Matrimonium', 1949, pp. 320–22 = *Sociétés et Mariage*, 1980. pp. 55–8.

kyrios and her fiancé. But there is an enormous difference between a Greek woman of eighteen, married without giving her formal legal consent, and a Roman girl less than twelve years of age giving herself to a man of thirty at her father's request.

The anatomical errors made by the Roman doctors, which were contested by Soranus of Ephesus, himself from the Greek world, could only be the result of girls being deflowered before puberty, as he repeatedly pointed out to these physicians. These Roman doctors imagined that the vagina was completely sealed internally and that this, plus the hymen, made the first act of intercourse very painful. According to this theory the man had the privilege of opening up the passage for the menses. Roman law confirmed the custom of marrying very young girls. In the days of the Republic they were never present when the matron, the mother of the family, went to help the men in the fields.[43] Roman custom did not change on contact with the Greeks, when the Mediterranean was conquered or under the Empire: at twelve a girl who was married could be called a wife, *uxor*.[44] Sometimes she had been married at a much earlier age.[45] Soranus' account of the Romans' ignorance of the normal formation of the vagina tells us that girls experienced intercourse before their first period and that the practice was sufficiently widespread for the doctors' misconception to go uncorrected. And perhaps Roman mothers did not teach their daughters to carry out the investigations which taught Greek women so much about their own anatomy and about the normal and abnormal changes which the uterus and cervix might undergo. If Roman women had been more familiar with the nature of their own bodies, Roman doctors would not have debated the point and Soranus would not have had to try to convince them of their mistake by referring to the experiences of Greek girls and recommending dissection.

Greek women liked to think that intercourse made it easier for menstrual blood to pass through the vagina,[46] perhaps because they felt that their periods were less painful once were married and had started sexual relations. Aristotle stated that all women suffered during menstruation, an error which probably stems from the attempts of women to keep men at a distance during their periods. Soranus mentions only a reduction or moderation of sexual activity and says that women

---

[43] R. Villers, Le statut de la femme à Rome jusqu'à la fin de la République, 1959, p. 181.

[44] *D*, 23, 2, 4.

[45] M. Durry, 1955, p. 87, and Le mariage des filles impubères dans la Rome antique, 1955, pp. 253–72, and Sur le mariage romain, 1956, pp. 227–43 and reproduced in 1970, pp. 17–25 and 27–42. For the Christian period, see Cyrille Vogel, Facere cum virgia(–o) sua(–o) annos . . . L'âge des époux au moment de contracter mariage d'après les inscriptions paléochrétiennes, 1966, pp. 355–66.

[46] *Gen.*, IV, 2.

should be allowed to dictate the frequency and nature of sexual relations at this time according to their habits and the discomfort caused by their periods.[47]

Medical theory seems to have taken hold of these notions and developed them in such a way that men were given a central role in maintaining women's health. The doctors were faced with an insoluble contradiction. On the one hand their theory led them to hold that sexual activity was essential once a girl showed the first signs of puberty, and on the other they noted that early pregnancies were very damaging to the female body. Aristotle advised that girls should be carefully supervised when they reached puberty because at that time they were strongly attracted by heterosexual pleasures. He was referring of course to Greek girls who were not married until after they had reached puberty. But Aristotle also noted that women aged quickly once they were married, which is not hard to understand when one reads the *Hippocratic Collection* and appreciates the frequency of their pregnancies. Aristotle noted that 'women have milk until they become pregnant again.'[48] Despite numerous recipes for potions to bring about miscarriage, which Fontanille shows contained substances which often caused sterility, Greek women seem to have had a large number of pregnancies, if not always a large number of children.[49] Prolapse was a frequent complaint according to the *Hippocratic Collection*. Aristotle said of the female animal that 'when it is free from the mother, on account of its weakness it quickly approaches its maturity and old age.'[50] He made the point even more strongly with reference to the young girls of his time. Their bodies, he said, ceased to develop 'because it seems that the body ceases to grow after it has produced three children . . . Once they have reached the age of twenty-one women are fit to produce children, while men still need to develop further.'[51] If the Greek girl, married at sixteen or eighteen, suffered adverse effects from pregnancies which stunted her growth, the situation must have been even worse for the Roman girls observed by Soranus and Rufus of Ephesus. Indeed Soranus suggested that fathers should not give their daughters in marriage until they had menstruated, generally around the age of fourteen.[52] The title of his eighth chapter,

---

[47] *Gyn.*, I, 26.

[48] *HA*, 587 *b*, and *Gen. An.*, 727 *b*.

[49] Fontanille, *Avortement et contraception*, has shown that many of the substances used in ancient times to bring about abortion were capable of producing permanent sterility. But our texts show that Greek women had numerous pregnancies although recipes for abortifacients abounded.

[50] *Gen. An.*, 775 *a*, tr. Peck.

[51] *HA*, 582 *a*.

[52] *Gyn.*, I, 20.

'Until what age should girls be kept virgins?', makes it clear that he was addressing fathers. In order to placate these men he suggested physical exercises and a diet to induce menstrual periods 'spontaneously and if possible before the first experience of intercourse'.[53] He recommended walks, passive exercise, massages with oil, not too much gymnastics, a bath once a day but no more, and a good deal of entertainment so as to relax the body. Rufus wrote that girls had 'a fiery nature' at puberty.[54] He remarked that in his time girls did not work as much as men, and that whereas Hesiod thought that the girls of his day should be married at eighteen, after four years of nubility, he, Rufus, considered it dangerous for girls who lived a life of leisure not to be married at the first sign of puberty. Firstly the body of a girl who lived a life of ease aged rapidly. A young girl felt a strong desire for sexual relations, and if she were not married, she would run the risk of a serious plethora and the problems this caused. Besides, sexual intercourse made menstrual periods easier, and the doctors even feared that the uterus would not function normally if the woman did not begin sexual relations soon after puberty.[55] Rufus, like Soranus, noted that babies born to very young mothers were weak and that the mother, 'wearing herself out before her time, would suffer the consequences and would soon sustain lesions to the womb'. Soranus noted that these very young mothers experienced tearing of the uterus during childbirth.[56] In cases of very early pregnancy he recommended abortion.[57] Some girls, he said, had become pregnant before they had their first period.[58] Rufus had probably seen young girls married and deflowered before puberty in the Greek and Alexandrian societies for which he wrote. But neither Rufus nor Soranus really thought that their advice would be followed, as indeed it was not. All that happened was that the Greeks, who wanted to marry their pubescent daughters at the same age as the Roman girls, gave their daughters the treatment used for amenorrhoea in mature women, which consisted of dangerous medicines which often caused miscarriage. Rufus was forced expressly to forbid the use of emmenagogues to treat virgins.[59]

Soranus advised that girls who were married very young and immediately became pregnant should be made to abort. Girls who were allowed to remain virgins until the age of sixteen or eighteen were given a special diet, which Rufus explained was necessary in order to avoid the

[53] Ibid., I, 25.
[54] LI, 2.
[55] Gyn., I, 31
[56] Ibid., I, 33; IV, 4.
[57] Gyn., I, 60.
[58] Ibid., I, 28.
[59] LI, 2.

plethora, in other words excessive weight gain. Girls should be put on the diet at the earliest signs of puberty and their appetites should be carefully watched even before they were separated from boys. After that they would be brought up away from boys and they would not be allowed meat, wine or anything fattening. They should go for walks, run and do gymnastics. Choruses which involved singing and dancing, and energetic ball games were considered excellent. The lifestyle proposed for young girls – diet, exercise, and not too many warm baths – was thus the equivalent of that recommended for adolescent boys.

It is clear that although men wanted very young wives, they wanted them to be fertile immediately. Rufus listed the signs which indicated that a girl would reach puberty early or late, and he also pointed out that a girl who had just reached puberty was rarely fertile. In short, he recommended that from both the father's and the husband's point of view it was best to wait. These men wanted children, indeed needed children, for since Augustus' time the law obliged them to have children,[60] unless they chose not to receive any legacy or inheritance but were willing to see relatives who had children receive half of the estate that should have come to them from a relative who had died leaving a will or intestate.

Augustus' measures were aimed at those men who instead of legal marriage, chose to live in concubinage with women whose status in Roman law was inferior, even if they were free women of noble birth. The law recognized concubinage and set out rules relating to the relationship: those who chose this state lost their right to inherit according to the *lex Papia* and the *lex Julia*. They were no longer considered as married men. Children born to a couple in concubinage could not inherit from their parents, and concubines could not adopt. Only marriage and the production of legitimate heirs entitled one to inherit, so fathers forced reluctant sons into arranged marriages. Sons rebelled, but daughters, who were subject to the same laws, agreed to marriages that would not be consummated. But with the *lex Papia* Augustus forced couples to have children once they were married. Some might plead that they had been forced into marriage, but the jurists replied that once a son was married, even against his will, he had given his formal consent to the marriage. Opposition to a father's will could not bring about the legal annulment of a marriage, but if both fiancés wished to cancel the marriage this was possible.

[60] There are a number of works dealing with Augustus' caducous laws. Many of them are listed in R. Astolfi, I beni vacanti e la legislazione caducaria, 1965, pp. 323–36, and Note per una valutazione storica della lex Julia et Papia, 1973, pp. 187–228. Also by R. Astolfi, *La Lex Julia et Papia*, 1970. Among earlier works, R. Besnier, L'application des lois caducaires d'Auguste d'après le Gnomon de l'Idiologue, 1949, pp. 93–119. More recently, R. Besnier, Pline le Jeune et l'application des lois démographiques, 1979, examines the Emperor's provisions for exempting certain people from the effects of the law.

As far as succession was concerned, a legatee could not claim his inheritance until he had fulfilled the necessary conditions, in other words until he was married and had at least one child, but the legacy could be held for him until the conditions were fulfilled.[61]

This then is the socio-political background against which we must consider the gynaecological works of Soranus and of Rufus of Ephesus in the first half of the second century. It explains why they considered so carefully how to choose a girl who, if she had not reached puberty, showed signs of being fertile. It explains their advice on how to make sure that intercourse was followed by conception, and finally it explains the care taken of a woman during pregnancy and the measures to ensure the survival of the baby. These last two points have generally been considered as a credit to Soranus' humanity, and the considerable progress made in gynaecology in ancient times.

There was no doubt in ancient times that the most fertile phase in the female cycle was that which immediately followed the menstrual period. Indeed Greek women thought that intercourse before the end of the menstrual period was the most likely to result in conception. They noted that that was when the cervix was softest and most open. Menstrual periods were thus considered as essential to conception,[62] and Galen stated that a woman could not conceive without having had a period. As far as we can tell from the *Hippocratic Collection*, for Greek women the question of choosing the most fertile moment only arose if a woman feared she was sterile. Following her first experience of sexual intercourse a woman would be pregnant with her first child, and then, towards the end of the second year of breast-feeding she would know she was pregnant again when her milk dried up. Sometimes she would choose to have an abortion, but in general the attention a woman paid to her periods did not indicate that she was anxious to become pregnant or that she was afraid of becoming pregnant. It was simply a natural process that women accepted.

Amenorrhoea, in the oldest texts, was thus considered a sign of very serious genital disorder. In Greece a woman would complain of amenorrhoea if she was still of child-bearing age and had resumed her periods after weaning a child, or if she was sterile. In such cases female tradition prescribed a long course of treatment, consisting of emmenagogues which were also used as abortifacients, and also a certain number of local treatments, the longest and most complex of which were a series of genital fumigations, pessaries, douches and baths. Amenorrhoea was linked with fatal genital disorders and was considered so serious that a

---

[61] R. Astolfi, I beni vacanti, Note per una valutazione, and *La Lex Julia et Papia*.

[62] *Med. Coll.*, XXII, 3, Galen, and 8.

woman would agree to undergo unpleasant treatment lasting several months.

Soranus' Roman work on gynaecology does not reflect the same fear of fatal female disorders at the mention of amenorrhoea. The Roman women he wrote for did not breast-feed their children. Their menstrual periods occurred regularly throughout their adult life. Whereas in the Greek world attention was devoted to the question of the relative importance of the menstrual flow and female sperm in the production of an embryo, in Rome the question was whether periods were essential firstly to health and second to conception. Soranus' answer was that they were necessary for conception.[63] Some authorities went so far as to compare menstruation to a wound which was injurious to health. Soranus considered amenorrhoea as a frequent and clearly identified phenomenon occurring for example among singers or women who engaged in sport a great deal.[64] If they wanted children he advised them to change their lifestyle. In contrast to other authorities, Soranus stated that in terms of women's health menstrual purgation was the equivalent of gymnastics for men.[65] So, as we have seen, attempts were made to encourage the early appearance of periods in young girls who had not yet reached that stage. If older women had very irregular cycles or suffered from amenorrhoea, this did not give rise to fears for their life, for amenorrhoea was no longer considered a sign of impending death. Something as simple as a long journey might lengthen the cycle.[66] Soranus described what he considered to be true amenorrhoea: it was accompanied by the sensation of fuzziness in the head, impaired vision, pains the joints (part of the premenstrual syndrome[67]), discomfort in the sinuses, faintness and nausea. None of this recalls the accounts of amenorrhoea as a sign of serious illness given by the Greek doctors in the *Hippocratic Collection*. It bears more resemblance to Soranus' account of the temporary indisposition caused by periods themselves.[68] Sexual activity and pregnancy sometimes cured dysmenorrhoea in virgins and also in widows who remarried.[69] So Soranus, in his Roman practice, advised against the old treatment using drugs,[70] and, as Galen was to do,[71] recommended the scarification of the ankle so as to draw blood into the lower part of the body, which he considered the equivalent of the menstrual flow. Herodotus, a Greek

---

[63] *Gyn.*, I, 28–9.
[64] Ibid., I, 22–3.
[65] Ibid., I, 27.
[66] Ibid., I, 22.
[67] Laffont, *Manuel de gynécologie*, p. 206.
[68] *Gyn.*, I, 26.
[69] Ibid., I, 31 and 42.
[70] Ibid., III, 12.
[71] *Med. Coll.*, VII, 2.

doctor of the third century AD,[72] used cupping. Soranus explained that the cupping-glasses should be applied to the scarified pubis.

The Roman attitude to amenorrhoea does not mean that doctors were henceforth unconcerned with female genital disorders, but simply that amenorrhoea was considered separately from the other symptoms, whereas in the *Hippocratic Collection* it was, quite correctly, associated with them. What it indicates is that Roman noble women suffered frequently from amenorrhoea without any apparent serious consequences, or rather that they were alarmed each time that their periods were late, which was not reflected in earlier medical works. It was doubtless for these women, and at their suggestion, that the doctors identified two new female disorders: atony and paralysis of the uterus, the principal symptom of which was aversion to sexual intercourse. Neither of these disorders was mentioned in the *Hippocratic Collection* or in Galen's works, although the *Hippocratic Collection* did note that Greek women rejected their husbands' advances in certain circumstances, generally when they were suffering from vaginal discharge. But Soranus considered that these disorders of the uterus were linked with miscarriages or repeated abortions. Women who could not retain male sperm were also thought to be suffering from one of these conditions. Miscarriages and also too frequent pregnancies, a particular problem among Roman noble women who did not breast-feed, were considered harmful to the mother's health, and therefore also to any baby she might wish to have.

It was therefore essential to prepare for the conception of a child. As we have seen, the prospective father must abstain from sexual relations and from all excesses in order to produce thick and abundant sperm. The doctors were quite convinced that frequent sexual activity was harmful to health and to the quality of the sperm produced. The same applied to women: if a woman did not lead an ordered life and observe moderation in her sexual behaviour she was to blame if she was sterile. If a man wanted to produce a healthy child he was called upon to look after his wife: 'Women who are trying to have children must be allowed a gap between successive pregnancies for those who continually become pregnant damage their constitution and spoil their figure and they produce children who take after them.'[73] It mattered little to the husbands whether their wives had wanted to have sexual intercourse or not. Aristotle's theory that women conceived without reaching orgasm was developed by Soranus in writing clearly not aimed at women: 'For even if some women who were forced to have intercourse have conceived, one may say with reference to them that in any event the emotion of sexual

---

[72] Ibid., VII, 17.
[73] *LI*, 7, Athenaeus.

appetite existed in them too, but was obscured by mental resolve.'[74]
Pleasure on the part of the woman was not one of the conditions Aristotle
considered necessary for procreation. Soranus went further and ruled out
the need for conscious desire. But he made it clear that a man should
never make a woman drink before getting her pregnant because a child
conceived while the mother was in a drunken haze would receive from
the mother's blood a troubled *pneuma*.[75]

And yet elsewhere Soranus states that unhappiness and fear are causes
of sterility in women: 'The passions of the soul affect the body and can
make it rebel against its natural function. If the body feels no sexual desire
it seems to suffer just as the spirit does, and although it may passively
accept what is being done to it, it will submit to coitus without the
consent of the spirit.'[76]

The gynaecological writings of Soranus and Rufus of Ephesus were
manuals on fertilization written for husbands. The tradition of female
experience collected and passed on by women, which had been handed
over to the Greek doctors and integrated into their theories, had become a
tool to help men retain control over their family life and even to help
them establish an ascetic way of life for themselves whereby they could
fulfil their duty and produce an heir, but could, in their private life,
withhold their vital spirit for contact with the divine.

The aim was to achieve one single act of intercourse which could be
relied on to be fertile so that the woman became pregnant. This required
concentrated male sperm, and in cases where intercourse had not resulted
in pregnancy doctors from Aristotle on considered it necessary to analyse
the man's sperm.[77] If the sperm sank to the bottom of a receptacle filled
with water it was of good quality and fertile. All these preparations for
conception did not indicate any anxiety about sterility; they were
considered normal within the average Roman marriage. Soranus makes
this clear. In his book *On Hygiene* he covers sexual relations from the
man's point of view and from the woman's. In his *Gynaecology* he
specifies that he will only be dealing with sexual relations as far as they
concern women, in other words intercourse with the aim of producing a
child.[78] Once the preparatory measures had been taken and the best
conditions for fertile intercourse chosen, success would be indicated by
the suppression of periods. But sometimes earlier confirmation was
sought, either so that the pregnancy could be brought to an end or so that

---

[74] *Gyn.*, I, 37, tr. Temkin.

[75] Ibid., I, 38 and 39.

[76] Soranus, *Gynaecia*, 64, in Caelius Aurelianus, '*Gynaecia*'. *Fragments of a Latin version
of Soranus 'Gynaecia' from a thirteenth century manuscript*, Ed. Miriam F. Drabkin, 1951.

[77] *Gen. An.*, 746 *b*.

[78] *Gyn.*, I, 40.

it could be protected. Women claimed that during the very act which resulted in conception they could feel the uterus pulling in the man's sperm. Galen held that this could be confirmed by male experience: 'Often men feel that their penis is being drawn into the womb as if by a cupping-glass.'[79]

Soranus held incorrectly that the cervix was dilated during pregnancy.[80] But Galen[81] correctly stated that the cervix was closed, supple[82] and not painful, in contrast to that of a woman who was feverish as a result of a genital inflammation when the cervix was closed but also hard and painful.[83] It was not the woman herself but a midwife who would carry out these examinations and confirm the pregnancy which she would then supervise. Spontaneous abortion had to be avoided. Greek women had noted the link between violent movements and miscarriage. The *Hippocratic Collection* advised women not to lift heavy weights, to avoid receiving a blow, not to jump or to expose themselves to shocks, sudden cries or passions.[84] Jumping was in fact one of the ways of provoking an abortion: Hippocrates used this method to terminate the pregnancy of a slave whom one of his friends had hired to entertain at banquets. The girl had become pregnant and was afraid she would not be able to serve her mistress properly.[85] Soranus mentions this case[86] as does Antyllus,[87] so it was well known throughout the ancient world from the fifth century BC to the fifth century AD. The text on the care of pregnant women which Oribasius quotes, which may be by Rufus rather than by Galen as the manuscript indicates, recommends that women should avoid shouting, becoming angry, tired, upset or frightened, and advises them not to jump, lift heavy weights or bend down. But in fact the young women of the noble classes for whom these works were written had little occasion to make these violent movements. The type of woman described by Athenaeus[88] was not the Roman aristocrat: he advised her, even when she was not pregnant, to spin wool and do a certain amount of housework – supervising the baker and even kneading the dough, making beds and keeping an eye on the whole household. Simply worrying about things, which Hippocrates referred to as 'the soul taking a little exercise', would not keep her in good health: what she needed was physical exercise or

[79] *LI*, 6.
[80] *Med. Coll.*, XXIV, 31.
[81] *Nat. Fac.*, III, 3.
[82] And *Gyn.*, 43.
[83] *Med. Coll.*, XXII, 3, Galen.
[84] *Dis. Wom.*, 25.
[85] *Nat. Ch.*, XIII.
[86] *Gyn.*, I, 60.
[87] *Med. Coll.*, VI, 31.
[88] *LI*, 5.

activity designed to make her fit when she went into labour.[89] He recommended spinning wool, and going for walks, but she should not take baths during the first stage of pregnancy, and she should take moderate exercise to avoid putting on too much weight which could cause the plethora. This text advised women not to have intercourse too often while pregnant. Doctors still had the idea that intercourse brought on menstrual periods, which went completely against all female experience as described for example in the *Hippocratic Collection*. Indeed the bleeding, referred to as menstruation, which indicated that a pregnancy was at risk, was attributed to sexual intercourse. Yet the same text stated that intercourse from time to time did not endanger a pregnancy or the foetus, provided that it did not occur too often. Soranus, on the other hand, expressly forbade sexual activity.[90] Galen advised against sex while a woman was breast-feeding her child, though it must be said that this advice came in a chapter on wetnurses, women who would lose their livelihood if their milk dried up because they became pregnant.[91] Needless to say the advice was not addressed to the wetnurse herself, but to her masters whose child would have to be found a different nurse in such circumstances. Nevertheless, the nine months of abstinence which Soranus called on the mother to observe must have led to a very unequal sexual relationship if the abstinence was not observed by both spouses.

A woman was supposed to remain very calm and sensible throughout her pregnancy. If she did not, she was told she risked not simply miscarriage, but even producing a deformed or retarded child.[92]

Nowhere in the *Hippocratic Collection* is there a reference to any unpleasant effects caused by pregnancy. The pregnant woman could have intercourse, except perhaps during the eighth month which was considered to be a dangerous period,[93] but she was positively encouraged to have intercourse during the ninth month so as to make it easier for the baby to pass through the birth canal. A few precautions should be taken, but that was all. The only peculiarity ascribed to pregnant women was cravings.[94] Aristotle, who said that women felt exhausted during their periods,[95] wrote that 'most women felt unwell during pregnancy'[96]. 'There are, however, a few women who feel better (than usual) when they are pregnant.' Rufus, Soranus, Galen and Athenaeus all stressed nausea, vomiting and abdominal pain, but noted that women of the lower classes,

[89] Ibid., 6.
[90] *Gyn.*, I, 46 and 56.
[91] *LI*, 14.
[92] *Gyn.*, I, 47.
[93] *LI*, 6.
[94] *Dis. Wom.*, 3.
[95] *HA*, 582 *b*.
[96] *Gen. An.*, IV, 6.

who worked, seemed not to suffer from these ailments, just as they did not seem to have difficult deliveries, 'because they do not adopt a gentler lifestyle since they can not do so while fulfilling their duties, neither do they eat too much as it is all they can do to find enough to eat.'[97]

According to Galen,[98] nausea combined with an absence of periods was a sign of pregnancy, but in chapter VI of Oribasius' *Libri Incerti* (from Galen or Rufus) it was when a woman felt nausea at the very moment of conception that she could be sure she was pregnant. After the second month, nausea, abdominal pains and vomiting were very frequent and called for a special diet. Nausea and vomiting became more or less a normal feature of pregnancy[99] in aristocratic circles under the Roman Empire (among the Greeks as well as among the Romans).

As rich women seemed to suffer more during childbirth than poor women who worked for their living, the doctors compared their way of life and advised rich women to take exercise which would be the equivalent of the work carried out by poor women. The main problem was running out of breath when it came to pushing out the baby because a woman needs to pant at the end of her labour.[100] Aristotle added that 'giving birth is even more difficult if, during the labour, women lose control of their breathing when they need their breath to push'. They needed to hold their breath when it came to pushing the baby out.[101] This was the basis for the advice on how to prepare for childbirth. Supervision of pregnancy in the Roman Empire had the same final aim as in the Greek world: to avoid miscarriage and to produce a healthy baby. But there were other concerns, more closely related to the woman. We can not of course say that a Roman woman did not take an interest in the child she was carrying, but she was concerned about her own body in a way that it does not seem Greek women were, as far as we can tell from the *Hippocratic Collection*. There was general agreement about the damage done to the mother's body by numerous pregnancies. But whereas Greek women simply noted the effects of pregnancy, Roman women refused to accept them. Just as they had not been allowed to eat excessively during adolescence, they were advised by their doctors not to eat for two when they were pregnant.[102] They were told to exercise their muscles gently, but sufficiently to ensure that their abdominal muscles would work during the expulsion of the child, even though two helpers would press the mother's abdomen to help in the expulsion. They tied down their

---

[97] *LI*, 6, Galen or Rufus.
[98] *Med. Coll.*, XXII, 3, *Commentary on the Aphorisms*.
[99] *Gyn.*, I, 48.
[100] *Dis. Wom.*, 34.
[101] *HA*, VII, 9.
[102] *Gyn.*, I, 49; Galen, *Uses of the Body*, XI, 11.

breasts, loosening the bands a little towards the end of the pregnancy.[103]
Soranus recommended that they support their swelling abdomen with
another band. They refused to breast-feed their babies and Soranus
prescribed medicaments to dry up their milk.[104] Above all, they wanted
to avoid becoming fat. It was not simply the wish to avoid the medical
condition of plethora that made them wish to remain slim and beautiful.
Gaining excess weight and ruining her figure were expressly stated as the
enemy of the pregnant woman. When Soranus recommended that women
remain continent he was replying to an objection: 'Among women we see
that those who, on account of regulations and service to the gods, have
renounced intercourse, and those who have been kept virgins as ordained
by law are less susceptible to disease. If, on the other hand, they have
menstrual difficulties and become fat and ill-proportioned this comes
about because of idleness and inactivity of their bodies.'[105]

The Roman women described by Soranus and later by Galen agreed
reluctantly to have intercourse and felt sick during their pregnancies.
Some refused to admit that they were going to be mothers right up to the
birth of their children, and Soranus offered advice to midwives who had
to deliver women who would not cooperate.[106] Nevertheless, they were
made to have at least one child. But in a society where it was so easy for
couples to separate, as it only needed the wish of one of the partners who
did not even have to give a reason, why insist that a girl who was too
young should have a baby? Marriages were arranged, with the verbal
consent of the girl, to ensure inheritance and to create alliances between
families. A child had to be produced by such a marriage. Throughout the
period spanned by the Roman Empire the legal and particularly patrimonial
ties between a mother, her family and her children, which did not exist in
ancient Roman law, continued to increase.[107] A child was the sign of a
union between families, even if his parents' marriage was dissolved by
divorce or repudiation. The child was necessary, but once he was born,
his mother was free.

She was free, above all, to terminate any future pregnancy. Women
wanted abortions[108] and would ask their doctor or midwife for the
recipes which Greek women passed to one another. According to
Soranus, there were only two reasons for a doctor to refuse to help a
woman abort: when the child was the product of adultery and when the
woman's only reason for wanting an abortion was to preserve her

---

[103] *Gyn.*, I, 49.
[104] Ibid., II, 8.
[105] Ibid., I, 32, tr. Temkin.
[106] Ibid., IV, 2.
[107] On the legal ties between a mother and her children, see R. Villers, *Rome et le droit privé*, 1977, p. 476.
[108] *Gyn.*, I, 65.

beauty.[109] The one case in which abortion was considered essential on medical grounds was when the woman was so young that her uterus was too small. In cases that fell between these extremes, Soranus gave recipes for abortifacients, but he advised against using the ancient and traditional methods.[110] A number of these recipes were reproduced by Oribasius, both in his *Medical Collection* and in the résumé he made of this work, which was a sort of manual intended for fathers of families, known as the *Euporista*.[111] Soranus advocated contraception as preferable to abortion, and the chief method he recommended was periodic abstinence.

It is astonishing that throughout the whole of antiquity no one realized that an error had been made in relation to women's fertile period. To suggest, as Soranus did, that one single act of intercourse just after the menstrual period could ensure conception would have required ovulation very close to the menstrual period and very vigorous spermatazoa. But Soranus clearly stated that if a woman wanted to avoid pregnancy she must avoid intercourse in the days immediately following her period. If the safe-period method had been used as much then as it has been in the twentieth century then the Romans would have discovered more accurately the timing of a woman's fertile period.

The other method of contraception used was withdrawal – by the woman. She was told by the doctor that when she guessed that the man was about to ejaculate she must hold her breath and 'draw herelf away a little, so that the seed may not be hurled too deep into the cavity of the uterus'.[112] Then after that she should squat down, sneeze and wash out her vagina. Moreover, before intercourse she should place on the cervix pessaries and plasters which acted as a diaphragm.[113]

All of these factors – male asceticism, arranged marriage with the aim of producing between one and three legitimate children as the law required, error as to the fertile period in the menstrual cycle, contraception and the opportunity for a man to avoid touching his wife and yet have sexual relations without fear of legal risk – combined to limit the number of births among the Roman aristocracy. Abortion completes this list. But when Soranus reveals that prolapse had become rare in this society,[114] this shows us that as well as fewer births there were also fewer pregnancies. This was still the case at the end of the fourth century, for Oribasius reproduces a text[115] which shows that 'sometimes the uterus prolapses'.

[109] Ibid., I, 60.
[110] Fontanille, *Avortement et contraception*, includes a very fine study of all these recipes.
[111] Oribasius, *Euporista*, CMG, VI, 3, 1931, and in the Daremberg edition, vol. VI by A. Molinier, with a Latin translation.
[112] *Gyn.*, tr. Temkin.
[113] Ibid., I, 61.
[114] Ibid., IV, 35.
[115] *Med. Coll.*, XXII, 3.

Frequent abortions would have killed women as much as it reduced the number of births. But all the evidence points not to a high mortality rate among women but to a reduction in fertility.

By using abortion, by refusing to have intercourse, in other words by negative means, Roman girls who had been married by the age of fourteen and sometimes much earlier, once they were mothers, regained control over their own bodies. Whereas up until then their bodies had been prepared and groomed to serve their fathers' political manoeuvrings and their husbands' need for heirs, now they could concentrate on keeping their bodies slim and attractive. As for the children brought into the world by these women, it was recognized throughout the Mediterranean that their mothers cared very little for them.[116]

---

[116] *Gyn.*, II, 44.

3

The Bodies of Children

His parents had entered into marriage in order to produce him. His mother's pregnancy had been supervised so as to ensure his survival: she had been denied exercise, food and sex for his sake. He was wanted, expected, indeed he was essential to the continuance not only of the family but also of its inheritance. Whether he was a first, second or third child, he was wanted and necessary, all the more so if his older siblings had died young. The estate denied unmarried men and married men without children was shared between the other men of the family in proportion to the number of their children. The extent to which spouses could bestow gifts on one another – and men married women from their own class – also increased in proportion to the number of their children. It was necessary to have at least one child who survived, in the case of a girl to the age of twelve, in the case of a boy to the age of fourteen. Two children who had died before the age of three were sufficient proof of good intentions as far as the state and the law were concerned. Three babies who had died after nine days showed that the parents had tried to meet the law's requirements and it was considered that fate had prevented them from fulfilling the conditions which would entitle them to receive their inheritance. According to Rufus, girls who were too young gave birth to weak children or indeed were unable to carry babies to term. All the medical and social efforts to prevent miscarriage and perinatal mortality need to be examined in the light of these laws of succession.

It was not simply a question of a woman choosing to become a mother or wanting to have a baby. Nor did the fact that a couple chose to have intercourse during the woman's fertile phase mean that they would refrain from sexual activity at other times because they had learned to control the desires of the body, but rather it reflected the very real necessity to procreate so as to fulfil the rigorous conditions relating to the laws of succession.

This is why women were careful to look out for any sign of impending miscarriage – bleeding during pregnancy, known as periods,[1] a shrinking

---

[1] *Gyn.*, I, 23.

of the breasts, a cold feeling in the thighs, a heavy feeling in the small of the back.[2]

Furthermore, the prospective father would take steps to determine the sex of the child. From the time of the *Hippocratic Collection* on, it was believed that the uterus consisted of two cavities, just as women were thought to have two testicles like men. Naturally a male child was produced by the better side, the right,[3] so he would be the result of sperm from the father's right testicle becoming embedded in the right side of the womb.[4] But if the male sperm was not thick enough, female sperm might win, so the doctors advised men who wanted to produce a son to bind their left testicle so that only the right testicle would produce sperm[5] and vice versa if they wanted a daughter. During the course of the pregnancy there would be indications of the sex of the foetus, but by that stage nothing could be done to alter the sex.

When they gave birth to girls the women of antiquity said that they had had a bad pregnancy, and when they had produced boys they said they had had a good pregnancy. Soranus pointed out that one could not generalize in this way, but the women themselves were sure that they had felt sicker and had had more unsightly marks of pregnancy[6] when they were carrying girls, and also that their delivery had been more painful.[7]

Thanks to the detailed descriptions given by Soranus[8] and Galen[9], and before them the *Hippocratic Collection*, we can reconstruct the kind of delivery women would have experienced at the time. Throughout labour the woman would remain lying down, and she would be surrounded by other women. Soranus recommended that those present should speak to the woman gently and quietly so as to calm her fears. All the women present must keep to themselves any remarks which might increase her fears and her discomfort. Use was no longer made of the violent procedure known as succussion, which consisted of tying the woman to her bed, tilted until it was vertical, and then dropping her onto a bundle of sticks designed to break her fall. This procedure had been used to speed up a lengthy delivery.[10] The woman in labour would use what were described as frequent breaths, probably a series of short breaths similar to

---

[2] Ibid., I, 46 and 60; *Med. Coll.*, XXII, 2, Rufus, and *LI*, 6, Galen or Rufus.

[3] *Med. Coll.*, XXII, 3, Galen.

[4] The right-left opposition, and the association of masculinity with the right side, is already found in Parmenides: Abel Rey, *La science dans l'Antiquité*, II: *La jeunesse de la science grecque*, 1933, p. 493.

[5] *Superf.*, 31.

[6] *Gyn.*, I, 45, Hippocrates; *Med. Coll.*, XXII, 3, Galen; *Bar.*, 216.

[7] *Med. Coll.*, XXII, 3, Galen.

[8] *Gyn.*, II, 5, 5, 6.

[9] *LI*, 12.

[10] *Dis. Wom.*, 68.

the panting used nowadays to prevent the diaphragm pressing on an extremely sensitive uterus. The woman would sit for the last stage of the birth, and Soranus advised her to 'breathe deeply without crying out, rather than moaning and holding her breath'.[11] When the midwife, who had been assessing the dilation of the cervix, judged that the time had come to push out the baby, the woman would be made to sit on a special gynaecological seat, or, if this was not possible, on the knees of a very strong woman. Three helpers would press her abdomen, and the midwife would kneel, taking care not to gaze too fixedly at the woman's genitals so as not to embarrass her and make her retract the baby with a muscular contraction. She would assist dilation by applying warm oil, and when the cervix was fully dilated she would pull the baby after each contraction of the uterus, so as not to damage the uterus. She would receive the baby into her hands and lay him on the floor. Soranus specified that a midwife's hands should be soft, with short nails, and that the midwife should not be in the habit of working wool (which would make her hands rough) and that she should lay a soft cloth over her hands so that the child did not slip. The lighting should be soft[12] so as not to hurt the baby's eyes. He said that the light in the baby's room should also be shaded. No one should shout near the newborn child, indeed everyone should be silent in his presence.

So as not to add to the shock of the birth itself, the cord would not be cut immediately. Soranus described in detail how much of a shock birth was to the newborn. While the child was still attached to his mother, before the placenta had been delivered, it must be remembered when regulating the temperature of the room and the bathwater that the baby had just emerged from a soft, warm and protected environment.[13] Soranus has been hailed as a great gynaecologist because of the effort he made to understand the experience of childbirth, revealed by this care of mother and baby, even though the motives, at least of the father who hired the doctor and midwife, were entirely interested. But the nature of the events that followed the birth was rather different. While the newborn baby was allowed to remain attached to his mother, and while she remained seated in the position in which she had delivered, waiting for her baby, the midwife would examine the child to see if he was worth raising.

She would make signs to indicate whether the child was a boy or a girl; then she would carry out her examination, taking into account the mother's health during the pregnancy and the length of the pregnancy. The child's first cry was important: it gave cause for concern if the child

[11] *Gyn.*, II, 6.
[12] Ibid., II, 31.
[13] Ibid., II, 12.

gave a feeble cry or if he did not cry for some time. Then the midwife would see whether the baby was physically perfect. She would check his limbs and orifices. Aristotle[14] had noted that a premature baby, born at seven months, whose ears and nostrils had not yet opened, rarely survived, but that if he did survive the orifices opened in due course. Soranus instructed midwives to check the natural orifices, the joints, the size and shape of the child, and the feel of his skin. Everything was examined. Only after this examination would the midwife cut the umbilical cord four finger breadths from the baby. Why was the examination carried out before the cord was cut? Galen[15] described the same sequence of events and made clear the link between the condition of the baby and the cutting of the cord: 'The umbilical cord shall be cut at a distance of four fingers from the stomach of the newborn, that is of course if he is perfect in all respects . . .'

What then happened to the child who was not perfect? We are not told. What is clear is that the medical profession had full responsibility for making the decision. But the midwife could not kill the child simply by failing to cut the cord. The lungs would already be functioning and spontaneous clotting in the cord would generally enable the child to survive as a separate entity. The delivery of the placenta would take place normally. Failure to cut the cord would not necessarily result in the death of the child by producing hypoxia or anoxia and thus brain damage, so it could only be a symbolic gesture. Perhaps it is to a text by Ammianus Marcellinus that we must turn to discover what the medical writers do not tell us. The Emperor Julian's wife, Helena, had been the victim of the machinations of her sister-in-law, the Empress Eusebia. Constantius II, who had made Julian a Caesar and then a few days later married him to Helena,[16] had wanted to ensure that Julian would have no heir. But Helena had given birth in Gaul where she had followed Julian. Ammianus writes:

> When she had borne a baby boy, she lost it through this machination: a midwife had been bribed with a sum of money, and as soon as the child was born cut the umbilical cord more than was right, and so killed it; such great pains and so much thought were taken that this most valiant man might have no heir.[17]

This then was considered to be a sure way of killing a newborn child: Soranus stressed that even when the cord was cut at a distance of four

---

[14] *LI*, 5.
[15] Ibid., 12.
[16] Amm. Marc., XV, 8, 18.
[17] Ibid., XVI, 10, 19, tr. Rolfe.

fingers from the baby, a tight knot must be tied to prevent haemorrhaging. This was probably the method used to dispose of handicapped children at birth. Helena's midwife was thus able to cast doubt on the child's condition at birth and invoke her right to prevent malformed children from surviving. The medical texts make it clear that the decision whether or not a child should be allowed to live was purely a medical one.

The father's decision to raise the child,[18] that is to take him in his arms and consider him his own, would come after the cord had been cut. The medical writers do not refer to this. The midwife would have signalled the child's sex as soon as it had been delivered, and a girl would not be raised up by her father. But a son who was taken into his father's arms in this way would be safe from the threat of abandonment thereafter.[19]

There were thus two levels at which decisions about the child were made: the medical decision concerning his normality as defined by society, and the father's decision on whether he should be accepted into the family or abandoned and cast out of the house. This practice was only condemned by the law in AD 374,[20] probably under Christian influence, and when one compares the number of girls and boys who received public assistance under Trajan, it appears as if girls must have been exposed fairly frequently.[21]

The mother had no say in the matter. In any case the texts say no more about her after the birth, except to give recipes for concoctions which would dry up her milk. Attention passed to the child and his nurse. There was no advice on care of the breasts for the mother who breast-fed her baby, and it was the fear of ruining the shape of their breasts which made

---

[18] Nicole Belmont, Levana ou comment 'élever' les enfants, 1973, pp. 77–89, uses the ancient texts collected by G. J. Witkowski, *Histoire des accouchements chez tous les peuples*, 1887 (Ovid, Varro, Tertullian, Suetonius, Augustine), but no medical writers, which is understandable since one only expects to find 'medicine' in doctors' writings. Where the literature says *auspicaretur rectus esse*, Belmont thinks that there is a notion of verticality, the father lifting the child from a horizontal position to a vertical one in a symbolic gesture. She prefers to translate *rectus* as *droit* (upright) and thinks that it is extrapolation to translate 'to see if he is deformed' (or infirm), p. 87. Witkowski gives the correct order of events for the child was 'raised up' after he had been examined to see whether or not he was normal. Raising up had nothing to do with the child's condition.

[19] On the exposure of children, see *Recueils de la Société Jean-Bodin*, XXXV; *L'enfant*, part 1, 1975: Louis R. F. Germain, L'exposition des enfants nouveau-nés dans la Grèce ancienne, aspects sociologiques, pp. 211–46, argues that children were not exposed except for reasons of eugenics (*contra*: Vatin, *Recherches sur le mariage*, chapter V and bibliography on the infanticide of girls); for Rome, see Maxime Lemossé, L'enfant sans famille en droit romain, p. 259.

[20] *CJ*, 8, 51, 2 and 9, 16, 7.

[21] J. Carcopino, La table de Velleia et son importance historique, 1921, p. 299, and *Daily Life in Ancient Rome*, tr. E. O. Lorimer, 1941 and 1956; p. 90 in 1978 Penguin reprint.

Roman women unwilling to feed their children. No one cared what happened to the wetnurse.

The principal concern of the medical writers when they came to discuss the cutting of the cord was not the elimination of handicapped babies but the Roman taboo against using any metal object for the purpose. Soranus and Galen both insisted that midwives should stop using pieces of broken glass, reeds or crusts of bread and should instead use a knife. To these Greek doctors this was an ancient Roman custom which had to be abandoned. The doctors then recommended that the child be rubbed gently with fine salt. The custom was to use dried myrtle leaves and powdered oak bark, which Soranus and Galen considered astringent and of no value. They condemned the practice observed by foreigners and some Greeks of washing the baby in cold water.[22] Soranus claimed that some perfectly viable babies had been killed by a cold bath. He advocated using tepid water. The navel would be bandaged so that it would be an attractive little hollow, and the bandages used must not have any selvage or seams which might hurt the baby's skin. They must be neither too narrow nor too broad in case they cut the skin as they creased. Doctors differed in the advice they gave, but all advocated swaddling the baby. Antigenes recommended the method used by Thessalian women: they would place the baby on a mattress of straw or hay in a hollowed out log, cover him with cloths and bands and tie him down with laces passed through notches in the log.[23] Soranus described this method as cruel. The Thracians and Macedonians tied babies to a board, which flattened the back of their head, a feature which the Romans considered hideous and, as we have seen, the sign of a poor constitution. Instead Soranus recommended that a good pillow be placed in a cradle or a trough and that the baby be wrapped and placed on the pillow. His fists would be open, with the fingers straightened and bandaged 'so that they would not be twisted as the child moved his hands in an unco-cordinated manner'. The arms would then be bandaged, with particularly tight ties at the wrists and elbows, then the legs from the toes up, with extra pressure on the insteps and ankles, then the trunk. Girls would have their chests bandaged especially tightly but their hips would be bound more loosely. The arms would then be stretched along the body and the child would be bandaged again from head to foot, with a cloth between his bottom and the bandage. The head would be bandaged separately. The child would

---

[22] *Gyn.*, II, 12, and *Med. Coll.*, X, 7, Agathinus.

[23] This is shown in a Gallic sculpture in the museum at Beaune, a photograph of which is to be found in H.-P. Eydoux, *La France antique*, 1962, fig. 200. Other photographs in R. Etienne, La conscience médicale antique et la vie des enfants, 1973, 'Enfants et sociétes', pp. 15–46.

thus be prevented from moving for two months or more[24] to ensure that he had a straight, well formed body, according to Soranus and Galen, though the latter gave fewer details about the method of bandaging.

Bandaging a child in this way was quite a lengthy procedure which would surely not have been adopted by those who, following the advice of Mnesitheus of Athens, bathed the child three times a day, or even twice a day on Galen's advice. Soranus, having given instructions for this lengthy bandaging, ordered that a child should only be bathed once a day. Moreover, when the baby was in the bath his bladder would be pressed to make him urinate so that his bandages would become less wet later on, thus avoiding the need to give him a second bath. Nurses resisted this advice on bandaging, and covered the baby's torso with wool, leaving legs and bottom naked.[25] They bathed the baby three times a day. The doctors accused them of refusing to bandage babies through laziness and of bathing them in order to make them sleep.[26] According to the doctors, these women thought that if they made sure they were disturbed as seldom as possible by the baby in their care they would be satisfying their master. The physicians were appalled by these baths, which were in their view too hot and too frequent, and which softened a body which was already soft and moistened a body which was already wet. This was nothing short of medical heresy. Here then was this baby, tightly wrapped in his bandages, soaked in urine and excrement, his skin irritated by the wool rubbing against it (the physicians having forbidden the use of linen which shrank when wet). So for a few days, while his sores healed, he would be allowed the freedom of wearing just a vest.[27]

One might think that the Roman baby at least had one moment of freedom once a day, at bathtime. But nothing of the sort. The water was indeed tepid, and there was equipment at hand to warm it up if need be. But as soon as he was taken out of the bath the baby would be held by the ankles, head downwards, so as to separate his verterbrae.[28] Then he would be massaged and moulded on his nurse's lap, following the advice given by Soranus, Rufus and Galen. Soranus gave the most explicit instructions concerning this moulding that the nurse should carry out. She must begin by loosening the joints, making the baby's feet touch his bottom, bringing his left foot over to touch his right hand and vice versa, moving the kneecap around – a whole sequence of gymnastic manoeuvres which tradition has kept alive right down to our own day. But she went further, to satisfy the aesthetic fashion of the time, or perhaps rather to

[24] *Gyn.*, II, 42.
[25] Ibid., II, 15.
[26] *Med. Coll.*, X, 7, Agathinus, first century BC.
[27] *Gyn.*, II, 42.
[28] Ibid., II, 32; *LI*, 20, Rufus.

satisfy the desire to dictate, while his body remained pliable, the physique the child would have in later life. The aim was to flatten the concave areas of the knees, mould the ankles and push in the area around the buttocks. Finally she would turn her attention to the points which called for most care – the head, the nose and the penis. As we have seen, the head should be round. Long heads would be reshaped, indeed all babies' heads would be reshaped to make them conform to the desired shape. The nose would be corrected. The nurse would lift up flat noses, and press down aquiline noses, bringing out the nostrils. And as we know that the men of ancient times were very particular about the shape of their penis, which would be seen by a great many people every day at the baths or at the gymnasium, the nurse would gently stretch the end of the foreskin every day, and would sometimes tie the end with a little piece of wool so that it always covered the glans properly. The scrotum would also be massaged, having first been protected with a flock of wool. To make sure that the child would not be left-handed the right hand would be unbandaged first, especially when the bandages were finally removed little by little. For the same reason, the nurse always had to begin feeding a baby with the right breast so as to keep the baby's left arm still and leave his right arm free. But for the first two months the baby, wrapped in his bandages, could never touch the breast that was feeding him. Children must have had very unpleasant memories of bathtime and the manipulation which followed:

> When children are older (about a year old?) and can be made to obey by the use of blows, threats, reprimands and admonishments, there are two moments of the day when it is most appropriate to give them a bath and massage. The first and best time is when they awake in the morning and after playing for a while ask to be fed. This is the best time to tackle them and drum into them habits which will make their bodies healthy and attractive and their characters docile and obedient, by telling them that they will be given no food unless they have their massage and their bath without making a fuss.[29]

So the nurse influenced and shaped the child's body. The ethic was, quite openly, one of obedience and docility. The nurse had a decisive role in a child's upbringing until he reached school age, at six or seven.[30] In Rome, putting a child into the care of a nurse was in no respect a disguised form of infanticide. On the contrary. The physicians of the *Hippocratic Collection* discussed women, mothers and sterility. The selection of Galen's writings which Oribasius called 'On the manner of

[29] *LI*, 17, Galen.
[30] Ibid., 21.

bringing up children'[31] was intended for mothers. Oribasius' fourteenth chapter, taken from Galen, refers to the woman who feeds a child, without saying whether she is his mother or a nurse, and says simply that another nurse should be sought 'if the woman breast-feeding the child should conceive': this suggests that it might be the mother herself who is pregnant. Chapter 15, taken from Mnesitheus of Cyzicus, advises mothers to employ Thracian or Egyptian nurses. Galen (chapter 16) says that the milk, doubtless the mother's, should be examined before another nurse (or several nurses, if the family is rich) is sent for. And in chapter 17, based on Galen, it is a nurse who is referred to as bringing up the child. Mnesitheus of Athens (chapter 19) also refers to the care of a nurse. Rufus' long passage (chapter 20) does not once mention the person who will be carrying out the instructions he gives for the care of the child. The custom, so well described by Soranus, of entrusting the Roman child to a nurse was still flourishing at the end of the fourth century, and Soranus' chapters on choosing a nurse were translated into Latin and included in the summary of his work on gynaecology. But the practice of putting a child in the care of a nurse did not originate in medical theory. It was a social custom, and what the physicians were called upon to do was show that the custom was not harmful to the child. Soranus likened it to gardening. The mother was the seedbed; putting a child out to a wetnurse was like planting out a seedling. The physicians did, however, have some reservations. Damastes and Apollonius said that nature had intended a baby to be fed with his mother's milk.[32] Mnesitheus of Cyzicus[33], who recommended Thracian nurses, said that the best nurses were 'mothers themselves, or if this is not possible, their close relatives or women who are physically very like them'. Soranus[34] considered it natural that a baby should be fed by his mother, but thought that it was better to let the mother recover her strength first since the tiredness which followed pregnancy and childbirth would affect the quality of her milk for the first twenty days. Needless to say, the fact that the nurse was herself a mother was mentioned nowhere.

Mother's milk, which, as we have seen, Soranus held to be harmful for twenty days, and which Mnesitheus considered harmful for forty days, was thought to be too rich in casein and too heavy for the baby to digest. Soranus recommended instead that for the first two days the baby should be given either nothing at all or some hydromel, and that after that he should be fed on goat's milk sweetened with honey rather than his mother's milk. If absolutely necessary, the child could be given his

[31] Ibid., 12.
[32] *Gyn.*, II, 17.
[33] *LI*, 15.
[34] *Gyn.*, II, 17.

mother's milk, but she should first feed an older child, who would take off the most indigestible part of the milk. After this initial period, Soranus said, mother's milk was the best and breast-feeding also strengthened a mother's love for her children. Oribasius does not report Soranus' detailed description of the good nurse, but copies a chapter by Mnesitheus which lays more emphasis on examination of the breast milk than on the appearance of the breasts.

The nurse should be solidly built, with breasts of average size – heavy breasts would stifle a baby – and the skin of the breasts should be soft and not wrinkled. The breasts themselves should be soft and free from lumps. The breasts and nipples should be examined and palpated, and then milk should be expressed from them and examined. The quantity produced should be checked and a glass of milk should be kept and examined and tasted the following day. This advice from Mnesitheus of Cyzicus and Soranus was intended for fathers. Even if the father did not carry out the examination himself, he should see that it was carried out and supervise the way in which it was done.

Soranus recommended that each child should have several nurses at a time so that if a nurse was ill or died the baby would not be affected so badly by the change. Galen confirmed this advice. The nurse would live in the family's house, in the child's small room. She was advised not to take the baby into her bed in case she suffocated him in her sleep.[35] The woman chosen would be one who could abstain from sexual relations.[36] The texts make it clear that the nurse had to be strong enough to breast-feed the baby, get up to him at night, and also do a servant's work during the day: tidying, drawing water, winnowing and grinding grain, kneading bread and making beds. Galen said that she should grind and sift the grain, and also weave. The aristocratic mother who was breast-feeding her child herself should exercise at the gymnasium, play ball games and go for walks and rides in a carriage as this would be equivalent to the house work carried out by poorer women. The doctors stated that nursing women should not support their breasts while they were working, so that the breasts might draw nourishment from the rest of the body. Mnesitheus was less demanding, but perhaps his advice to support the breasts with loosely tied strips of bandage was intended mainly for breast-feeding mothers.

The women of the popular classes refused to follow the advice of the physicians. They bathed newborn babies day and night, they refused to wrap them in bandages, they rocked them in their arms when they cried, and even put them to the breast to soothe them, which was heresy to the

---

[35] Ibid., II, 37.
[36] LI, 14, Galen; 15, Mnesitheus of Cyzicus; Gyn., II, 19.

doctors.[37] The physicians said babies should be fed according to a timetable. A baby should not be fed until he had completely digested the previous feed, particularly at night. He should be left to cry after his bath, for it would be harmful to feed him straight away. In any case, crying strengthened the respiratory organs and aided digestion. Only if the child cried for a long time after a feed should his nurse comfort him by taking him in her arms, talking to him and singing lullabies.

Here then was the noble child, often in the care of one or more women of the lower classes, who were employed both for their milk and their strength, and kept busy all day with housework in addition to feeding and bathing the baby. Their own child, who would have been weaned, would be fed elsewhere on cereal without any milk. When Soranus accused women of laziness if they gave six-week-old babies cereal instead of breast-feeding them, he was perhaps referring to those women who sought to hire themselves out as wetnurses. When people of ancient times tried to explain why there were more bow-legged people in Rome than in other towns, they laid the blame on the dampness of the ground and the immorality of mothers. Soranus blamed mothers who were ill prepared to care for their children. But perhaps the cause of rickets in children was rather the fact that mothers of the popular classes had to work so hard, sometimes as wetnurses, and also the lack of sunlight in the blocks of dwellings in which they lived.

Nevertheless women chosen as nurses had to show devotion and affection to the babies in their care. Soranus added that Greek nurses should be hired so that children would hear the finest of all languages from the earliest age. Thus a child would be consoled in Greek for the harsh treatment imposed on him by Greek doctors in the service of Roman families.

After two months in bandages, the child would have his bandages removed little by little. Drops of oil would be put in his eyes as the doctors were always anxious to protect them. His room would be softly lit and a veil would be placed over his head. At around six months the child would begin a mixed diet of breast milk and cereal. He would be given alternately a milk feed and a feed of cereal soaked in milk or hydromel, soup or eggs. At six months the doctors ordered that the child should be given sweet wine or wine sweetened with honey, or water, either mixed with wine or not, or else bread soaked in wine.[38] Rufus wrote that children should never drink water and that a government which imposed this by law should not be trusted. Galen, who disagreed with Soranus and Rufus, said that children should on no account be given wine when they were weaned, but that they should be given fresh water.

[37] *LI*, 20, Rufus.
[38] *Gyn.*, II, 45; *LI*, 20, Rufus.

Great care must be taken in choosing the water, which should not be stagnant or cloudy, but must be from only the purest springs. It seems clear that his advice was not taken, for Oribasius repeats all the texts which prescribe wine. The one thing which must be avoided, by young children as by women, was putting on too much weight. The child's appetite must be controlled, he must be distracted from eating too much and the nurse's diet must be controlled so that her milk was not too thick.

The child would be helped to sit up and then to walk, and his progress would be followed by the nurse and the doctor up to the age of eighteen months or two years, when he would gradually be weaned 'when he was old enough to understand blows and threats . . .' as Galen said. Athenaeus, two centuries earlier, exemplified a gentle approach to the upbringing of children, in opposition to all we know of the pedagogical harshness of antiquity. He wrote: 'Small children who have just been weaned should be allowed to play and do as they please.'[39] I shall quote the passage at length because it describes very clearly the harsh system of upbringing adopted in Rome.

> From the age of six or seven, boys and girls should be put in the care of gentle and humane teachers; for those who are attractive to children, who use persuasion and encouragement and praise their pupils often, achieve better results and make their charges more enthusiastic. Their method of teaching makes children happy and puts them at their ease, and children who are relaxed and happy learn much. By contrast, those who force their pupils to learn by means of severe reprimands make children servile and frightened, and make them hate the subject they are being taught. These teachers beat children to make them learn and expect them to remember what they have learned when they are being beaten, when they have lost all presence of mind.

Athenaeus also said that the amount of time devoted to study should be reasonable, and should leave children time to play. In summary, then, whereas Athenaeus saw the role of education between the ages of six and fourteen as being to develop children's tastes, Galen expected it to instil in them 'docility and obedience'.

As young people emerged from childhood, the method of their education changed,[40] and girls and boys were treated in different ways. As far as girls were concerned, the main fear was that they might not be married as soon as they were of marriageable age. Their sexuality was a

---

[39] *LI*, 21.
[40] Eyben, Antiquity's view of puberty, 1972, pp. 678–97, reproduces observations on the physical changes affecting men and women at puberty.

cause for anxiety. It was thought that badly brought up girls felt sexual desire before they had menstruated,[41] and it was also believed that sexual intercourse made menstruation easier.[42] Plethora in a virgin who did not take much exercise was thought to cause serious illnesses. So if a young girl was not married, she must at least be made to use up a lot of her energy and she must not drink wine. After the age of fourteen, girls became women and we must turn to what Oribasius called *A Regimen for Women*, which he borrowed from Galen and Athenaeus.[43]

The doctors were all agreed that the female body was by nature cold and moist. Only men possessed the qualities of warmth and dryness, which produced the most airy *pneuma*. Children were born 'dribbling, nose running, wet in all respects'.[44] Their whole upbringing, based on these medical notions, was aimed at controlling the reduction of this wetness, a process which nature kept up until death.[45]

A boy's lifestyle during puberty was very different from that of his sister. He and his family would watch for the first signs of his sexual maturity. The appearance of pubic hair and his first ejaculations were a cause for celebration for the whole household, particularly the father. For a girl the day of her marriage would be the time when she left behind her toys and all the trappings of childhood, with the mixture of emotions that this was bound to bring. For a boy, however, the day when he celebrated his manhood was given over entirely to enjoyment, as a day devoted solely to his body. Whether this family feast day took place at the actual onset of the individual's puberty or was postponed until the *Liberalia* on the next 17 March so that it would be part of the general celebration of that age group, the recognition of a boy's virility was a joyful occasion. When he came to take a wife, his father would have to give assurances as to his son's virility, a kind of certificate that he was not impotent.[46] At these first manifestations of sexual maturity the young man would be the object of renewed attentions.

A regimen would be drawn up to take the boy through the transitional period up until he had finished growing, at twenty-one, when the ancients agreed that his sperm, which he had been producing from the age of fourteen, became truly fertile.[47] He should exercise his body, but with

[41] *Gyn.*, I, 33.
[42] *LI*, 2, Rufus.
[43] Ibid., 4 and 5.
[44] Ibid., 20, Rufus.
[45] On the theory of the dry and the moist, and the hot and the cold, see Rey, *La science dans l'Antiquité*, II, p. 487 et seq.
[46] C. Lécrivain, s.v. Matrimonium, *Dictionnaire des Antiquités grecques et romaines*, ed. C. Daremberg and E. Saglio; physical examination of a boy before marriage, Ulp. 11, 28; Gaius, 1, 186; Quintilian, 4, 2, 5; *IJ*, 1, 32.
[47] *Med. Coll.*, XXII, 4, Athenaeus.

moderation, for excessive activity would stunt his growth.[48] At the baths, the young man should go directly to the cold bath – not too cold though, or again his growth would be impeded.[49] The young man would be able to experiment with his new-found sexuality before marriage. The doctors took little notice of the circumstances or nature of the young man's first experiences of intercourse. They simply enquired, when examining a young man, whether or not he was sexually active. When Galen found that a youth's body was too dry he would 'deduce that he had been indulging excessively in intercourse' and would prescribe humidification of the body to treat this. He would then advise exercise after coitus. Galen took it for granted that a young man would be sexually active, and held that day to day health care should take account of this. Athenaeus, on the other hand, writing before the Christian era, advised that young people's energies be diverted towards sport, 'so that, by tiring both body and mind, they would be able to repress their desires from the start, for nothing hinders the development of the mind and the body as much as premature and excessive sexual activity'. So there were two traditions regarding the upbringing of young people and it is not easy to see how they coexisted.

Athenaeus hoped that young people would be keen to continue their studies. It was in order to ensure that their education would not be interrupted by adolescent outbursts that he advocated a gentle approach to schooling and to preschool education: 'Small children who have just been weaned should be allowed to play and do as they please; by means of little tricks and games, one should teach them to exercise their minds and also to rest them.' Athenaeus did not advocate that adolescents should ignore their bodies and devote themselves to study, but rather that they should achieve a balance between the two. Sexual intercourse was not solely a physical activity because it tired the spirit as much as the body. What the physician in fact recommended was exercising the mind and the body of the adolescent separately.

As we shall see, Galen was in favour of men and women remaining virgins. As a doctor, however, he recognized the disorders which could result from abstinence in those who chose to practise it. And yet, while he recommended restraining babies in layers of bandages, and training children by means of blows and threats, he let the young man indulge freely in sexual activity, which he considered purely physical. Could it be that Athenaeus was referring to a different kind of coitus? Was it homosexual passion that he wanted young men to curb in order to leave their minds free to study? If this is the case, the purely physical nature of the sexual behaviour studied by Galen – heterosexual in all the examples

[48] Ibid., VI, 15.
[49] *LI*, 18, Galen.

he gives,[50] reveals Roman brutality towards women. This is why, once he was satisfied, Galen's young man would have a free and rested mind.[51]

Mastery of the body, then, was important from birth right up to death. The newborn baby who was seen or felt to be deformed did not count; as far as his father was concerned, it was as if he had not been born. In the ancient world, these children, even if they were viable, were rejected and either eliminated at birth by the midwife, or exposed, that is to say abandoned in conditions which were such that many died.

Those who were accepted because they were well formed were required to resist the cold from the first moments of their life, even though the physicians advised against this practice. I have tried to convey the sensory aspect of the upbringing which small children received, something not recorded in histories of education. Certainly for a man in ancient times the education of the senses continued throughout life, in a way it does not in our day when, from the age of six, unless the individual has a very marked taste for this kind of pastime, the time devoted to physical activities such as gymnastics, music, singing, and the visual and plastic arts is gradually reduced. Lifelong education of the senses was, however, more a feature of Greek than Roman society. But it is interesting to know a little about the pre-school upbringing of the child whom we see entering school and studying the arts, sciences, gymnastics and music.

Those around him looked after his health. He was given filtered, boiled water to drink.[52] His food was cooked for a long time. He was taught to clean his teeth even though it was believed that honey would preserve them. His errors of pronunciation were corrected, if necessary by minor surgical operations,[53] and any abnormality of his foreskin was put right because it had to be long enough and supple enough to cover the glans with comfort.[54] And yet this obsession with physical appearance led to sensory deprivation for the first two months of life, which cannot but have marked the children of the great Roman families. Besides this, there is the fact that the child was left in the care of women who were obliged to carry out other work between the child's feeds. Of course we are told that if a child went on crying for a long time he would be rocked in his nurse's arms and soothed with songs, but this kind of upbringing where the child was constantly subjected to extreme treatment, left to cry one minute and

[50] Ibid., 8.

[51] Ibid., 8

[52] *Med. Coll.*, V, 1, Galen.

[53] Ibid., XLV, 16.

[54] Ibid., L, 1, Galen. The adult's power over the child's body is one of the elements analysed in Maud Mannoni, *Education impossible*, 1973, which includes a study of the restrictive education system created by President Shreber's father.

spoiled the next, and exposed at a very young age to the brutality of corporal punishment, foreshadowed the severity of the treatment he would face at school.

It is not surprising that the Roman conquest and the Empire should have spelled the end of the methods which Athenaeus advocated in Asia Minor. And yet while he called for children to have a gentle upbringing and teachers who made reasonable demands on them, he also called on young people to learn to attenuate the violence of the sexual desires of adolescence by diverting their energies into physical exercise so that they would be better able to devote themselves to studying. For Athenaeus, the joy of learning was the greatest pleasure of old age, and stopped a man from becoming bitter with those around him.

By oppressing the child from birth, society hoped to avoid having to repress him later on. While the Greeks, or at least the physician Athenaeus, sought to make a young man able to control himself, the medical profession which served the Roman nobility used its knowledge to impose restraints on the child as soon as he was conceived, if not before. Happiness was not a factor to be considered. Happiness is always relative in any civilization, and whether illusory or not, can exist in conditions which are foreign to us. The bands which imprisoned the young child might be the one thing which, all his life, would bring him back to thought as the source of truth. They might represent both reality and truth for him, as they did for the philosophy to which his youth would be devoted or to which the experiences of his adult life would convert him.

4

On Virginity and Hysteria

'The body sick with desire.'
Soranus, *Gynaecology*, I, 30

In AD 135–6, when Valentinus moved to Rome from Alexandria where he had already developed what he considered to be a Christian theology, Soranus was either just at the end of his life or had just died. Galen had been born in Pergamum in AD 130. Marcion was expelled from Rome ten years later, in AD 144, seventeen years before Galen moved to the city. Valentinus' and Marcion's disciples had a reputation for indulging freely in sexual activity, even outside marriage, in observance of their faith.

That they indulged freely in sexual activity outside marriage does not distinguish them from other men (though not women) of ancient times whose sexual activity was only limited by the freedom of their partner – rape was forbidden by law – and by the rights which another man might have over a woman. The only thing which Roman or Greek pagans found scandalous was allowing women the same freedom, in other words permitting adultery and *stuprum*. Indeed one of the ways of remaining strictly within the law was to refuse to marry.[1]

That their sexual behaviour should have been seen as part of their Christian faith does, however, require explanation. They did acknowledge a woman's sexual freedom, and, what is more, they considered their search for God compatible with homosexuality and paedophilia, both practices which had been common for centuries throughout the eastern part of the Roman Empire in areas which reflected the Greek influence, and which, in various forms, had been adopted in Rome.[2] As this sexual polymorphism was a social phenomenon, the fact that it was turned into a theory can not really be seen as representing any kind of sexual liberation.

[1] For an introduction to these questions, see H. Jonas, *The Gnostic Religion*, 1958, 1963, 1970; and J.-T. Noonan, *Contraception*, chapter III.
[2] See P. Veyne, *La famille et l'amour à Rome*, 1978, pp. 35–63.

If we describe this philosophy as dissolute, as some do,[3] we are giving it a moral colour which is entirely modern, or rather we are judging the morality of these Gnostics by the standards of Christianity, whether modern or ancient, and not in terms of the social and sexual norms of antiquity. The men and women of these sects were not rebelling against sexual oppression, they were integrating sexual freedom into their worship of the Christian God, in the same way as it was also a part of many pagan sects. The most significant point is the official nature of this integration of sexual behaviour into religion as a means of salvation, and the extension of sexual freedom to women. In producing theories affirming the urgent necessity and benefit of this freedom, the Gnostics were in effect carrying to the extreme the freedom which was already the rule in their society. We might call this a kind of theoretical sexualism.

The medical works of the time make no mention of these theories or practices. They contain no chapters intended to make life easier for those indulging in sexual activities which contemporary orthodox Christians considered unbridled. The advice on health care for those who led a fairly active sexual life might have been applied in these cases, but there is no evidence that the doctors devoted any attention to them. Nor are their ideas discussed in the medical works. One may conclude that the followers of Valentinus and Marcion did not seek medical advice for disorders or tiredness which they or their doctors would have attributed to their sexual activities.

All we find in the medical texts is a warning against sexual excesses, but not against any particular form of sexual life, although Rufus did state that heterosexual relations were less violent than homosexual relations. The only text which specifically refers to the harmfulness of over-indulgence in sexual activity is by Diocles (third to second centuries BC): 'Of the various parts of the body, the bladder, the kidneys, the lungs, the eyes and the spinal cord are particularly susceptible to lesions in those who indulge inappropriately in venereal excesses.' Galen[4] simply said, as Athenaeus had done, that sexual activity weakened the body, but he declined to give, as Rufus did, a regimen which would allow patients to be sexually active without suffering any ill effects.[5]

The only examples of venereal excesses we find in the medical texts are pathological, and relate to the disease which the ancients called satyriasis, which could affect men and women alike. Soranus, in his *Gynaecology*, says that he has dealt with this question in his work *On Acute Diseases*, which we know in the form of a Latin paraphrase made in the fifth or sixth century AD by Caelius Aurelianus. The disease was one which

---

[3] For example in Jonas, *The Gnostic Religion*.
[4] *LI*, 22.
[5] *Med. Coll.*, XXII, 2, Galen; *LI*, 21, Athenaeus; Ibid., 9, Rufus.

affected men more often than women, though women could suffer from it. The symptom of the illness was constant, violent, unquenchable sexual desire. Ejaculation brought a man only the briefest respite and a woman who had the disease would fall at the feet of any man she set eyes on. Both men and women, when affected, would constantly touch their sexual organs, which the treatment forbade. Freedom to touch one's sexual organs was, at least for Hippocrates, a condition of healthy living, and he considered that this partly explained the impotence which he was told afflicted the Scythians, who wore very tight fitting clothes.[6] The book *On Acute Diseases*, which deals with men as well as women, instructs that the patient be confined to a warm bedroom to which no young women or boys should be admitted, 'for the attractiveness of such visitors would again kindle the feeling of desire in the patient. Indeed, even healthy persons, seeing them, would in many cases seek sexual gratification, stimulated by the tension produced in the parts.'[7]

In cases of genital disease,[8] where a man or a woman experienced involuntary genital discharge, not accompanied by desire or tension in the genital area, the patient was advised to avoid erotic works of art and literature, which were sexual stimulants to the healthy as well as the diseased. So we learn that the presence of women or young boys generally aroused male desire and that erotic pictures or stories aroused desire in the normal woman. When a man or a woman could not have intercourse with a partner in order to assuage this desire, he or she would masturbate to obtain relief. Masturbation was only forbidden – on medical, not moral grounds – in cases of satyriasis and genital discharge. But Aristotle stated that when young people rubbed themselves to make themselves emit sperm during puberty, the satisfaction this brought was only relative because the rubbing might be painful.[9] In practice, if a woman was married as soon as she reached puberty, her sexuality would find an outlet within marriage, and, in classical Greece, it appears she would find satisfaction. If they could not find satisfaction within marriage, we learn from the comedies of the time that some women would use leather penises.[10] A young man, on the other hand, even if he were not married, was not obliged by social constraints to remain continent. As Galen said when referring to the philosopher Diogenes, masturbation was simply a source of relief when one could not do better.[11] In Roman and Greek

[6] See J. Clavreul's analysis in *L'ordre médical*, 1978, p. 61 et seq.

[7] Caelius Aurelianus, *On acute diseases*, III, 18, tr. I. E. Drabkin, 1960.

[8] Temkin, in his translation of *Soranus' Gynecology*, III, 45, p. 168, n. 80, accepts T. Puschmann's demonstration (in *Alexander von Tralles*, vol. I, p. 273) that the ancient concept of gonorrhoea covered spermatorrhoea and masturbation as well as gonorrhoea.

[9] *HA*, VII, 1, 581 *a*.

[10] Herondas, VI.

[11] *AP*, VI, 5.

society, there was no moral objection to the use of prostitutes or slaves or to the practice of homosexuality.

The ancients recognized that if a man did not have intercourse for a while he would ejaculate in his sleep. The anonymous physician of the Aristotelian writings noted down the confidences of women who spoke to him about their erotic dreams and their nocturnal emissions of female sperm.[12] Women told this doctor that they had 'dreamed they were having intercourse with a man', and that 'they had had erotic dreams'. There is no mention of a period of continence before these dreams. In the writings of Soranus passed on by Caelius Aurelianus, and then those of Galen reported by Oribasius, things were somewhat different. Galen was writing about men, but Caelius Aurelianus does not specify whether the subject is men or women. Soranus had devoted a chapter to nocturnal emission: 'On amorous sleep, which the Greeks call emissions during a dream.'

> Nocturnal emission is the discharge of semen in the course of a dream. The name [*oneirogmos*] is derived from this symptom, for the dream provides the venereal stimulation which gives rise to the emission. But, in general, nocturnal emission at the outset is not a disease or even a concomitant of disease; it is essentially a consequence of what the person sees [*phantasia*] while he sleeps, and results from a longing for sexual enjoyment, that is to say, from constant and uninterrupted sexual desire, or, on the other hand, from continence or a long interruption of sexual activity.[13]

The connection was no longer made simply with erotic dreams but also with unsatisfied sexual desire experienced by the individual during waking hours. This is also what we find in Galen's writings, although his analysis is different. Noting that some people were exhausted by love, appearing thin, with sunken eyes, but also that they might experience nausea and headaches as a result of continence, Galen concluded that their sperm was composed of bad humours. The proof of this, in his view, was the extent to which their nocturnal ejaculations during periods of continence weakened them.[14] This is quite new in medical literature: here we have men ravaged by desire who consult their doctor because they are ejaculating at night. Soranus told them that this was neither a disease nor the symptom of a disease.[15]

---

[12] *HA*, X.

[13] Caelius Aurelianus, *Chronic diseases*, V, 7, tr. I. E. Drabkin, 1960.

[14] *LI*, 10.

[15] See R. Jaccard, *L'exil intérieur, schizoïdie et civilisation*, 1975, for a bibliography and a consideration of the problem of nocturnal emissions and masturbation.

The end of the first century and the beginning of the second century BC saw the start of a great medical debate on the problems caused by continence. This highlighted the contradiction between the doctors' evident theoretical prejudice in favour of virginity or continence and the difficulty their patients experienced in following this path. The disorders caused by continence were known about from Hippocratic times, but only in cases of involuntary continence – young girls who were not married at puberty and women who were without a partner, usually widows – for these were the only obvious cases. Greek women had named these disorders hysteria,[16] although in young girls the condition was not true hysteria.

When girls approach the age of marriage but are not married they frequently undergo experiences, at the onset of their first menstrual period, to which they have not been exposed before. For at this time the blood travels to the womb as if to flow out of the body. Since the orifice by which it should flow out is not open, and as the blood arrives in ever great abundance as a result of the girl's diet and the rate at which she is growing, then the blood, having no means of leaving the body, rushes to the heart and the diaphragm. As these organs fill with blood the heart becomes sluggish; this gives way to numbness and then delirium . . . When these organs are full, shivering and fever set in. These fevers are called erratic. In this state the woman has a fit caused by the acute inflammation, she has murderous desires brought on by the putrid condition of her internal organs, fears and terrors when she sees shadows, and the pressure around her heart makes her feel that she wants to strangle herself. Her mind, which is confused and distressed because her blood has become corrupt, becomes in its turn deranged. The patient says terrible things. She has visions which tell her that it would be better or would serve some purpose to jump, to throw herself into a well, or to strangle herself. If she does not have visions she feels a certain pleasure at the thought of death which appears to her as something desirable. When their reason returns, women afflicted in this way make many offerings to Diana, in particular they give her their finest clothes on the orders of false soothsayers. They are only cured of this illness when the blood is no longer prevented from flowing out of the body. I would advise young girls who suffer in this way to be married as soon as possible; indeed if they become pregnant they are cured. If they are not married at puberty or shortly afterwards they will suffer from this disorder or

[16] *AP*, V.

from some other. Among married women, those who are sterile are most at risk of developing this disease.

Thus the symptoms were essentially hallucinations and suicidal tendencies the cure for which was marriage followed by pregnancy.

The chapter is short and its contents are not referred to elsewhere. No doubt the illness was a rare one largely on account of the ratio of girls to boys. C. Vatin has noted the absence of references to 'old maids' in comedy and in texts which describe the society of the time. The practice of killing girls at birth or abandoning them meant that girls from good families were scarce enough to be sure of finding a husband as soon as their *kyrios* wanted to marry them off. (Girl babies who were abandoned, if they survived, were liable to be brought up as slaves.) So the sort of adolescent crisis described in the book on girls' illnesses was doubtless as rare as were unmarried girls themselves.

But as soon as a girl was married she became a woman and she might experience periods of enforced continence. I shall set out here the scientific description of how continence leads to hysteria, a notion which is quite inconceivable to us because of the semantic development of the term hysteria. We have adopted the Greek word but have taken it out of the aetiological context in which it was created. Let us start with the symptom. In contrast to the variety of physical manifestations of hysteria according to modern terminology,[17] the ancients used the term to refer to one clearly identified phenomenon, which was recognized by society and known to be as dramatic and striking when it occurred as epileptic fits, which doctors taught people to distinguish from these hysterical fits. The *Hippocratic Collection* sets out the position quite clearly. If a woman was unable to speak and clenched her teeth, if her skin became dark and she fell into a sort of coma, her genital organs would be examined immediately. The pains caused by various gynaecological problems, in particular the abortion of an extra-uterine pregnancy, which were rediscovered in the twentieth century, were perfectly described in the fifth century BC. When told that a woman was experiencing intense pains in an area that might be far removed from the genital zone, the midwife would undertake a palpation of the vagina and would sometimes discover symptoms of some uterine disorder. A change in the colour of the skin was regarded as a sure sign of serious infection, which explains the term hysteria. Women accepted quite readily that the womb actually

---

[17] On hysteria and somatic manifestations in general, see Ilza Veith, *History of hysteria*, 1965; J.-P. Valabrega, *Théories psychosomatiques*, 1954, and *Phantasme, mythe, corps et sens*, 1980, where the author calls for a historical anthropological study of fantasy. R. Gori, L'hystérie, état limite entre l'impensable et la représentation, in *L'interdit de la représentation*, 1983. J. Clavreul, *L'ordre médical*, chapter 11, shows how the hysterical patient expresses herself through symptoms she has already heard the doctors speak of.

moved up to the heart, the liver or the throat, and this notion was very widely held. These genital pains were the sign of an incurable disease. What puzzled Galen was the fact that not all the women who experienced them died.[18]

Sometimes the vaginal examination revealed no sign of genital disorder, and yet the woman would be stiff and to all intents and purposes unconscious, although Soranus noted that she would remember the fit. The patient presented all the clinical signs of the most serious female genital disorders and yet she recovered. The *Hippocratic Collection* pointed out that this hysterical fit, named after its symptom, occurred mainly in women who were unable to have sexual intercourse,[19] unmarried girls or young widows who remained alone.[20] Thus the most common somatic expression of what *we* call hysteria occurring among the women of antiquity was the appearance of very serious genital disorders, of the illness known as hysteria, that is to say disease of the womb, correctly defined by observation of the clinical signs. Greek women had no legal right to make any decision regarding their own marriage: they could not ask a man to marry them, or even decide that they wanted to be married or to accept an offer of marriage, so it is perhaps not surprising that their impotent anger should take the form of a disease in which their womb was literally suffocating them. The expression of female desire in enjoyment of sexual intercourse was accepted because it was considered necessary for them to experience pleasure in order to conceive. When female desire was contained it would break out in symptoms of fatal genital disease.

Female desire was socially recognized, and the diagnosis put forward by the midwife and the patient's female entourage was clear: this was a serious illness which would lead to death if not cured by sexual activity and pregnancy.

Plato agreed with this position, referring to the womb as a dangerous animal roaming around the female body. Once dissection of the human body, or even of female monkeys, was practised, as Galen describes in his first book, *De Uteri Dissectione*, the scientists of the second century AD could no longer accept this. Galen even felt it necessary to make it clear that the seat of desire was not the uterus,[21] in other words he drew a distinction between desire and procreation. Aristotle, before him, had made this distinction and had come to the conclusion that female sperm did not exist.

It was impossible to dismiss the link, on the one hand, between a

[18] *AP*, VI, 5, on hysteria.
[19] *Dis. Wom.*, I, 7.
[20] Ibid., I, 127 and 137.
[21] *Uses of the Body*, XIV, 13.

hysterical fit and genital disorders, and on the other hand between a fit and frustration at enforced continence, that is to say in both cases between hysteria and the genital zone. Galen dismissed the notion that the womb moved around the body but retained the principle of a correlation between fits and the genital area, even when palpation revealed no sign of genital disorder. He concluded that there was a causal link between continence and hysteria: the womb must be suffering from retention of sperm, an explanation which was not possible if the existence of this sperm was denied. Galen justified his theory by reference to a single case which seemed to him to be ample proof that he was right. The case concerned a male patient:

> I also knew a man who refrained from sexual pleasure because of grief for his wife. Since he had previously enjoyed intercourse quite frequently, he became nauseated, could hardly digest the little food he consumed and evidently, if he forced himself to eat more, promptly vomited. He became despondent neither for this reason nor for another obvious cause, as do melancholic patients. This condition subsided, however, as soon as he took up his earlier habits.
>
> Scrutinizing these [observations] it appeared to me that the retention of semen does greater harm to the body than the suppression of the menstrual flow, [especially] in persons who have an abundance of poorly conditioned humours, who lead a lazy life, and who initially had indulged quite frequently in sexual relations but suddenly stopped their previous habit. I realized that in these patients their physical desire for seminal discharge was the cause [of the disorder], because all people of this type must ejaculate their abundant semen.[22]

It was not possible, of course, to study the effects of involuntary continence on free men as it was in the case of free Greek women. A Roman woman who was widowed or separated, living in the second century AD when Galen was writing, had more freedom to do as she pleased, with the formal approval of her guardian. Thus, as with men, all that could be observed in the case of such women was voluntary continence, except in the months which they were legally obliged to spend alone before remarrying. In any case, the doctors did not undertake studies of such subjects: their observations were made during consultations.

The hysterical fit described in the *Hippocratic Collection* and later in

---

[22] *AP*, VI, tr. Rudolph E. Siegel, 1976.

Soranus' and Galen's work is not reproduced in Oribasius' compilation as it has come down to us. Perhaps it was dealt with in one of the books which has been lost. There seems to be a reference to it in the chapters on treatment and remedies. Oribasius copies from the writings of Antyllus (second century AD) the vaginal fumigations recommended in the *Hippocratic Collection*. The woman would be seated on the chair used for deliveries, wrapped in blankets. A decoction would be set to boil beneath her and the vapour from this would be introduced into her vagina or even her uterus by means of a tube.[23] Antyllus would revive the patient by making her breathe in a strong smell such as castor soaked in vinegar, sulphur or burnt hairs. Garlic, which had been used routinely by Greek women, was no longer used in fumigations although it at least had the merit of disinfecting a uterus which was found on examination to be inflamed or suffering from some other affliction.

The *Hippocratic Collection* had expressly forbidden the use of garlic in fumigations to treat hysteria because the aim in such cases was to bring back to its proper place a womb which had moved into the heart or the throat. For this it was necessary to use sweet-smelling fumigations. Garlic was recommended, in conjunction with other repellents, to make a prolapsed uterus return to its proper place, because here the object was to repel the uterus, not to attract it.

A series of fumigations was regarded as efficacious against inflammation and was intended to prepare the patient to resume sexual relations. It was considered a good sign when she felt the desire to resume intercourse, which would have a beneficial effect on her health. Hippocrates stated that sex was beneficial to women's health because it helped to keep the womb moist, whereas if it became dry there was the risk of painful contractions.[24]

In short, Galen found it hard to rid himself of the simple notion, set out in his book on hysteria,[25] that sexual activity with the emission of sperm was necessary to human health and well-being. His theory on hysteria caused by continence was based on the example of a hysterical fit cured instantly by an orgasm brought about by a female attendant massaging a female patient's genitals with ointment. So Galen retained the Greek view that female hysteria could be cured by marriage and the resumption of sexual activity.

Soranus, writing half a century earlier, had put forward an opposing theory. He was against fumigations, and refused to recommend their use in pre-marital examinations. He also refused to use them as a treatment for hysteria, stating, before Galen's time, that the womb was not a wild

---

[23] *Med. Coll.*, X, 19 and 20.
[24] *Gen.*, IV, 2.
[25] *AP*, VI.

animal roaming through the female body.[26] Like Galen, he prescribed ointments. He also recommended rocking in a hammock and bathing the lower parts with soothing substances. But he also suggested bleeding or the use of cupping glasses without scarification on the pubis or the armpit, which was the treatment generally recommended in cases of amenorrhoea. In this case the aim was not to bring on a menstrual period, but to decongest the patient's genital organs. These contrasting methods of treatment reflect the different demands made of the medical profession by the Greek women of the *Hippocratic Collection* on the one hand and by the Roman men and women of the second century AD on the other.

It is Soranus who tells us of the debate carried on in the first century about female virginity or the non-marriage of girls.[27] One reason for this question being raised might have been a change in the ratio of girls to boys of the same age group and the same social class, in this case the privileged class. As we have seen, in order to receive any inheritances due to them men had to have at least three children, whose sex was not specified in Augustus' law, so if one or more of a father's first three normal children was a girl she would be accepted without difficulty. A second reason for this question being raised was the reticence on the part of men to take a legitimate wife, either because they preferred concubinage or casual affairs, or because they had decided to practise continence. It may also be that some girls tried to refuse marriage, an issue raised by young Christian girls. But Soranus does not mention any religious or philosophical ideas as having prompted the medical debate. He reports both sides of the debate. It appears that it was the problems encountered by those who chose to become continent after they had had their first sexual experiences which led to the view that virginity was preferable to depriving oneself of a pleasure which one had experienced. The adherents of this school held that 'the body was made sick by desire', and weakened by sexual intercourse, and that any emission of sperm was detrimental to the health of a man or a woman. In addition to this, a woman had to contend with the tiredness caused by pregnancy, and premature ageing. The doctors who belonged to this school claimed that men who abstained from sex were taller and stronger than other men.

The other school held that virginity only inflamed desire, whereas sexual intercourse quickly quenched it, leaving the spirit in peace. The doctors of this school felt that virginity was more harmful to women than pregnancy. It was claimed that cases of amenorrhoea had been noted among virgins, which proved that the absence of sexual intercourse

---

[26] *Gyn.*, III, 29.
[27] Ibid., I, 30–31; 32.

prevented menstruation. The fact that unmarried girls tended to put on weight was explained with reference to dysmenorrhoea.

Soranus sided with those who thought virginity preferable, repeating Epicurus' view that sexual intercourse was harmful in itself. He developed this point of view in a work on *Hygiene* which, like similar works by other writers, was a sort of medical *vademecum* designed to help families avoid the need to consult a doctor for every small complaint. He noted that women 'who, on account of regulations and service to the gods, have renounced intercourse, and those who have been kept in virginity as ordained by law are less susceptible to disease,'[28] and he made it clear that married women in Rome did not enjoy good health. Soranus argued strongly in favour of virginity for men and women, and refused to recognize the classical aetiology of hysteria. He held that it was necessary to see hysterical fits in the context of the patient's gynaecological history, and repeated the details given in the *Hippocratic Collection*, adding new observations of his own, but omitting the *Collection*'s reference to pains occurring some time after initial symptoms and in areas far removed from the uterus. He considered that hysteria might be the result of repeated miscarriages, a premature delivery, a long widowhood, amenorrhoea, the end of a normal pregnancy, or a swelling of the uterus. Given the conditions in which young Roman girls' first sexual experiences took place, they might well suffer miscarriages and premature deliveries often enough for the link to be made between these events and fits which involved fainting, the inability to speak, convulsive contractions of the extremities or extreme weakness.

It is not surprising that Soranus, who recommended speaking gently to these patients and soothing them, advised against treating hysteria by telling patients to resume sexual relations. We may see this as the confirmation, or rather the consequence of the view expressed by Plutarch in a text analysed by M. Durry who has studied the consummation of Roman marriages between mature men and young girls:

> The practice of the two peoples in the matter of giving their young maids in marriage conforms to their education of them in general. Lycurgus made them brides only when they were fully ripe and eager for it, in order that intercourse with a husband, coming at a time when nature craved it, might produce a kindly love, instead of the timorous hate that follows unnatural compulsion; also that their bodies might be vigorous enough to endure the strain of conception and child-birth, convinced as he was that marriage had no other end

---

[28] *Gyn.*, I, 32, tr. Temkin.

than the production of children. The Romans, on the other hand, gave their maidens in marriage when they were twelve years old, or even younger. In this way more than any other, it was thought, both their bodies and their dispositions would be pure and undefiled when their husbands took control of them.[29]

It was scarcely reasonable to expect Roman wives who were suffering from hysterical fits as a result of miscarriages or premature deliveries to turn to husbands who inspired 'timorous hate' in them.

Soranus compared accounts of organic hysteria, that is to say hysteria caused by uterine disorders, and hysteria caused by continence, from both of which he said women generally recovered very quickly, and explained that, as Roman married women were suffering from fits which until then had only been observed in Greek widows, it was no longer possible medically to maintain the existence of a close correlation between continence and hysteria.

Oribasius, writing fifty years after the Empire had become Christian, makes no mention of this correlation. But he does give one text by Galen on the effects of uncontrolled continence:

> Some young people become weak after intercourse; others who are not in the habit of having intercourse, experience head aches, fever, feelings of anxiety, loss of appetite and indigestion; we have observed that some of these patients, after abstaining from intercourse, have become sluggish and lazy, and that others have become bad tempered for no reason and depressed in the same way as those who suffer from black bile, and that all of these problems cease when the patient has intercourse. Reflecting on this fact, I have come to the conclusion that retention of sperm is very harmful to those who are young and strong, whose sperm is naturally abundant and composed of humours which are not entirely irreproachable, who lead a somewhat idle existence and who, after a period when they indulged frequently in intercourse, suddenly turn to a life of abstinence.[30]

So it was accepted at the end of the fourth century that continence might have adverse effects, but these were not associated with hysteria or the uterus. Galen's discovery had been completely superseded.

One may, however, ask whether the symptoms which had given hysteria its name still existed, whether in the Graeco-Roman world cases

[29] Plutarch, *Lycurgus and Numa*, IV, 1–3, tr. Bernadette Perrin; translated into French and analysed by Durry, Le mariage des filles impubères dans la Rome antique, p. 265.
[30] *Med. Coll.*, VI, 37.

of this somatic manifestation peculiar to continent women still occurred. If so, then it was medical theory, and Soranus as its principal proponent, which was responsible for the oblivion into which hysteria caused by continence fell. Of course, Soranus was practising in Rome, and his gynaecological theories were based on his observations of young women whose sexual lives were quite different from the sexual lives of the Greek women referred to by the *Hippocratic Collection* and by Galen. Most commentators have been rather critical of these Roman women of the Early Empire. J. Carcopino has judged them just as harshly as J. Marquardt. We are told that they went out a great deal, that even married women had lovers, and that they neglected their duties as wives, mothers and mistresses of a household. 'It is evident that the independence which women at this time enjoyed frequently degenerated into licence, and that the looseness of their morals tended to dissolve family ties.'[31] If we carried this argument to its logical conclusion, Roman women could be blamed for the fall of Rome without the scholars objecting. And yet we are told that these women were happy. Indeed Pliny, whose two previous wives had not been able to give him the child he needed in order to receive his inheritance, made excuses for his third wife in a letter to her grandfather, who held the powers of a father over her, and he asked his wife's aunt to help assuage the grandfather's displeasure. There was every reason to be critical of his wife: 'Being young and inexperienced she did not realize she was pregnant, failed to take proper precautions, and did several things which were better left undone,'[32] which led to a miscarriage. In his letter to Calpurnia's aunt, Pliny says that this was due to his wife's youthfulness. Moreover as her miscarriage had led her to the brink of death she should be pardoned. She had been punished enough. It appears that the child was needed as much by Calpurnia's family as by Pliny himself, perhaps even more as an imperial rescript granted him the rights of those who had three children[33]. 'Your desire for great-grandchildren cannot be keener than mine for children. Their descent from both of us should make their road to office easy; I can leave them a well-known name and an established ancestry.'[34] So his child-wife must be forgiven for not realizing that she was pregnant, and excuses should be made for her to her own grandfather who retained control over her (*manus*) and

[31] Carcopino, *Daily Life in Ancient Rome*, Penguin ed., p. 107; and the whole section on *Feminism and Demoralization*; J. Marquardt, *Das Privatleben der Römer*, 1886, vol. I, French tr. 1892, p. 82 et seq. In particular, see n. 4, p. 82, after giving examples of murders committed by women of the Roman upper classes: 'This was what emancipated women were like.'
[32] Pliny, *Letters*, VIII, X, tr. Betty Radice, 1969.
[33] R. Besnier, Pline le Jeune et l'application des lois démographiques, 1979, pp. 89–95.
[34] Pliny, *Letters*, VIII, X and XI, tr. Radice.

who, as her father was dead, had given her in marriage so that she would produce a child to unite their two families.

It seems that there were more urgent problems for Roman women than to find a sexual partner in marriage. Widows and divorced women had more freedom in Rome than in Greece, and did not necessarily have continence imposed on them by someone else. Further, marrying and producing children were not seen as the solution to insistent desire. Pregnancy was not the cure for the Roman woman's hysterical fits in the same way as it was the ultimate remedy prescribed by the Greek texts.

This is doubtless why, while Galen's writings referred to a single phenomenon known as the hysteria of continence, which could occur in men, the doctors quoted by Oribasius referred to a female condition known as hysterial suffocation, which had no link with continence, and their studies of the effects of continence, usually on men, were separate and occurred elsewhere in their works.

Doctors noticed that continence affected the body and also the temperament of the individual. They therefore held that continence should not be practised without certain precautions. Galen had described these precautions at the beginning of the second century AD. They constitute a regimen which is all the more interesting as it was designed for men, who we know must have chosen a life of continence of their own free will, unlike many girls who were kept against their will in a state of celibacy and virginity. Galen's advice was that of a physician who believed that moderate exercise of the sexual organs was necessary to good health: but he was prepared to use his knowledge to help those who did not share his opinion. A broad programme of sensory deprivation was drawn up in order to stem the tide of sexual desire. Where a patient was suffering from a disease involving excessive sexual desire the disorder was treated by visual, aural and tactile deprivation. When it was simply a case of the individual wanting to reduce or eliminate normal sexual activity the pagans began by limiting the patient's food. So the same medical scholar on the one hand confirmed the diagnosis of the hysteria of continence in women and on the other set out a suitable regimen for those who wanted to experiment with sexual abstinence. For Galen, as for Athenaeus three centuries before him, the chief disadvantage of sexual activity was not the risk of disease, tiredness or loss of vital spirit, but rather that nagging sexual desire disturbed the workings of the mind. Galen proposed to reduce the effects of this 'inconvenience' not by imposing a daily routine, although he did provide one for those who wished to follow it, but by a compromise which he called chastity: rapid male ejaculation, if necessary by masturbation, but preferably during sexual intercourse. This male ejaculation on the grounds of health quite deliberately ignored female desire, and taken together with the insight provided by medical writers into sexual relations within legitimate Roman aristocratic marriages, might very well explain why the hysteria suffered by Greek widows also occurred so frequently among Roman married women.

5

Adultery and Illicit Love

'The Atreidae are not the only men on earth who love their wives.'
D, 48,5,14, quoting the *Iliad*, 9, 340

Most experts in the history of law, to whom historians are indebted, agree
that Augustus' laws on marriage imposed severe restrictions on a
Roman's choice of wife to prevent men marrying beneath them.[1] Some
see this as the reason for the spread of concubinage during the early years
of the Empire.[2] The sons and daughters of senators were forbidden to
marry slaves, freed persons, prostitutes, procurers and procuresses and
their freed slaves, actors and actresses and their children, and persons who
had been publicly condemned, particularly those condemned for adultery.
In a world where fathers chose their children's first marriage partners that
left all the young men and women of free birth and good behaviour,
among whom there must certainly have been a number of families of
unequal rank. Therefore it can not have been solely to prevent unequal
marriages that Augustus felt it necessary to introduce such a severe law.

Free men who were not senators had more or less the same restrictions
imposed on them, but the only freedwomen whom they were forbidden
to marry were those of procurers. The texts do not state that they were
forbidden to marry prostitutes, as were senators, but this seems likely.

In short, the number of people with whom Roman citizens were
prevented from entering into a full marriage contract was quite small.
They fell into three basic categories: slaves, people involved in prostitution

---

[1] J. Gaudemet, La décision de Callixte en matière de mariage, 1955, pp. 334–44 = 1980,
pp. 106–7: 'Apart from the risk that Augustus' prohibitions might prevent a proposed
marriage, they restricted the individual's choice of partner to a considerable degree.' And the
same author, 'By his Lex Julia, Augustus banned unequal marriages', *Le droit privé romain*,
1974, p. 280.

[2] C. St. Tomulescu, Justinien et le concubinat, 1972, pp. 299–326, summarizes the
arguments relating to concubinage after Augustus' time and gives a full bibliography.

and those involved in the theatre. In addition, senators must avoid all freed persons.

Now legitimate, lawful marriage was essential in two areas which were clearly linked. By the same law Augustus stated that in order to receive a legacy or succession a citizen must be legitimately married and a father. Moreover, any child born outside a lawful marriage had no legal ties either with his father or his father's family. Therefore the simplest course, in view of the *lex Julia* on marriages and then the *lex Papia Poppaea*, was to take in lawful marriage the free and honourable daughter of a good family, and to make her a donation before marriage, according to custom, since no donations between spouses were valid in Roman law, and to receive a dowry from her father's patrimony. The contract specified what would happen to these possessions if the marriage should be dissolved. The wife no longer left her father's authority to come under that of her husband. During the Republic, all a wife had to do to remain under the control of her father's family was to spend three consecutive days in his house each year. This was no longer necessary under the Empire. The Roman was obliged by law to marry, but he was free to choose his wife, the mother of his legitimate children, from a wide social spectrum.

Setting aside marriage, what sexual freedom did the Roman man have during the classical period? He was not bound to remain faithful to his own wife. But if he accused her of adultery his own conduct would be examined by the judge, for 'it would be unfair if a husband demanded of his wife a standard of behaviour which he himself did not observe'.[3] Thus legal constraints on sexual behaviour might be imposed from outside the marriage. The law defined three crimes. Apart from incest, *stuprum* and adultery could lead to a man's losing his position in his family and in society.[4] Incest was more widely defined then than it is nowadays, and those who entered into an incestuous marriage or engaged in incestuous practices outside marriage were prosecuted unless they separated as soon as they discovered the existence of a hitherto unknown relationship. The law stated that any man who had sexual relations with a young boy, a girl from a good family, or a widow was guilty of *stuprum*,[5] and would be judged by the public courts. A man found guilty of *stuprum* with a young

---

[3] *D*, 48, 5, 14, Ulpian.

[4] Ibid., 48, 5, 35, Modestinus.

[5] Ibid., 48, 5, 35, Modestinus. Lécrivain's article, Stuprum, in *Dictionnaire des Antiquités*, ed. C. Daremberg and E. Saglio, needs to be revised, particularly where it deals with the question of freedwomen and with homosexuality. See Marcello Molè, Stuprum, *Novissimo Digesto Italiano*, XVIII, 1971, pp. 582–7. On incest, Roman law forbade all marriages between those connected by a direct line of descendancy, and also between uncles and nieces, and between first cousins, J. Gaudemet, *L'Eglise dans l'Empire romain, IVe-Ve siècle*, 1958, p. 527, and Justum matrimonium, 1980, pp. 59–64; on incest, Yan Thomas, Parenté et stratégies endogamiques à Rome. Etude d'une mutation, 1976, pp. 149–85.

boy was liable to receive the death penalty in former days, but under the
Empire he would receive the same punishment as adulterers.[6] In the case
of sexual relations with a girl from a good family who had been a virgin,
both the man and the girl were punished by having half of their
possessions confiscated, unless the girl could prove that she had been
raped. Sexual relations with widows, who retained the status of *matres
familias*, also counted as *stuprum*.[7] Modestinus[8] adds that a man could
not have sexual relations with a free woman, outside of marriage or
concubinage, without risking the penalty for *stuprum*. Even though
Modestinus goes on to define *stuprum* and adultery, mentioning young
girls, widows and married women, the term 'free woman' also includes
divorced or repudiated women, who retained the status of *mater
familias*.[9]

A man who became involved with another man's wife was also an
adulterer, as was the woman with regard to her husband. Moreover, a
relationship with another man's concubine was considered as adultery in
certain cases. It is important to define these cases in order to establish the
degree of sexual freedom enjoyed by the Romans. We know from
funerary inscriptions that concubinage was very widespread.[10] Was
concubinage a free union in which the partners renounced the right to
prosecute one another for adultery and to ask the tribunal to impose a
punishment?

This question is complex, as is the whole area of Roman concubinage,
and depends on the interpretation of texts of the *Digest*, that is to say,
fragments of legal works written for the most part before the fourth
century, and collected between 530 and 533 by a commission of jurists
appointed by Justinian.[11] The key text for present purposes is by Ulpian,
and shows that certain concubines could be accused of adultery, and that
their lovers would be condemned with them.[12] 'If it is not a wife who has
committed adultery, but a concubine, she can not be accused under the
law of the husband (*jure mariti*); but it is possible to lodge against her an
accusation according to the law of the stranger (*jure extranei*) provided
that she has not lost the name of matron, for example the woman who is
her master's concubine.'[13]

[6] *D*, 48, 5, 9 and 11.
[7] Ibid., 48, 5, 11.
[8] Ibid., 48, 5, 35.
[9] K. Visky, Le divorce dans la législation de Justinien, 1976, p. 241, and n. 5.
[10] See the second, and soundest, part of J. Plassard, *Le concubinat romain sous le Haut
Empire*, 1921.
[11] Villers, *Rome et le droit privé*, pp. 130–1.
[12] *D*, 48, 5, 14 [13].
[13] There is general agreement that a freedwoman who was her master's concubine was a
matron.

So in order to appreciate how many women, other than their own concubine, were out of bounds to a man, we need to know which concubines were not regarded as matrons, or mothers of families. First of all there were those who could never have been matrons, that is to say honest women whose sexual relationships were official and respected[14] but 'free'. Neither these women nor their lovers could be considered guilty of adultery or depravity. Prostitutes, actresses and actresses' daughters came into this category. They could become the concubines of free men of any class, but they would never be *matres familias*. Their partners in concubinage could never accuse them of adultery, or demand that the penalty for adultery be applied to them or their lovers. This is why Ulpian wrote: 'I agree with Atilicinus that the only women one can take as concubines without fear of committing a crime are those with whom one can not be committing *stuprum*.'[15] He goes on to add: 'If a man takes as a concubine a woman condemned for adultery, he is not exposing himself to the *lex Julia* on adultery as he would be if he had married her.' This is clearly the chief concern of the legal texts, to answer the questions of the anxious Roman who asks: 'If I marry or take a concubine or have a temporary relationship with someone, how can I be sure that I am not falling foul of the laws on *stuprum* or adultery?'

A woman who had been found guilty of adultery, and even one who had been caught *in flagrante delicto* but not condemned, could never be legitimately married to a Roman of whatever social rank, and had lost the status of matron. She no longer had *conubium* even if, having been caught *in flagrante delicto*, she had not been found guilty.[16]

In his important study of Roman concubinage, Jean Plassard held that only freedwomen who were the concubines of their master could attain the status of matron. This is not the case. The texts clearly show that this status was attained by all respectable concubines (that is to say those who were not prostitutes, actresses or the freedwomen of procurers), but that they forfeited this status if they left their master-concubine against his will, just as they lost the status of matron if they repudiated their master-spouse.[17] But they did at least have the right to repudiate their partner, and such a separation was effective,[18] because all ties between a man and a woman ceased as soon as one party withdrew his or her consent to the relationship.[19] E. Volterra imagines, with reason, that the *repudium*

---

[14] *D*, 40, 16, 46, 1.

[15] Ibid., 25, 7, 1, 1.

[16] Ibid., 48, 5, 30, 1. Gaudemet, Justum Matrimonium, 1949 = 1980, p. 73.

[17] *D*, 23, 2, 41, Marcellus.

[18] *D*, 24, 2, 11.

[19] M. Andreev, Divorce et adultère dans le droit romain classique, 1957, pp. 7–8; E. Volterra, *Istituzioni di diritto privato romano*, 1961, p. 671.

came most often from the husband or the male partner in a concubinage and that in such cases the freedwoman would be at liberty to marry again.[20]

It appears then that only a fairly small number of concubines were denied the status of *mater familias*.[21] It would help us to be more precise if we knew whether a freedwoman who became the concubine of a free man other than her master, with the latter's agreement, was a *mater familias*. As the text on adultery committed by a concubine does not make this clear,[22] and the text which states that a concubine loses the status of matron emphasizes the lack of agreement on the part of her master, it may be that this is the only condition that really counted. These women could in any case, even without their master's approval, marry the man of their choice or enter into concubinage, if they had been freed by *fideicommissum*,[23] in other words if their deceased master had charged the executor of his will to free them, which was the most common means of granting freedom.

The list of women with whom a Roman man could have a temporary sexual relationship without incurring the penalties for adultery or *stuprum*, setting aside slaves,[24] thus comprised prostitutes and actresses, procuresses and their freedwomen and women found guilty of adultery, even if any of the above were the concubines of another man. It also included women who had been their master's concubine or wife but had left him for another man. In all other cases, a Roman could not have a sexual relationship with a free woman unless he asked her to marry him or become his concubine. Even in such circumstances he might run the risk of being accused of *stuprum* or adultery if he took as wife or concubine a woman who was a *mater familias*, a matron, and not a young virgin, the daughter of a good family, given in first marriage by her father. That men were anxious about these risks is reflected by the number of chapters of the legal code which relate to accusations of *stuprum* or adultery against men who have just entered into marriage or concubinage.

The problem arose because of the lack of formal acts to register the events of private life. For instance, if a man married a woman who, it was later discovered, had had casual relationships with other men, he could accuse her of adultery if he knew that she had had lovers: the fact that she

---

[20] E. Volterra, Sulla *D*, 23, 2, 45, 6, 1972, pp. 325–7.

[21] On this point I disagree with Plassard who feels that only the freedwomen who were their masters' concubines were *matres familias*.

[22] *D*, 48, 5, 14 [13].

[23] Ibid., 23, 2, 50, Marcellus.

[24] A free man was not entitled to have sexual relations with someone else's female slave as this was considered as damaging her owner's property.

was married made her a matron and she therefore had a duty to be faithful. But if the husband died, the woman could not then be accused of *stuprum* even though she was a widow. She would now have a status which should have been ascribed to her before.[25] So although there was a register of prostitutes, there remained doubts about the status of certain other women.

Whereas it was safe enough to marry a widow or a virgin, it was advisable to make enquiries before marrying a single woman who appeared not to depend on any other person, such as a woman who had gained the rights of those who had had three children and so no longer had a guardian.[26] She may have been divorced by common accord, or repudiated by her former husband, but she might equally well have broken off her previous relationship unilaterally. How could one be certain that the former husband would not bring an action for adultery?

It appears that even if a woman moved into a house which belonged to her and was therefore living apart from her husband, she still had a duty to be faithful to him. If he discovered a lover in her house he could kill him with impunity. Such a lover was guilty of adultery.[27] Moreover, even when spouses lived in separate homes, the law considered them as married and they were allowed to make no donation *inter vivos*.[28] What was important in the eyes of the law therefore was less the fact that the spouses were separated, which was in general impossible to prove, than the nature of any new sexual relationship which the separated woman might have.[29]

The law stated that a man who had repudiated his wife could not thereafter accuse her of adultery if she remarried.[30] And even if the first husband could prove that he had not sent a letter of repudiation, the

---

[25] *D*, 48, 5, 14, 2, Ulpian.

[26] Riccardo Astolfi, Note per una valutazione storica della 'lex Julia et Papia', p. 189. From Hadrian's reign on, they could count their illegitimate children, in other words those born in concubinage.

[27] Eva Cantarella, Adulterio, Omicidio legittimo e causa d'onore in Diritto Romano, 1972, p. 262.

[28] *D*, 24, 1, 32, 13, Ulpian. Andreev, Divorce et adultère, p. 7. This article's most important contribution is its study of the insecurity created by the lack of formal separation procedures for Roman couples; in some cases separation was considered official, in others it was not: whether or not a person could be accused of adultery depended on this point.

[29] Andreev considers that the fact that doubts were expressed about the validity of some separations shows that the text of the *Digest* which required a partner to deliver the letter of repudiation in front of seven witnesses did not apply to all cases of repudiation after the enactment of Augustus' law. But he still feels, rightly, that this procedure involving witnesses dates from the first century, although he can find no satisfactory reason why informal divorce and repudiation by letter should have existed side by side.

[30] *D*, 48, 5, 17, Ulpian.

second husband would not be considered as an adulterer.[31] In short, the second marriage was proof that the first had been dissolved.

So if he married a woman who claimed she had been divorced or repudiated, even if there was no proof that the earlier marriage had been dissolved, a man could not be accused of *stuprum* or adultery. But if he preferred to enter into a relationship which had no implications with regard to inheritance, namely concubinage, was he running the risk of being accused of adultery? It is in this light that we must consider the following text by Marcianus (second century): 'The following women may be taken as concubines: another man's freedwoman, a free woman, and especially women of obscure birth or those who sell their body . . . But if a man prefers to enter into concubinage with an honest woman of free birth . . . he is not committing adultery by taking her as his concubine.'[32] Plassard feels that adultery here should be taken in the sense of *stuprum*, so that the passage means that an honest and decent woman might become a concubine without risking a charge of *stuprum*. But it means more than that, and we must retain the strict interpretation of the word adultery, since the texts distinguish quite clearly between *stuprum* and adultery.

Marcianus says that a man is not guilty of adultery in such a case. He can only be adulterous if he has sexual relations with another man's wife or concubine. This text should be considered alongside a passage by Modestinus, who was Prefect of the Watch (*Praefectus vigilum*) in 244: 'A man who has a sexual relationship with a free woman without marrying her is committing *stuprum* unless he takes her as his concubine.'[33] If she has been divorced or repudiated, he is not committing *stuprum*. If she is allegedly married and comes to live with him as his concubine, that is not adultery in the way that a casual relationship would be. Just as one marriage cancels a previous marriage, so concubinage breaks a woman's matrimonial ties with another man.

The essential point is thus the fact that the woman has moved into a man's house as his wife or his concubine. Only by becoming spouses or concubines can a free and respectable man and woman avoid being accused of adultery. No woman can take refuge, even temporarily, in a man's house in order to escape from a husband whom she wishes to repudiate, and no man can shelter in his house a married woman who wishes to be separated from her husband, even if he does not have a sexual relationship with her. Hadrian decided to banish for three years any man who took a woman into his house and made her send a letter of

---

[31] Ibid., 48, 5, 44, Gaius. On this text and the interpolations it has undergone, see Andreev, Divorce et adultère, pp. 3–4.
[32] *D*, 25, 7, 3.
[33] Ibid., 48, 5, 35.

repudiation to her husband from his house.[34] The text does not refer to such a couple as spouses or concubines, which might have protected them from charges of adultery.

The only casual relationships a Roman man could have without running the risk of being brought before the public tribunals were thus with slaves, actresses, prostitutes and some women who were other men's concubines, and who were denied the rights of matrons. In all other cases, if a man and a woman wanted to have a relationship but did not intend it to be a very lasting one, they were nevertheless obliged to marry or to show that the relationship was serious enough to constitute a concubinage which involved fidelity on the woman's part and cohabitation. Without the commitment to a lasting relationship implied by marriage and concubinage, a man who had a relationship with a married woman or a concubine was exposing himself to the vengeance of the woman's father or to an accusation brought before the public tribunals by anyone other than a slave,[35] as Augustus had made adultery a public crime.

Augustus' law on adultery, which was commented on and modified throughout the course of the Empire, but never repealed, pre-dated by more than twenty years any laws on marriage. As we have seen, there were very few restrictions on marriage in Rome. The law placed no restrictions on separation. Ties were dissolved if one of the spouses or concubines desired this. There might be consequences related to inheritance, as we shall see, imposed sometimes as a penalty for unmotivated repudiation, but the separation was still valid and the dissolution of the relationship definitive. What the *lex Julia* on adultery set out to prevent was casual relationships entered into by free women who were considered respectable, daughters of good families, *matres familias*, wives, widows or divorcees.

According to penal law, the partners in such a relationship were committing a crime, and if the woman was married, they were committing adultery. Cases of adultery and *stuprum* were heard by the public courts and involved the full judicial process, which explains why the law and the legal commentators went to such lengths to define what constituted the crime, which crime was involved, who might make the accusation, and what the co-respondents' responsibilities were. The great legal writers all commented on the law and set out the risks involved and the means of protecting oneself against charges of contravening it. All the quotations from jurists collected in the *Digest* are replies to questions by men: the men responsible for registering accusations, husbands, fathers, lovers of accused women, friends of the lovers, and individuals outside a

---

[34] Ibid., 24, 2, 8, Papinian.
[35] Ibid., 48, 2, 4.

family who were making accusations. The writers answered their anxious enquiries just as they replied to the queries of those who were taking as concubine or wife a woman who had been married, and who were worried lest they be accused of adultery.

Above all, the law set out to ensure that all adulterers were punished. It began by punishing those who should have denounced lovers but had not done so. The father of an adulterous woman only fell under suspicion if the adultery took place under his roof or if he had surprised the couple at his son-in-law's house. In this case he had the right to kill his daughter's lover providing that he also killed his daughter, or could prove his intention to kill her by showing that he had seriously injured her or had genuinely pursued her.[36] He would not be charged with murder if he had killed in such circumstances. Moreover, he was not obliged to kill the couple on the spot, but could kill them once his initial fury had abated. If he did not seek to kill his daughter, he could not kill her lover, but must then make a public accusation within two months of learning of the adultery.

A husband could kill the lover but not his wife, and the conditions imposed by the law ensured that he did not kill while in the grip of passionate fury: before dealing the fatal blow he must establish that the lover was either a slave, an *infamis* (i.e. a free man who had lost the rights of a citizen) or a freedman. Moreover the law gave the lover twenty hours to prove his innocence with the aid of witnesses.[37] A husband could not kill his adulterous wife, but while the law would find him guilty of murder if he killed his wife or a lover who did not fulfil the necessary criteria, it would commute his punishment in view of his justifiable anger and, in the third century, taking into account his social class.[38] Our purpose, however, is not to examine the penalty incurred by a husband who committed murder, but rather to examine the risks taken by a man who became the lover of a Roman married woman. The law made provision for cases where the father or the husband did not immediately use violence against the offending couple. They would have sixty days to accuse one or other of the lovers (both would in any case be brought to trial) before the public courts. After this time, any person who knew of the adultery had a duty to bring a charge within four months, and must also charge with procuring the husband who had turned a blind eye to his

[36] On the execution of lovers by the woman's father or husband, see Eva Cantarella's fine article, Adulterio.

[37] Cantarella, Adulterio, p. 252. *Infames* were defined by their profession: they were gladiators who fought other gladiators and those who fought wild animals, actors, dancers, singers, procurers and prostitutes.

[38] G. Cardascia, L'Apparition dans le droit des classes d' 'honestiores' et d' 'humiliores', 1950, pp. 305–37 and 461–86.

wife's misconduct.[39] If the couple were found guilty, the husband would then be sentenced alongside them. The father, the husband and any other accuser would be charged with 'calumny' if they made a false accusation, and would then have to pay the costs of the trial, which were set out by the texts, and which mainly involved the cost of slaves belonging to the wife, her husband or the lover, who had died as a result of being tortured on interrogation.[40]

Adultery was thus a serious misdemeanour in the eyes of the penal law as well as in moral terms. Any person held to have been an accomplice to adultery, by making it easy for a couple to meet even if he did not provide the place where their criminal relationship was carried on, suffered the same penalty as if he had committed adultery.[41] But the legislation taken as a whole seems to have been designed principally to prevent husbands from allowing their wives a degree of sexual freedom which they themselves enjoyed, or even from keeping a wife once she had committed the most short-lived of infidelities. For this reason the law made the most detailed provisions as to the husband's obligations. He must first of all repudiate his wife as soon as he suspected her of committing adultery. This was the only case where repudiation was obligatory, and the husband must be able to prove to the court that he had complied with the law, or else he risked severe punishment. This is doubtless why the *lex Julia* on adultery provided for formal repudiation with the letter of repudiation being read in front of seven witnesses. In every case where a woman and her alleged lover were accused of adultery the judge enquired whether the husband had repudiated the wife. During the reign of Septimius Severus a *clarissimus* (senator of the highest rank) who brought a charge against his own wife was found guilty of procuring because he had failed formally to repudiate her.[42] In some respects it was in the husband's interests to bring the charge himself, as this was virtually the only way he could repudiate his wife and still keep a part of the dowry as well as the donation he had made her before their marriage. If he repudiated her without bringing a charge, she could begin an action to recover her property. If a woman's case had been dismissed she could, if she wished, remarry her husband if it was he who had brought the case against her, or consider that the marriage was not dissolved if it was someone outside the family who had made the accusation.[43] But if she wished, even if the husband repented, she could consider the repudiation

[39] *D*, 48, 5, 2 and 27, Papinian.
[40] Ibid., 48, 18, 6 and 48, 5, 28.
[41] Ibid., 48, 5, 9, Papinian, and 10, Ulpian.
[42] Ibid., 48, 5, 2.
[43] Ibid., 48, 5, 14 [13], 9.

as having taken effect and her marriage as dissolved.[44] If he had repudiated her on the basis of a false accusation of adultery, and if the accusation had been withdrawn before a judgement had been made, she could recover her property. No one could accuse her of adultery if she then remarried.[45] If she had been accused but had not yet appeared before the court she could even become another man's concubine providing that man was not her alleged lover.[46]

If a husband had no wish to kill or even accuse his wife's lover, he was nevertheless obliged to charge him with adultery or else he himself ran the risk of being accused of procuring if a third party should make against his wife the accusation he had declined to make. Lovers therefore had only one chance of escaping judgement and that was to seek a general pardon which cancelled all charges being considered and also sometimes, by *indulgentia*, any judgements already pronounced. The reference to this public pardon in Papinian's commentaries on the *lex Julia de adulteriis* shows that adulterers, like other accused people apart from slaves, could receive the amnesty accorded by this pardon. Only under the Christian Empire were they excluded from receiving it.[47] Trajan allowed a period of thirty days following the celebrations which had given rise to the amnesty during which time, if the accuser wished, he could re-introduce his charge.[48] But the husband was no longer obliged to institute proceedings for fear of being accused of *lenocinium*. It was perhaps with a view to such cases where amnesty had been granted that the law made provisions for women who had not been condemned although they had been caught *in flagrante delicto*: they could not remain married to a Roman nor could they marry any other respectable citizen.[49]

We do not have the exact text of the *lex Julia* on the punishment of adulterers, but Justinian's *Institutes* which refer to this law, indicate that the penalty for adultery was death by the sword,[50] as it was for sexual relations with young boys.[51] The punishment for *stuprum* laid down in the same text of the *Institutes* distinguishes between rich and poor (*honesti* and *humiles*), as does the text of the *Digest*.[52] This distinction

[44] Ibid., 24, 2, 7, Papinian.
[45] Ibid., 48, 4, 17 [16], Ulpian.
[46] Ibid., 25, 7, 1, 1 and 2, Ulpian.
[47] Fausto Goria, Ricerche su impedimento da adulterio e obbligo di repudio da Giustiniano a Leone VI, 1973, p. 308.
[48] D, 48, 16, 10, Papinian.
[49] Ibid., 23, 2, 43, 12, Ulpian.
[50] IJ, 4, 18, 4.
[51] Goria, Ricerche, pp. 292–4, n. 27, doubts whether the *lex Julia* demanded capital punishment and notes that this penalty was rarely applied, particularly to women, until the time of Constantine.
[52] D, 48, 19, 6, 2.

dates from the end of the second century and applies to the punishments of Severus' rule as, probably, do the *Sententiae Pauli*.[53] Rather than trying to establish the punishments laid down by Augustus' laws on adultery, it is more relevant to examine the evolution of the law up to the period at the end of the second century and the beginning of the third century for which we have accurate texts.

It is clear that the official sentence was the death penalty, but it is equally clear that this was not always implemented. In any case, it was not applied to those women in relation to whom the numerous legal texts set out the conditions in which they might live after their trial. Men found guilty of adultery were disgraced.[54]

At the end of the first century, Domitian declared that the law on adultery, which dealt more generally with what constituted respectable behaviour on the part of free women, must be strictly applied.[55] In the second century, two extensions of the law reveal that this policy was being followed. A husband who had caught his wife *in flagrante delicto* was not to kill her, on pain of being charged with murder, just as he was not allowed to kill her lover if the latter was a free and respectable man. But these murders were common enough for the Emperors to feel it necessary to introduce legislation on this point. Antoninus and his two successors, Marcus Aurelius and Commodus, reduced the penalty for husbands who committed murder from the death sentence, which normally applied to homicide, to exile for rich husbands and a life sentence of hard labour for those who were poor. Some decades later, Alexander Severus mentions no other penalty than exile.[56] If the lover killed by the husband had been a slave, an *infamis* or a freedman, there was no need for a murder trial. So the authorities clearly sought to soften the punishment meted out to a husband who had killed his wife and her lover.

Severus' laws, coming after those of Augustus and before those of Constantine, were the most prolix in this area.[57] When Dio[58] began his first term as consul under Septimius Severus (193–211), he found that there were two thousand trials for adultery under way.[59] Septimius Severus' legislation was not calculated to reduce the number of trials. He

[53] *Sententiae Pauli*, 2, 26, 14.

[54] *D*, 23, 2, 43, 12, Ulpian.

[55] T. Mommsen, *Le droit pénal romain*, II, in *Manuel des Antiquités romaines* by T. Mommsen, J. Marquardt and P. Krüger, French tr., 1907, p. 417, n. 2.

[56] *CJ*, 9, 9, 4. Cantarella, *Adulterio*, pp. 260–1.

[57] I do not propose to deal here with the law of the Christian Imperial period; on this, see Clémence Dupont, *Le Droit criminel dans les Constitutions de Constantin*, II: *Les peines*, 1955, and F. Goria, *Ricerche*.

[58] Dio, 76, 16.

[59] Mommsen, *Le Droit pénal*, II, p. 423, n. 1.

even declared that a fiancée could be prosecuted by her future husband according to the *jus extranei*.[60] And it was he who had a husband condemned for procuring because although he had brought the charge of adultery against his wife he could not prove that he had repudiated her,[61] even though the man in question was a *clarissimus* and no one had accused him of prostituting his wife.

The laws relating to the pecuniary fines to be imposed on adulterers probably date from Severus' time. Under the Republic, on separation the husband could keep one sixth of his wife's dowry if she had committed adultery, one eighth if she had behaved badly but not committed adultery.[62] It is clear that a woman found guilty of adultery always had some of her property confiscated. The most explicit text on this point is to be found in the *Sententiae Pauli*.[63] The penalty for *stuprum*[64] gives us the best indication of the size of the fine imposed on an adulterer. In the case of *stuprum* committed with a virgin or a respectable widow, if the guilty parties were *honesti*, half of their possessions would be confiscated and they would be banished. If they were *humiles*, the penalty was corporal punishment and banishment. Caracalla had the idea of making the collector of taxes responsible for adultery trials, doubtless so that the State might take part of the dowry and possessions of the guilty lover.[65] So if the lovers were not fortunate enough to have the charge against them cancelled by a general pardon, they might lose half of their property, be banished if they were rich and sentenced to hard labour for life if they were poor, unless an *indulgentia* annulled the judgement against them. The *lex Julia* on adultery was thus still being applied in Severus' time, even though exile had replaced capital punishment, and indeed it was being more widely used. But although adultery was always strictly dealt with, Alexander Severus declared invalid the clause in matrimonial agreements which penalized the spouse who initiated a repudiation.[66] The financial obstacles to unilateral repudiation were thus removed, and a woman who had been abandoned by her husband could now repudiate him without difficulty.

Young senators were not keen to marry. Perhaps marriage was too serious an undertaking. If they did not wish to adopt a life of asceticism,

---

[60] *D*, 48, 5, 14.

[61] Ibid., 48, 5, 2.

[62] Cato, in Aulus Gellius, 10, 23; Ulpian, *Regulae*, 6, 12.

[63] G. Branca, in the article Adulterio, *Enciclopedia di Diritto Romano*, quotes Mommsen, *Le Droit pénal*, II, p. 426, as if this was the range of penalties imposed by the *lex Julia de adulteriis*. We do not know if this is so.

[64] *IJ*, 4, 18, 4.

[65] Mommsen, *Le Droit pénal*, II, p. 423 and vol. I, p. 322.

[66] *CJ*, 8, 38, 2.

rather than marry they preferred a long-term relationship with a Greek freedwoman, an actress or an actor's daughter. This relationship would be either an illegitimate marriage, or a concubinage. Augustus decided to impose legal disqualifications on those who entered into such a marriage. The marriage would not be void; it was simply considered contrary to the law and the disqualification related only to patrimonial matters. The most important disadvantage of such a marriage was that, like those who were unmarried, neither party could receive any succession in its entirety. There was no dowry and a concubine who had property in her own right could recover it in the event of a separation. Any children belonged to the woman and did not become part of the husband's family or receive any inheritance from him. However, donations could be made between concubines, which was not the case within a legitimate marriage, and they remained valid even if the parties later married one another legitimately.[67] Studies have been made of the ways in which senators escaped the duty to marry imposed on them by Augustus. We know that fathers forced their sons to marry because sons argued against their fathers in court to have these marriages annulled. We also know that couples consented to artificial marriages which were never consummated in an attempt to win the right to inherit.[68] But perhaps we should examine the law in relation to the length of time during which it actually affected the life of a senator or a woman from a senatorial family. The law demanded marriage and children. It urged the widowed or divorced man or woman to remarry and treated them as unmarried people if they refused to fulfil their duty. The *lex Julia* on marriage required a widow to remarry within ten months, and a divorced woman within six months. The *lex Papia* extended this period to a year.[69] But in fact there was no hurry. If they had legitimate children, those who were widowed, divorced or repudiated could wait until they were due to receive an inheritance before entering into another marriage, and in the mean time they could live in concubinage, which was an official and respectable condition.

Particularly if the other party in a concubinage was a freed slave, an actress or actor, concubinage had the advantage of leaving intact the rights of any legitimate children already born, of not giving them any brothers or sisters, and not altering in any way the arrangements for succession. This was the view of Marcus Aurelius after the death of his wife Faustina, who had given him twelve (or thirteen) children of whom only six

---

[67] Plassard, *Le concubinat romain*, pp. 36–7.
[68] Unconsummated marriages: *D*, 23, 2, 30, Gaius; a father's power to force his son to marry: Ibid., 23, 2, 21; *CJ*, 5, 4, 12 and 14; on ways of getting round the law, see Astolfi, Note per una valutazione, pp. 212–15.
[69] Astolfi. Note per una valutazione, p. 198.

reached marriageable age. He refused to marry Fabia, but took her as concubine 'so as not to give all those children a step-mother'.[70]

Those who wanted to marry had a wide range of people to choose their partners from. While freed persons, actresses and prostitutes were forbidden, that still left plenty of respectable free-born individuals, so that any illegitimate unions must have been the result of deliberate choice on the part of senators and not the result of unbearable constraints imposed by the law. If the senators did not marry it was because they did not want to. And in general, since they were urged to marry and have legitimate children, the end of a marriage, whether as a result of the death of a partner or repudiation or divorce, led not to a second marriage, as the State desired, but to concubinage either with a man or woman whom a person of senatorial rank could not marry, or with a free man or woman who accepted this status perhaps for the same reasons as the other partner.

The general rule was therefore one marriage and subsequent concubinages. But if we examine matters from the woman's point of view we will have a better understanding of sexual relations in the society.

[70] *Scriptores Historiae Augustae*, ed. and tr. D. Magie, vol. I, Marcus Antoninus, 29. See Plassard, *Le concubinat romain*, pp. 182–3. On Marcus Aurelius' children, see M. Manson, Le temps à Rome d'après les monnaies, in Aiôn, Le temps chez les Romains, *Caesarodunum X bis*, published by R. Chevallier, 1976, pp. 183–96.

6

Separation, Divorce and Prostitution

In Rome many girls were still children when they were married. We might wonder whether the fact that girls under twelve were allowed to have sexual relations should be counted as a measure of the freedom enjoyed by women or of that enjoyed by men. However this may be, these little girls, who were given, with their consent, to men who were always older than themselves, were considered responsible for their actions. The law was the same whether the girls were entering into concubinage or marriage: legally, they only became concubines or wives, in other words matrons, once they were twelve years old, even if they had been given away before that age.[1] The legal writers of the time were called upon to advise husbands and concubines who wanted to bring charges of adultery against partners of less than twelve.[2] If they wanted to denounce and accuse the girl's lover then they had to accuse the girl herself. The question asked by the husbands and concubines of these young girls – in all seriousness and with reference to actual cases – concerned procedure and not the girl's responsibility. There was no question as to whether a girl of that age could be held to be guilty of adultery. It was perhaps in cases such as these that the woman was accused but not condemned, only the lover being found guilty. These were probably also the cases where the husband re-married his wife, having accused her only because he could not have pursued her lover without doing so. In any case, the tie between the two partners had not been broken (providing that the wife had not been caught *in flagrante delicto*) because the husband could not bring an action against a wife who was a minor using the *jus mariti*, as he was not yet legally her husband, but had to use the *jus extranei*.[3] The obligatory repudiation only remained valid if the wife wished it. One imagines that these cases often involved girls who had been freed by their master to become his concubine and who later wished to leave him for a

---

[1] *D*, 25, 7, 1, 4.
[2] Ibid., 48, 5, 14, 8.
[3] Ibid., 48, 5, 14, 8, Ulpian, and 23, 2, 34, Papinian.

man of their choice. These women would never again be matrons; their gowns would show that they were classed as prostitutes and owed no duty of fidelity to anyone.

Just as a wife who was a minor was considered capable of being guilty of adultery, so also was a lover who was a minor.[4] Any relationship between adolescents in a master's household was forbidden by the law. A girl could be held to be guilty of adultery from the time of her betrothal, a boy from the time he actually reached puberty.

Although there are texts which show that some girls under twelve, probably all freed slaves, began their sexual life as concubines, for most Roman girls their first sexual relationship was marriage. One has to be careful because an examination of the laws of the time can lead one to believe that there were separate categories of Roman women – those who were married, those who were concubines, those who were widows and those who were divorcees – whereas in fact any woman might be all of these at different times in her life. She might be married as a young girl of twelve, widowed a year later, and then re-marry so as to serve the political interests of her father. At twenty, having given her husband two children, she might agree to a divorce which allowed her to recover her own property. She might become a concubine for a while, and then marry yet again in order to be entitled to receive an inheritance left her by her uncle. She might then look for a way to repudiate her husband without losing her dowry or the donation he had made her before their marriage.

A study of male sexual freedom reveals the degree of freedom women had in the eyes of the law. But can one refer to a sexual relationship in which a woman could not choose her partner as freedom?[5] Can we say that slaves and prostitutes enjoyed sexual freedom in this sense when we know that the *leno*, or procurer, took them to the ports when he heard that a ship had arrived? We should not imagine that all the young girls who were abandoned and then brought up to be slaves or prostitutes or both, and later freed by a procurer, were *demi-mondaines*, although the latter certainly existed in Roman society. Some free women who could receive visitors in their houses without any difficulty, would officially register themselves as prostitutes so as to avoid being accused of *stuprum*,[6] or else, if they could, they would take a job in the theatre, which gave them the same security with regard to the law.

On the whole, this was not the path chosen by or for the free woman in Rome. She risked being accused of *stuprum* if she entered into a heterosexual relationship outside marriage or concubinage (female homosexuality is not referred to in the laws of the time) and so she sought

[4] Ibid., 48, 5, 37.
[5] P. Grimal, *L'amour à Rome*, 1963, Chapter V and p. 120.
[6] D, 48, 5, 11.

satisfaction within marriage or concubinage. If it was considered that she had not chosen her first marriage partner, and if she was not happy in her marriage, then she could obtain a separation even without her husband's agreement. If he agreed, then the matter was simple. If her husband repudiated her without good reason, which meant essentially without her having committed adultery, he was obliged by the marriage contract and by the laws to return the dowry which he had managed while the marriage lasted, and to give up part of the amount he had given his wife before their marriage. But he kept any property he had inherited in his own right. Things were different for the wife. She had the right to leave her husband, but if she repudiated him without reason she might lose part of her dowry and might have to return the donation made to her by her husband before their marriage. This was generally set out in the marriage contract.[7] If it was not, then the husband could even claim the donation together with any increase in its value between the time of the marriage and the separation.

A wife could not justify her desire to leave her husband by accusing him of adultery, even if he was legally guilty of the offence not because he had been unfaithful to his own wife but because he had had an affair with another man's wife. In Rome, a woman could not bring a case of adultery before the courts.[8] Now if she lost her dowry a Roman woman of the middle classes lost everything that constituted her inheritance. If she wanted to repudiate her husband she needed to have other financial prospects, or be able to work for her living.[9] In practice, she needed to have a proposal of concubinge or re-marriage without a dowry. So it was much more difficult for a woman to exercise the right to repudiate her partner than it was for a man.

A woman who had not been maltreated by her husband but simply deserted, particularly after she had given him the child who was needed to ensure the preservation of the family heritage and the union between the two families,[10] had no reasons with which to justify her repudiation of her spouse. The husband might have short-lived or more lasting affairs with slaves or women 'with whom he was not committing *stuprum*', or he

---

[7] Ibid., 24, 1, 57.

[8] Ibid., 48, 2, 1.

[9] Iro Kajanto, On Divorce Among the Common People of Rome, 1970 = *REL*, 47 *bis*, pp. 99–113; J. Le Gall, La 'nouvelle plèbe' et la sportule quotidienne, 1966, pp. 1449–53, shows that the majority of the population of the Urbs was made up of salaried workers and not clients who depended on the *sportula* distributed by their patron.

[10] Fontanille, *Avortement et contraception*, p. 182, refers to work carried out by N. Mallard, University of Bordeaux, 1970: 109 couples had only 161 children in all. More than half the couples had only one child, more than a quarter had two. Fontanille links this low fertility on the part of legitimately married couples with the use of abortifacients which resulted in sterility.

might adopt a life of abstinence. He might even have one or more concubines, but his wife would still not be considered as having grounds for a unilateral repudiation.

Only the *Sententiae Pauli*, which we now know were written in the fourth century, and are therefore Christian in period, state that a Roman could not be married and have a concubine at the same time: 'If a man has a wife he may not have a concubine.'[11] The *Sententiae* are introducing a Christian element here,[12] for all the other documents show that the opposite was the case in previous centuries. It is clear that the second union did not have the same consequences for husband and wife. If a woman had a sexual relationship with someone other than her husband while she was living with him then she was committing adultery. If she set up home with another man then this was a marriage or a concubinage and cancelled her first marriage. But if a man took another wife before his first wife had left the marital home, that is any of the residences owned by the husband, then the second union was considered invalid, but it was regarded in law not as adultery but as a concubinage.[13]

We can not regard this concubinage as adulterous, as Plassard has done.[14] This notion was foreign both to Roman society and to Roman law. To use the term harem, as do Plassard and Carcopino, is to suggest that multiple concubinage was a sexual practice reserved for a few deviants of Roman upper class society,[15] the best known example of which was Commodus whose 'large harem consisted of three hundred young people and three hundred concubines, matrons or prostitutes'.[16] In practice, the only way for a father to prevent his daughter from having to share her husband with one or more concubines was to have a penalty clause written into the agreement drawn up before marriage. Papinian, when asked about the validity of this clause, replied that it was in keeping with standards of good behaviour and perfectly valid,[17] from which we may understand that husbands who were subject to this clause tried to have it nullified.

---

[11] *Sententiae Pauli*, II, 20, 1.

[12] It was one of Constantine's laws, *CJ*, 5, 26, 1, which introduced this prohibition.

[13] The Roman legal works do not draw this parallel because they do not distinguish between texts relating to men and those relating to women. Plassard is the most accurate on this point, quoting, among others, Cicero, *De Oratore*, I, 40. See J. Plassard, *Le concubinat romain*, p. 166.

[14] Plassard, *Le concubinat romain*, p. 45 et seq.; p. 176 on Actè, who was Nero's concubine when he was still married to Octavia; p. 187 on Panthea, concubine to Lucius Verus while he was married to Lucilla.

[15] Plassard, *Le concubinat romain*, pp. 167 and 183; Carcopino, *Daily Life in Ancient Rome*, Penguin ed. p. 117.

[16] *Scriptores Historiae Augustae*, vol. I, *Life of Commodus*, 5; Plassard, *Le concubinat romain*, p. 183.

[17] *D*, 45, 1, 121, 1, *Responsa* XI.

Besides a legitimate wife whom he married in order to unite their two families and to make it possible to pass on the family wealth, a Roman might choose one of his female slaves, sometimes less than twelve years old, and free her to be a concubine, a free and respectable woman, whom no other man could approach without committing the crime of *stuprum*, which was not the case with a slave. In this way he kept her for himself. He could repeat the process if his attachment to the freed slave did not last. He could consent to her living with a free man, one of his freedmen, or even with a slave, as numerous inscriptions reveal. Plassard has found a number of inscriptions which refer to the concubinage of a man and a woman who bore the same name and had therefore been freed by the same master. Freed persons could marry legitimately, and if they were concubines the reason might be that the woman had left her master (perhaps against his will?) and thus lost the rights of a matron. A freedwoman had to rely on what she could earn by working if she did not have the favour of her former master. If she left her master against his will she was in an even more exposed position than a wife who left her husband without her father's agreement.

The fact that it was easier to bring a concubinage to an end and to show the legal dissolution of the relationship than it was to dissolve matrimonial ties did not make it any easier for those who were dependent to this degree on a man's decisions.

In practice it was not in a Roman man's interests to dissolve a relationship unless he himself wanted to enter into one that was more useful on political grounds or to break his ties with a family which was no longer politically useful to him or indeed with which it was dangerous for him to be associated. The political marriage was an alliance, necessitating a wife and a child. Alongside this, a man could seek pleasure or affection or both in casual affairs or in a stable concubinage which did not interfere with his freedom. This means that except where a husband was particularly happy with his legitimate wife, for every man there might be one or more women deprived of sexual relations, deserted, and yet in such a position that any sexual relationship they might enter into would be counted as adultery and punished by the courts.[18]

The Roman citizen of the upper class could thus with impunity take as concubine one of his freedwomen who was still a virgin, or even the wife of a free man, for instance one of his own freedmen, without committing adultery. Like marriage, concubinage cancelled a woman's previous relationship.

One of the key questions on which Plassard sheds light is the respectability of concubinage, a relationship which was chosen by many

---

[18] The patron was quite entitled to accuse his freedwoman concubine of adultery and once she had been condemned she would have to wear a prostitute's clothes.

free-born men and women who could apparently have entered into legitimate marriage. It seems quite natural to find relationships between a man and a female slave, or between a slave and a freed man or woman, which could not legally have been counted as marriages, described in inscriptions with all the warmth of conjugal love. But Plassard refuses to believe that a man who was buried between his wife and his concubine could have had both relationships simultaneously.[19] In his eyes, it was the respectability of the relationship which justified concubinage between two free-born individuals whose condition, as far as we can see, did not bar them from marriage. In a spirit of great generosity and broad-mindedness he wrote in 1921:

> It is a notion which dates from the period in question rather than from our day that the customary respectability of Roman concubinage was a result of the lack of secrecy surrounding the relationship.
> Nowadays, public opinion is indulgent towards shameful or immoral behaviour providing it is kept hidden from the public eye, but mercilessly condemns any unconventional relationships which are carried on in public. A man whose base behaviour is common knowledge but is nevertheless clandestine will be welcomed in the most exclusive circles, while another will be excluded because of a liaison which is publicly acknowledged, even though it may be a respectable and lasting relationship.[20]

One element is missing from this analysis, namely those cases where, although marriage was possible on the grounds of the social status of the individuals concerned (freed slaves, free-born citizens etc.), it was legally impossible, for example because the man was already married. (If it was the woman who was married then the new relationship did not come into this category since concubinage cancelled any previous ties on the part of a woman though not a man.) Funerary inscriptions show us men who, having erected a tomb for their legitimate wife, did not then marry their concubine. She might be free-born or freed; the problem was the same since the inscriptions are by men who were not senators. By itself, the respectability of concubinage can not explain such cases. In some cases marriage between free-born individuals or between a free-born man and a freedwoman was legally impossible, for example, where a free-born woman or a freedwoman had lost *conubium*, the title of matron, which the inscriptions would obviously not mention. Whereas the inscriptions do refer to the acting profession, they do not mention that of

---

[19] *CIL*, X, 1267.
[20] Plassard, *Le concubinat romain*, insists on the respectability of the relationship.

prostitution. The fact that a woman was or had been a prostitute of free birth could very well explain a concubinage described in the inscriptions in terms of great affection and appreciation. A woman or a man who had been convicted of adultery might find lasting happiness in concubinage, which the surviving partner might wish to record on a tombstone. The most common case, however, must have been that of the freedwoman who had been her master's concubine and then lost *conubium* when she left him.

Thus it was not enough to be free-born or a freed person in order to have the right to enter into a legitimate marriage: it was probably because legitimate marriage was not open to them that many of those described in the inscriptions entered into concubinage, rather than from desire for a free relationship, which Roman concubinage did not in any case constitute.

The only case where Roman concubinage provided a free union would have been that of a woman who agreed to her partner's wish to make no changes to the composition of his family or to his will. Such was the case of Fabia, a free-born woman from a noble family, who became Marcus Aurelius' concubine after Faustina's death.

Whereas the young master of a household would have a wife chosen for him by his father and would abandon her as soon as he had done his duty to his family, other couples would be attracted to one another within the *domus* and with the master's approval would form a relationship, as happened throughout the lower classes in Roman Italy. Such couples might consist of a free man and a slave, or, more commonly according to the inscriptions, a slave and a free woman; or else between freed women and male slaves or vice versa, or free-born men and freed women or slaves. These relationships would have been quite public, and their legal status as either marriage, concubinage or *contubernium* (between a free person and a slave) was of no consequence in society. Children born to concubines bore their mother's name but had steles engraved to both parents, who would be buried in the same tomb.[21]

Marquardt and Carcopino have ascribed the number of concubines to a laxity in moral standards, except where the social status of the individuals in question made legitimate marriage impossible. Plassard tried to show that Roman concubinage was a publicly recognized and honourable union. Armed with modern, even feminist ideas, it is tempting to see concubinage as a liberating institution, a more equal union than Roman marriage, and one in which a woman retained control of her own property and could leave her partner without financial loss. But this would be a quite inappropriate application of present-day notions to a very different era. Apart from those cases where Roman concubinage was

[21] *CIL*, VI, 7304 for example.

simply marriage without its disadvantages (although we can not be sure that it was seen this way in Rome), entered into by two individuals who did not have *conubium*, it constituted a form of female dependence on men, whereby the woman associated her private life with her concubine's political plans, particularly if the male partner's marriage was a true alliance of families. A woman of the Roman Empire was only in a strong position if she had her own property, which meant that she did not have to consider the risk of losing her dowry if she repudiated her partner without his consent, and if she had a powerful father who was prepared to take her back into his household and help her to form another union which would satisfy both his daughter's wishes and his own social ambition.

From the point of view of female emancipation, Roman concubinage may be seen as representing progress towards the right to enjoy a less unequal relationship. In fact, a Roman woman could not, on moral grounds, use this right unless her social status or the social position of her partner in concubinage placed her above criticism. Women who were concubines were essentially women who could not marry or whom men did not wish to marry, in the same way as people who were citizens of a nation under Roman dominance were primarily people who were not Roman citizens. In order actively to take advantage of the economic benefits of concubinage, a Roman woman needed to have a very independent nature. For a legitimately married woman to repudiate her husband without specific grounds required even more moral courage. The women who were genuinely free to act as they pleased were not those who had repudiated their husbands, but those who had been repudiated themselves without having committed adultery, or who were widows with three children (four if they were freed women), and no longer had a guardian and so could look for a new partner without any constraints being placed on them. Of course their freedom might be compromised if they found a man who was only interested in the political advantages of an alliance with their family. As for those wives who were abandoned after producing a child, and who had no support from any one else, no father who would help them to initiate a repudiation without grounds, is it surprising that they became the new hysterical women of the Mediterranean?

All that we have said so far only applies to those men and woman who were subject to Roman law. In the second century AD most of those living in the Empire were not Roman citizens but were subject to the laws of their own country.[22] Although in the third century all those who lived

---

[22] J. Modrzejewski, La règle de Droit dans l'Egypte romaine (Etat des questions et perspectives de recherches), 1970, sets out the main points relating to the difficult question of local laws in the Roman Empire, and gives a bibliography.

in the Empire became citizens of Rome, following Caracalla's Constitution, they still continued to organize their private lives according to local laws. For example, according to the Greek law which was in force in Egypt, the conditions relating to marriage and the separation of spouses, which have come down to us in the form of contracts written on papyrus, were completely different from those imposed by Roman law. According to the Greek contracts, a husband agreed not to install a concubine in the matrimonial home, or even, according to later contracts, in a second home over which his wife had no control.[23] So if he had a lasting relationship with a woman other than his wife, the latter could repudiate him and demand the return of her dowry, and in addition, sometimes, a sum of equal value.[24] A wife had a certain amount of power over her husband if she could make such a claim, since the threat of being divorced and having to give back the dowry plus an equal sum of money might well persuade him to end an extra-marital affair. It was thus in the interest of both spouses to arrive at an amicable divorce, on the grounds of incompatibility, since neither was allowed to be unfaithful, apart from a few casual affairs in which the husband, but not the wife, was allowed to indulge. We find an amicable separation agreement recorded on a late papyrus dating from AD 569:

> We were married at an early age, and set up home together intending to have legitimate children, and in the hope and belief that we would live together in good companionship till the end of our days. Instead, we find that for a reason which we do not know, our hopes have been confounded and, because of an evil and perverse demon, we must part. Thus we have decided to divorce one another, but we declare that neither of us has any grievance against the other, nor will we have any in future for whatever reason . . .[25]

Because of the great difference that existed between local and Roman laws in the Empire, we must be careful to consider the rules of the Christians only in the legal context in which they were drawn up and put forward.[26] Three texts give us an idea of the problem debated within the

[23] Vatin, *Recherches sur le mariage*, p. 204.

[24] R. Taubenschlag, *The Law of Greco-roman Egypt in the Light of the Papyri*, 332 B.C.–640 A.D., 1955, pp. 121–3; J. Modrzejewski, Zum hellenistischen Ehegüterrecht im griechischen und römischen Aegypten, 1970, p. 64.

[25] *P. Flor.*, I, 93, FIRA, III, no. 22; French tr. J. Gaudemet, *Le Droit privé romain*, 1974, pp. 297–8.

[26] Thus H. Crouzel, *L'Eglise primitive face au divorce*, 1971, pp. 48–9, in order to shed light on Hermas, turns to Chrysostom, Jerome, Ambrose and Basil who wrote at the end of the fourth century and two of whom were eastern in origin. On the other hand, Gaudemet, La décision de Callixte, pp. 334–44, uses the law and Christian authors writing in Latin at the time of the papal decision.

Church in Rome with regard to the conditions relating to sexual life which should be imposed on those wishing to be baptized or take communion.

Hermas' *Shepherd*, written during the first half of the second century, is presented in the form of visions and commandments, but in fact tells us a great deal about contemporary practices within the Church in Rome.

> He said: 'I command you to remain chaste and not to allow into your heart desire of another woman (than your wife), or of any kind of fornication or of any similar vice. For if you did so, you would be committing a great sin. Always remember your wife and you will never sin. If such desires come into your heart you sin, and if any other evil thoughts occur to you that is also a sin. For a servant of God to have such desires is a great sin. If a man performs this sinful act, he is preparing his own death. Take care, then, and abstain from such desire, for iniquity should not come into the heart of a just man, which is the home of holiness.' I said to him: 'Sir, allow me to ask you a few questions.' 'Speak', said he. 'Sir', I said, 'if a man has a wife who believes in the Lord, and if he discovers that she is committing adultery, is he sinning by living with her?' He said: 'As long as he does not know of her adultery, he is not sinning; but if he learns of her sin and if she persists in her adultery instead of repenting, then the husband shares her sin and takes part in adultery if he continues to live with her.' 'What then should the husband do, Sir, if his wife persists in this passion?' He said: 'He should send her away from him and remain alone. But if he sends his wife away and then marries another woman, he too is comitting adultery.' I asked: 'And if, Sir, the wife repents after having been sent away, and wishes to return to her husband, should he not take her back?' 'He should,' said he. 'If the husband does not take her back he is committing a grave sin, for one must take back a sinner who repents, but not too often. For the servants of God, there is only one repentance. It is because his wife may repent that a man should not remarry. This applies to the woman as to the man.'

The Shepherd tells a man to repudiate an adulterous wife, just as Roman law commands, but the work introduces two important new elements. The first is the fact that not only may the adulterous wife repent, but the husband may then forgive her and take her back. This would have been impossible according to Roman law, for it would have involved dissimulation of the wife's adultery, followed by a physical separation of the two spouses living in different houses. It would have meant that there had been no accusation in front of the court following a repudiation on grounds stated before seven witnesses. If the husband wished to retain the right to take back his wife, he ran the risk of being prosecuted for connivance and procuring if he had not brought an accusation against her, or else his wife might repudiate him without giving reasons if she wanted to regain her freedom completely and claim the return of her property. Hermas' command requires the husband to do rather more than strive to remain chaste while he waits for his adulterous wife to return; it requires him to have the courage to risk being prosecuted for *lenocinium*, which would mean that he would be publicly disgraced for having pardoned adultery and might even be exiled or sentenced to hard labour if because of his complicity he was condemned to serve the same sentence as those who committed adultery.

The second new element is the notion that adultery could be committed by a husband who was unfaithful to his own wife.[27] The text affirms that everything that applies to a man applies to a woman as well, and so a wife could not live with an adulterous husband. In taking back an adulterous husband who repented of his sin, a wife risked nothing. Repudiating him was more difficult. If she brought an action to recover her property she would have no legal grounds for repudiation. Her dowry could only be restored to her if the matrimonial agreement did not contain a clause penalizing the partner who initiated the *repudium*. Nevertheless a wife who repudiated an adulterous husband could marry him again without falling foul of the law, as the law made clear. But if neither the husband nor the wife had recourse to the various types of legal separation available, it was still possible for them to have an informal separation and the wife remained subject to her husband's wishes on the matter and also financially dependent on him. Wives who followed this command, without help from their father or their family, had to turn to the Church for assistance.

The two other texts both concern concubinage and both date from the first quarter of the third century. They set out the position of two adversaries, the Pope Calixtus and the Roman priest Hippolytus. We know of Calixtus' decision regarding concubinage through Hippolytus' *Philosophumena*, which criticizes it.[28] The *Apostolic Tradition*, also by Hippolytus, bars from communion all those who were denied the right to marry legitimately because of their profession, all those who were *infames*, all homosexuals and those who had emasculated themselves.[29] It

[27] H. Crouzel, *L'Eglise primitive*, sees this, but not from the point of view of the legal risks.

[28] Gaudemet, La décision de Callixte, loc. cit., corrects the text and the translation of this fragment. But he is wrong to say (p. 114) that concubinage was not an obstacle to baptism: it was for men.

[29] Chapter 16 of Hippolytus' *Apostolic Tradition* deals with those who were not accepted for baptism. Into this category fell all those who, according to Roman law, were *infames*:

also sets out the conditions on which concubines might be baptized, giving rules which were probably applied by the Church of Rome at the beginning of the third century.

Although these texts all deal with concubinage, they can not be viewed as homogeneous. Chapter 16 of the *Apostolic Tradition* covers the rules for the baptism of female slaves who were concubines and of men who had concubines. Calixtus' decision concerns girls from noble families who took as concubine a slave or a free man of inferior birth. These situations, which were all referred to as concubinage, were nevertheless very different. We might compare the position with that relating to citizenship without the right to suffrage. The rich Roman woman who was the concubine of an inferior man was in a similar position to a Roman citizen who went off to found a Latin colony: when he was in Rome he could assume the rights of a full Roman citizen. The female concubine who was a slave or freedwoman was like the foreign city raised to the rank of *municipium*. The comparison is not a trivial one: the slave girl who was a concubine could never leave her concubine master against his will without losing the right to marry, even if she was freed. The rich Roman woman could simply decide to leave her concubine for another or in order to marry someone of higher class. So the term concubinage covers very different circumstances. This is what the *Apostolic Tradition* has to say: 'A concubine, who is a slave and has reared her children, and has been faithful to her master alone, may become a hearer, but if she has failed in these matters she must be rejected. If a man has a concubine, he must desist and marry legally; if he is unwilling, he must be rejected.'[30]

The first sentence must refer to a woman who was concubine to a pagan, otherwise the Church would have demanded that he free her and marry her (which would have been impossible if he were a senator), or that he part with her and marry another woman. Chapter 15 states, moreover, that a Christian's slave must be presented by his master. The Church thus required a concubine slave not to leave her pagan master, or at least required that she should not have had any other sexual relationships and should not have any others in future. Even though she had been abandoned for another woman, whether or not she was slave, if she wanted to be baptized she had no other course than to remain alone.

---

procurers, actors, coachmen and actors in the games, gladiators who fought one another and those who fought wild beasts, and male and female prostitutes. Also included were those who organized shows at the theatre and the amphitheatre, magistrates, soldiers and those who took part in the pagan cult, as well as sculptors, painters and teachers. B. Botte (French tr., *La tradition apostolique*, 1968) translates *qui se abscidit* as 'mignons', but I prefer to translate the phrase as 'those who had emasculated themselves'. A Gallus (a eunuch or priest) of Cybele could never be baptized into the Christian faith.

[30] Hippolytus of Rome, *Apostolic Tradition*, tr. Burton Scott Easton, 1934.

She must also have brought up her children in order to be eligible, which amounted to saying that she must reject abortion although this was often demanded by masters, as we see from the account of Hippocrates himself helping at a slave's abortion on her mistress' orders. She must also have brought up her children, which went against the socially indisputable authority of a father over his children, and of a master over his female slave's children who were slaves like their mother. This was asking a great deal of a slave who had a pagan master. Furthermore, the Church required a baptized woman not to have known more than one man; it did not ask her to leave a pagan for a Christian.

A free man, on the other hand, was called upon to 'marry legally'. He could not be excused for living in concubinage, but must find a woman who was entitled to marry and whom he had the right to marry. In fact a senator gave his rank to any free woman he married. The only women eligible for marriage whom he could not legally choose were freedwomen. Thus the concubine whom he could not marry was, if she was a Christian, expected to resign herself to solitude so that her concubine might marry another woman and be baptized.

Calixtus' decision shows that free women of noble birth could not always find a husband from their own social class, which would allow them to retain their rank. Unlike men, they did not raise their spouse to senatorial rank. There were daughters of noble families for whom their fathers could not find a senator's son, but an *oratio* by Marcus Aurelius and Commodus forbade them to marry anyone else. So as senators' sons quite often married girls from a lower social class, that meant there were fewer husbands of the right class for senators' daughters. It was in relation to these girls that Calixtus raised the question of a concubinage that might be compatible with Christian baptism. Clearly it was not so much concubinage itself that posed a problem for the Church, as concubinage when chosen by men and women who could have entered into legitimate marriage. Girls from noble families could have married beneath them even though this would have meant losing their rank, so Calixtus was envisaging making an exception in order to accommodate them. It has been said that this was in order to allow them to live with a Christian slave rather than with a free pagan of whatever class, in which case this reflects Calixtus' personal weakness given that he had himself been a slave. The reproach that Hippolytus made was that this encouraged the usual consequences of such unions: these women who had not wanted to lose their class did not want to have children by the men they took as concubines, for they did not want these relationships to be public knowledge, so they had abortions. There was, however, a procedure for allowing exceptions to the law which stated that girls of senatorial class who married beneath them lost their rank. We find this in the *Life of*

Elagabalus[31]: a group of matrons put to the Emperor a list of those women who they thought should be exempt from the law. Calixtus' decision thus related to those who wished to avoid the need to appear before this committee, presumably because they did not wish to have to explain their choice of partner.

There is a clear contradiction between the decision requiring a free man to leave his concubine and that allowing an aristocratic woman to live in concubinage with a free man of inferior birth or with a slave. All other cases, whether relating to legitimate marriages or concubinage or a union with a slave (*contubernium*), are dealt with in chapter 15 of the *Apostolic Tradition*:

'If a man has a woman, or a woman a man, let the man be instructed to content himself with this woman and the woman to content herself with this man.[32] But if a man is unmarried, let him be instructed to abstain from impurity, either by lawfully marrying a wife or else by remaining as he is.' The Latin terms are general: man and woman, not husband, wife or concubine. The only exception to this rule about having a sexual relationship with one person alone is that of the free man who is able to marry legitimately and is therefore required to leave his concubine. The Church thus favoured legitimate marriage except where it was prepared to protect the rank of senators' daughters. A wife or a female concubine was called on to endure loneliness if she was abandoned, or if, as a legitimate wife, she was obliged to repudiate an adulterous husband. Thus from this point on solitude endured by women within marriage or concubinage in Rome represented a deliberate choice and their continence was voluntary. All this was accepted as part of the path chosen by a Christian woman convert, whose personal life could not be shared by a pagan husband or concubine.

---

[31] *Life of Elagabalus*, IV, 3.
[32] Here again I disagree with Botte's and also Easton's translation; it is not husband and wife, but *mulier et vir*, man and woman, without reference to the law. The rest of the passage is quoted in Easton's translation.

7

Salvation by Child Sacrifice and Castration

Even before the birth of Christian asceticism, at a time when Christians were suffering torture and execution, the accusations which were levelled at the new religion and its adherents reflected practices within the pagan religion which, together with the ancient myths on which it was built, brought to life the fantasies which haunted the collective imagination, in an attempt to make sense of the Creation and of human birth and death.

> I am told that under some idiotic impulse they consecrate and worship the head of an ass, the meanest of all beasts, a religion worthy of the morals which gave it birth. Other say that they actually reverence the private parts of their director and high priest, and adore his organs as parent of their being. This may be false, but such suspicions naturally attach to their secret and nocturnal rites. To say that a malefactor put to death for his crimes, and wood of the death-dealing cross, are objects of their veneration is to assign fitting altars to abandoned wretches and the kind of worship they deserve. Details of the initiation of neophytes are as revolting as they are notorious. An infant, cased in dough to deceive the unsuspecting, is placed beside the person to be initiated. The novice is thereupon induced to inflict what seem to be harmless blows upon the dough, and unintentionally the infant is killed by his unsuspecting blows; the blood – oh, horrible – they lap up greedily; the limbs they tear to pieces eagerly; and over the victim they make league and covenant, and by complicity in guilt they pledge themselves to mutual silence. Such sacred rites are more foul than any sacrilege. Their form of feasting is notorious; it is in everyone's mouth, as testified by the speech of our friend of Cirta. On the day appointed they gather at a banquet with all their children, sisters, and mothers, people of either sex and every age. There, after full feasting, when the blood is heated and drink has inflamed the

passions of incestuous lust, a dog which has been tied to a lamp is tempted by a morsel thrown beyond the range of his tether to bound forward with a rush. The tale-telling light is upset and extinguished, and in the shameless dark lustful embraces are indiscriminately exchanged; and all alike, if not in act, yet by complicity, are involved in incest, as anything that occurs by the act of individuals results from the common intention.[1]

Such were the public rumours spread about the Christians and which two Christian writers felt it necessary to refute. Tertullian, writing in 197, shortly before or shortly after Minicius Felix, reported similar accusations, indicating that both child sacrifice and group sex were said to take place at the initiation ceremony. 'We have been in existence for almost two hundred years, and during that time there have been so many criminals among us, so many crosses deified, so many children massacred, so many loaves of bread soaked in blood, so many lamps overturned and couples united in random embraces.'[2]

The rhetorical device used by both authors, in Minucius Felix's *Octavius* and Tertullian's address *Ad Nationes* and his *Apology*, is to list the accusations made against the Christians and then to attribute the practices to pagans of various sects or ethnic groups. But though they refer to the myth of Saturn, it is not the African practice of sacrificing children to Saturn which they put forward as the equivalent of the crimes imputed to the Christians.

Yet you are infanticides..., you who kill your newborn children ... The fact that your murders do not form part of a rite and are not carried out by the sword makes no difference. Indeed they are all the more cruel, for your children die of cold or hunger or are eaten by wild beasts if you expose them or suffer the slowest of all deaths if you drown them.[3]

The incestuous revelry becomes the Egyptian custom of brothers marrying sisters and the Persian custom of mothers marrying sons. Both writers claim that the Romans' own sexual freedom puts them in danger of committing incest without realizing it. 'Each act of adultery, each illicit relationship, each act of debauchery conducted in your houses or in the street, results in another mixing of blood and thus another path leading to incest.'[4]

[1] Minucius Felix, *Octavius*, 9, 3–7. This passage and all others from the Octavius. tr. Gerald H. Rendall, 1931.
[2] Tertullian, *Ad Nationes*, 1, 7, 10.
[3] Ibid., 1, 15; see Minucius Felix, *Octavius*, 30, 2.
[4] Tertullian, *Ad Nationes*, 1, 16, 11; see Minucius Felix, *Ocatvius*, 31.

This amounts to saying that there was no clear parallel; the practices of which Christians were accused or allegedly accused, the ritual sexual orgies and child sacrifice, were not openly attributed to pagan cults. Two other practices were attributed to the Christians: veneration of the priest's sexual organs, referred to as the father's organs, and worship of an ass. The first of these accusations is transferred to the pagans, in the form even of fellatio, and the second is linked with the worship of Egyptian gods and with some of the pagan myths. Minucius Felix, who was a lawyer in Rome, but originally came from Cirta (now Constantine), could doubtless have found a pagan equivalent to the child sacrifices and ritual banquets which, like Tertullian, he says a Roman rumour, started by an African, accused the Christians of practising. Tertullian, who was born in Carthage, made frequent visits to Africa, at least up until 197 when he wrote the *Apology* and the address *Ad Nationes*. Thus the only two Christians writers who report this body of accusations were Africans, and the accusations were apparently brought to Rome by a pagan from Cirta, himself an African therefore, Marcus Aurelius' tutor, the orator Fronto.[5] Now it so happens that in Africa, the cult practices of the Libyans included what was called the night of error, which could be compared with the incestuous orgies described above, while the Punic rites, which we know were adopted by the Berbers, included the sacrificing of children, generally young babies.

Tertullian, in his *Apology*[6], reports that the Roman authorities had banned these practices, but close study of his text leads us to believe that the measure in question was introduced either by Tiberius in the first century AD or by the proconsul called Tiberius in the second half of the second century.[7] Writing at the end of the second century, Tertullian claims, and he is the only writer to do so, that child sacrifices were still part of the cult of Saturn and were being practised secretly. Minucius Felix apparently did not wish to level at his countrymen the accusations he reports as having been made against the Christians. Writing in Rome,

---

[5] Minucius Felix, *Octavius*, 9, 6 and 31, 2, 3. On the accusations made against the Christians in this context, see Jean Beaujeu's text and French translation of Minucius Felix's *Octavius*, 1964, André Schneider's splendid French translation of Tertullian's *Ad Nationes*, 1968, and the text and French translation of Tertullian's *Apology* produced by J. P. Waltzing with Albert Severyns, 1971.

[6] Tertullian, *Apology*, 9, 2.

[7] G. Charles-Picard, *Les religions de l'Afrique antique*, 1954, pp. 132–3. All the same, the series of children's urns found in the sanctuaries ends in the first century (see Charles-Picard, p. 104). Carcopino, Rome et les immolations d'enfants, in *Aspects mystiques de la Rome païenne*, 1941, p. 42, n. 3, considers that the ban dates from Tiberius' time. M. Leglay, *Saturne africain, Histoire*, 1966, p. 319, says he is quoting Waltzing's translation of Tertullian, but in fact follows that of Charles-Picard who, in *Les religions de l'Afrique antique*, p. 61, n. 1, shows the difficulties facing translators.

he preferred to find other sources for these stories. The practice of incest he lays at the door of the Persians and Egyptians. But, like Tertullian, he refers to the real risks of incest in Rome because of the practice of adoption and more generally because it was possible to have casual sexual relations with certain women, which meant that men might one day have an affair with daughters they had fathered years before without knowing it.

He tells us that the night of error, when each man took hold of a woman in the dark, horrified the Romans because of the risk of incest and *stuprum*. Carcopino has shown that this practice was described in Augustus' time by Nicholas of Damascus, himself a pagan, as a rite of the Dapso-Libyans, who happily adopted the cult of Demeter.[8] In the second century AD Pausanias described this rite of the cult of Demeter taking place in certain backward areas of Greece. It is a fertility rite, or rather a fertilization rite, for fertility has different stages from the sowing of the seed up to the harvest. This night of love doubtless became part of the cult of the *Cereres* which was imported from Sicily into Carthage and from there passed on to the Numidian Africans and which became in Africa the cult of the goddesses Tellus and Korè.

Carcopino thought he had found in a passage by Sallust proof that the cult of Tellus and Korè had been adopted in Numidia by Massinissa's time (238–146) or at least by the time Numidia gained independence, whereas the first epigraphic reference to this cult in Numidia dates from 2 BC and comes from Vaga (Beja). This would mean that the cult of the goddesses, which would have been more readily acceptable in Numidia because of the Berber night of error, had arrived via Carthage rather than as a result of the Roman conquest. Sallust's text gives an account of the massacre of Italians living in Vaga:

> After arranging matters among themselves, they appointed the third day from that time, because it was observed as a holiday all over Africa and promised entertainment and festivity rather than danger. However, when the appointed time arrived, they invited the centurions and military tribunes and even the prefect of the town himself, Titus Turpilius Silanus by name, to their several homes. There all except Turpilius were slain while feasting.[9]

The Latin says that the appointed day was *diem tertium*, the third day, and the activities that took place on the feast day are evocatively referred to as *lascivia*. Carcopino corrected *diem tertium* to *diem Cererum*, the

---

[8] Carcopino, Le culte des *Cereres* et les Numides, in *Aspects mystiques*; Charles-Picard, *Les religions de l'Afrique antique*, p. 11 and p. 182 et seq.
[9] Sallust, *Bellum Iugurthinum*, LXVI, 2–3, tr. J.C. Rolfe, 1980.

day of the *Cereres*, arguing that there might have been some confusion when the Carolingian lower case letters were copied by the scribes who produced the eleventh-century manuscripts, the only surviving texts of Sallust. Yet he compared the celebrations described by Sallust, in which games, obscenities and feasting were the main activities, with the Syracusan thesmophoria, also imported into Carthage. His main reason for wanting to change *diem tertium* to the day of the *Cereres* was that the third day did not seem to him to make sense, but it was the description of the feast which made him think of this comparison. Why then correct Sallust's text, when we know that the thesmophoria lasted three days, and that the third and last day was given over to feasting, making obscene remarks and performing sexual acts to commemorate the fact that Iambè or Baubo, servant to the queen of Eleusis, made Demeter laugh by showing her sexual organs to the goddess who was grieving over Korè's abduction.[10]

Yet Sallust was writing in about 30 BC. He knew Africa, where he had served Caesar from 47 BC onwards and had been governor of *Africa Nova*, which was eastern Numidia, in 46 BC. The cult of Ceres certainly existed in this territory and the destruction of Carthage in 146 BC can not have destroyed it completely. The cult of Korè-Persephone and Tellus was re-introduced in the new Carthage rebuilt under Caesar.[11] One of the city's first aediles, Marcus Caelius Phileros, built at his own cost an *aedes Telluris*, a temple to Tellus, probably between 44 BC and 40 BC, when he was *apparitor* to T. Sextius, the governor of Africa.[12] The inscription was carved in Italy. But in Carthage itself, in the suburb of Malga, two plaques have been found which have been linked with the imperial cult Augustus allowed to be introduced in the province of Africa.[13] The star on Caesar's forehead on one of the plaques appears to refer to the divinization of Caesar in Augustus' time. We might also link the building of the *aedes Telluris* by Caelius Phileros with one of the themes of the Malga plaques which represents Tellus. The other plaque has at its centre Mars, known in Africa as Hadad, Lord of Mother Earth, and so of

[10] Charles-Picard, L'épisode de Baubô et les mystères d'Eleusis, 1927, p. 122 et seq. Carcopino, *Aspects mystiques*, p. 26, says in a note that it is also possible to restore *In diem tertium [Cererum]*, in other words it is possible to leave the text as it is and not correct it. He adds, p. 27, 'Sallust's text, restored to its original form, contains the only account we have of the celebration of the *Cereres* in Africa, which tallies with what we can deduce about the Syracusan thesmophoria on which it was modelled.'

[11] S. Gsell, Les premiers temps de la Carthage romaine, 1927, pp. 225–40.

[12] Ibid., p. 229; Carcopino, *Aspects mystiques*, p. 17.

[13] Gsell, Les premiers temps de la Carthage romaine, pp. 235–6; and Gsell, Les statues du temple de Mars Ultor à Rome, pp. 37–43; The bas-relief of Tellus, known as the bas-relief of the Three Elements, is in the Louvre; Héron de Villefosse, *Musée africain du Louvre*, pl. VIII, fig. 1.

Tellus.[14] All of this makes it clear that it was Caesar's policy to support the continuity of the cult of Tellus in *Africa Vetus*, Old Africa, which included the former territory of Carthage.

In Numidia, which Sallust knew from his period as governor in 46 BC, the position is less clear. When Sallust was there (and Vaga came under his control), Caesar had only just created the province, although Italians had been in the area for a long time.[15] It was inevitable that any account of the December celebrations in Vaga sixty years before, which included feasting and sexual amusements, should draw on the terms used to describe the equivalent celebrations in the hellenized world of southern Italy and Carthage. Sallust's text simply tells us that in Numidia at the end of the second century ritual practices took place after the winter wheat had been sown, and that these practices might provide a favourable background to the adoption of the cult of Korè and Tellus as it was practised in Carthage. Perhaps this had already happened, as Sallust would seem to suggest.

It was during this sexual feast that the inhabitants of Vaga, who were determined to reject Roman occupation and remain loyal to Jugurtha, decided to massacre the Roman officers they had each invited into their houses. Sallust explains that this feast day aroused expectations of entertainment and not feelings of fear, on the part of Italians that is. There is nothing to suggest that the goddesses who presided over these Numidian festivities were solely concerned with peaceful reproduction. Indeed, at Scillium[16] we see Ceres associated with Jupiter Omnipotens, and perhaps with the African Saturn, and when Perpetua and Felicitas were made to enter the arena at Carthage to fight raging cows, their tormentors wanted to make them don the robes worn by the priestesses of Ceres, just as their male companions in martyrdom were being made to wear the robes of the priests of Saturn.[17] When they refused, they were made to enter the amphitheatre naked. Nudity was in any case part of some of the rituals associated with the cult of the Punic Ceres, for the representation of a priestess at the banquet shows her wearing only a brassière.[18]

We only know of the night of ritual love-making in Libyan Africa through the brief allusion made to them by Nicholas of Damascus. In a

[14] M. Benabou, *La résistance africaine à la romanisation*, 1976, pp. 349–50.

[15] On Italian immigration in Africa at the time of the Roman republic, see J.M. Lassère, *Ubique Populus*, 1978 chapter II.

[16] On Jupiter Omnipotens associated with Ceres in Scillium see *BAC*, 1943–5, p. 365, no. II; and Benabou, *La résistance africaine*, p. 341 and Leglay, *Saturne africain*, p. 234, n.5.

[17] G. Charles-Picard, Les *sacerdotes Saturni* et les sacrifices humains dans l'Afrique romaine, 1948, pp. 117–23.

[18] G. Charles-Picard, *La civilisation de l'Afrique romaine*, 1959, p. 244.

few words he refers to the evening meal, the lamp being put out,[19] the search for a partner in the dark. Minucius Felix and Tertullian add the element of incest, the union in the dark of sons and their mothers, of brothers and sisters.

If child sacrifice, associated by Tertullian and Minucius Felix with the night of ritual love-making, had not been one of the rites practised by the Carthaginians, it would have been easy to imagine this notion resulting from a mistaken interpretation of the eucharistic rite, and the idea that the Christians practised incest stemming from the Christians' habit of calling one another brother and sister.[20] But in fact here we see that both these elements which were supposed to form part of the Christian initiation ceremony were among the rituals attributed to the Libyan Carthaginians. One simply wonders why Minucius Felix, writing in Rome, did not lay at the Africans' door the crimes which he says the Christians were accused of committing. Presumably he felt that the conversion of pagans in Roman society demanded a comparison with local customs rather than with African cults, so he compared child sacrifice with the practice of exposing children and with abortion. And on the religious level, he referred to the myth of Saturn rather than to a contemporary act of child devouring.

But Tertullian, writing in Africa, was quite aware that these sacrifices were part of the Libyan-Punic cults. In his *Apology*, which describes the night of incest and the child sacrifices of which he thinks the Christians are accused, he tells us that these sacrifices were still carried out at the end of the second century, a fact which no other writer mentions.

This is a chapter of the religious history of Africa about which it is almost impossible to discover more. We know from texts and archaeological discoveries that child sacrifice was practised until the first century AD in the Punic area and in the Numidian area of North Africa.[21] The burnt remains found in the urns kept in the sanctuaries of Saturn are those of children as are those found in great numbers by archaeologists digging at Salambo's tophêt (sacrificial shrine) in Carthage. The question is whether the practice was continued under Roman domination. Carcopino, who like many humanists believed in the civilizing role of the Romans, presented two papers which strengthened this conviction.[22] He tried to show that human sacrifices, which Tiberius had banned, had been replaced by animal sacrifices, and that moreover the Emperor Claudius,

[19] On the ritual significance of lamps, see Leglay, *Saturne africain*, p. 344.
[20] Claude Lepelley, *L'Empire romain et le christianisme*, 1969, p. 38.
[21] Charles-Picard, *Les religions de l'Afrique antique*, p. 104; Leglay, *Saturne africain*, p. 314 et seq.
[22] Carcopino, Rome et les immolations d'enfants and La réforme romaine du culte de Cybèle et d'Attis, in *Aspects mystiques*.

by making the cult of Attis official in Rome, had prepared the way for a ban on castration which those faithful to this god practised on themselves. None of the Europeans who love Africa, as did those who wrote its history, could be unaffected by the practice of child sacrifice if it continued to be carried out in the period of Roman control. And whereas historians seek to show the land and people of North Africa in a sympathetic light, pointing to the originality they retained despite successive occupations, it is hard to be positive about a resistance to cultural change which manifested itself in celebrations involving child sacrifice.[23]

According to Tertullian, child sacrifices were public affairs,[24] paid for and organized by the community, until the Romans banned them, after which they were carried on in secret. And yet the sanctuaries reveal no more child skeletons, but rather the burnt remains of animals from this time on. Archaeology, then, does not prove that human sacrifices to Saturn were carried out under the Empire. We can not simply say that whereas official sacrifices were effectively abolished, private sacrifices were tolerated.[25] The official sacrifices in Carthage took place in front of an assembly of the whole populus, as Diodorus Siculus describes: 'The number of these victims was not less than three hundred. There was in Carthage a bronze statue of Kronos with his hands stretched out, palms facing upwards and sloping down towards the ground so that a child placed on them rolled and fell into a pit full of flames.'[26] It seems the children had first been slaughtered at the hands of the priest. Private sacrifices existed before the ban. In any case, funerary urns contained the ashes sometimes of several children, sometimes of only one;[27] in other words they had not been thrown into the flames so as to make it difficult to identify the bones. One couple sacrificed their first child, who was handicapped, when they had a second, healthy child. If private sacrifices had really been tolerated by the Romans, we would have found remains of children, not animals, in the urns placed in the sanctuaries during the Roman period.

[23] F. Decret and M. Fantar's index in *L'Afrique du Nord dans l'Antiquité*, 1981, does not include the term *molk* or even the word *sacrifice*. Human sacrifice is not mentioned, Benabon, *La résistance africaine*, mentions Saturn but not the rites associated with his cult.

[24] One may wonder how public sacrifices, which meant official sacrifices held for the whole community, could be carried on in secret. F. Paschoud, Entretiens de la Fondation Hardt, XIX, *Le culte des souverains dans l'Empire romain*, 1973, p. 34, notes that the official cults (of the Roman Empire) were only celebrated properly if the State met the cost. After they had been banned by the Christian Emperors they could no longer be celebrated in the proper manner. Thus, if there were private sacrifices, these were not a secret continuation of an official cult.

[25] Leglay, *Saturne africain*, p. 322.

[26] Diodorus Siculus, *Bibliotheca historica*, XX, 14, 4–6.

[27] Leglay, *Saturne africain*, p. 320, n. 3.

If child sacrifices did continue to be practised, then as the sanctuaries contain no trace of this except for the reference to the substitution of an animal *pro vicario*, the remains of the children sacrificed can only be in the necropoles, the animal remains having been placed in the god's sanctuary to show that the human sacrifice had been carried out. This is only a hypothesis, but it is based in part on the observations made by P.-A. Février and R. Guéry at the necropolis of Sétif, which was used from the first to the fourth century AD. There is a very high percentage of children: '16.67% of children did not reach term or died at birth, 38.60% did not live to the age of one and . . . only 20.18% survived to adulthood.'[28] Thus 41.22% disappeared between the ages of one and twenty-one. If this sample is valid, this reveals a population almost incapable of maintaining itself.

Setting aside the myth of Saturn devouring his children, it is the texts by Tertullian and Minucius Felix, not those which deal with paganism but those which list the ceremonies said to be performed by Christians, which describe human sacrifices in Africa in Imperial times. They are private and clandestine sacrifices, whether real or imaginary.

The child was placed on a table and covered with flour. In Rome an animal which was to be sacrificed was covered with a mixture called *mola salsa*. One may also recall the *dealbatio*, the whitening of 'Saturn's stones', which was part of the ritual sacrifice to Saturn although Leglay does not know at what point in the ceremony it took place.[29] We should perhaps remember the stone covered in tongues which Rhea made Saturn eat instead of the child Zeus, and which she then helped him to vomit up again. Having been covered in flour, the child would be slaughtered by the neophyte. All those present would then dip pieces of bread in his blood and eat them, according to Tertullian. Minucius Felix, on the other hand, says that the child was eaten by the whole community. It is this above all which makes one disinclined, in the absence of any other accounts, to believe that this type of sacrifice was really a part of any religion. As we lack any documentary proof other than these two texts in which child sacrifice is presented as a wicked calumny on Christian practices, it might be just as wrong to attribute these practices to another cult.

Moreover, child sacrifice is described as being part of an initiation ceremony, and nothing, apart from the *dealbatio* and the slaughter of the child, is closely comparable with the Punic practice of sacrifice which was adopted by the Libyans. Even if this is not a case of an actual pagan

[28] P.-A. Février and R. Guéry, Les rites funéraires de la nécropole de Sétif, 1980, pp. 91–124; I wish to thank Professor Biraben and J.-P. Bocquet for the information they provided on this question of infant mortality.

[29] Leglay, *Saturne africain*, p. 349.

custom being imputed to the Christians, it was certainly to the fund of pagan mythology that the collective imagination turned to find crimes, such as the night of love and child sacrifice, to lay at the Christians' door.

How should we regard the two other accusations, namely adoration of the priest's sexual organs and worshipping an ass?[30] No document relating to the African cults refers to the adoration of sexual organs, or to the fellatio of the priest's penis by one of the faithful as described by the pro-Christian part of the *Octavius*. It may simply be a rumour, perhaps linked with the first stage, representing male fertilization, of some fertility rite like the night of love of Tellus, Mother Earth. It may be relevant to note that the word used for fellatio in the second century AD was phoenicize.[31] Could this have been a Phoenician practice imported into Carthage? Elagabalus celebrated the festival of flowers in this way with his lover Hierocles,[32] so it could have been a ritual part of some fertility religion, with all the nuances of interpretation added in the second century.

Ass worship is thought to have been a form of mockery, and has been linked with a graffito in the Roman catacombs representing a man with an ass's head hanging on a cross.[33] Another figure, which has not previously been used to clarify this text, was found on a sheet of lead inscribed with imprecations, discovered in the underground part of the great amphitheatre at Carthage.[34] It shows a demon with a man's body and an ass's head considering prayers requesting that one of the hunters at the games should fail and therefore be killed.

Again, it is the Christian texts which provide information about the use of the games to perpetuate human sacrifice. It has been noted that the fact that the martyrs of 203 were supposed to put on the robes of the priests of Saturn and the priestesses of Ceres shows that human sacrifice was being carried out in the context of the games.[35] It is probably relevant that the imprecations seeking the death of the *venatores*, the hunters in the games, were found in a room of the great amphitheatre at Carthage. None of the sheets requests that a hunter be spared, although as the hunters were not

---

[30] Fellatio: Minucius Felix, *Octavius*, 9, 4; 28, 10. Tertullian, *Apology*, 9, 12; *Ad Nationes*, 15, 6–8. Ass worship: Minucius Felix, *Octavius*, 9, 3; 28, 7; Tertullian, *Apology*, 16, 1; 16, 12; *Ad Nationes*, 1, 11, 16 and 1, 14, 1.

[31] Lucian, *Philopseudolus*, 28.

[32] *Scriptores Historiae Augustae*, Life of Elagabalus, VI, 5.

[33] For references to studies dealing with this point, see Schneider, *Le premier livre 'Ad Nationes' de Tertullien*, p. 242 and pp. 259–63.

[34] A. Audollent, *Defixionum Tabellae*, 1904, pp. 333–4; see L. Poinssot and P. Quoniam, Bêtes d'amphithéâtre sur trois mosaïques du Bardo, 1951–2, p. 151.

[35] Charles-Picard, *Les sacerdotes Saturni* pp. 117–23, developing an idea suggested by Lukas Holstein and taken up by J.-P. Migne, see Lepelley, *Iuvenes* et circoncellions: les derniers sacrifices humains de l'Afrique antique, 1980, p. 268, n. 5.

fighting one another but animals the survival of one did not necessitate the failure of an opponent. The *Martyrdom of Perpetua and Felicitas* tells us that 'the hunter who had let the beast loose on Saturus was disembowelled by the animal and died a few days after the game': in other words the result was the opposite of what had been expected. It was professional hunters who led the animals into the amphitheatre and directed them towards those who had been condemned to be killed. They were also responsible for making them go back into their cages, so it was essential that they should survive. We see them lined up when the martyrs entered the amphitheatre at Carthage. It was they who carried out the wishes of the spectators, and whipped the Christians who insulted the procurator as they passed in front of his box. They were, in fact, tamers, but the animals were not there simply to be shown to the public, as can be seen from the bears of the peacock mosaic at Carthage which were called Cruel and Homicide.[36] Marcus Aurelius and Commodus made it illegal for prisoners who were condemned to death to be sold as combatants in the circus, which sometimes meant playing the role of hunters, unless the individuals agreed to this.[37] At Lyons, Blandina and some of her fellow slaves were pitted against the animals, but Blandina's mistress and the other Roman citizens were killed outside the amphitheatre. Only slaves and, at Lyons, the free men who were not Roman citizens, died in the amphitheatre in 177. The free men who were not Roman citizens, in other words foreigners, were condemned to be burned at the stake in the arena, but not to face wild animals.[38]

In Carthage in 202, Perpetua, Felicitas and their companions were condemned to face wild animals whether they were slaves or free persons. Yet the Gauls, like the Africans, liked to see contests where they knew in advance who would die, as was the case when condemned prisoners were disguised as combatants and made to fight wild animals or professional fighters. In any case, into the arena came combatants who were destined to die and combatants who were destined to win or who were there to lead the wild animals towards the victims.[39] It was without doubt these victims whose death the tablets requested, if necessary by invoking a divinity with an ass's head.

Tertullian, who is more precise than Minucius Felix, tells of a 'scoundrel who was hired to excite the wild animals and who held up in public a tablet with this inscription: God of the Christians, a race of asses.

---

[36] L. Poinssot and P. Quoniam, Bêtes d'amphithéâtre, pp. 145–6, fig. 8 and 9.

[37] A. Piganiol, Les *Trinqui* gaulois, gladiateurs consacrés, 1923, pp. 62–76.

[38] On the different punishments applied to persons of different social status, see A. Rousselle, La persécution des chrétiens à Alexandrie au IIIe siècle, 1974, pp. 222–51.

[39] Charles-Picard, *La civilisation de l'Afrique romaine*, p. 265, thinks that the hunts did not involve human deaths.

This god had the ears of an ass and a horn foot, carried a book in his hand and wore a toga.' In his address *Ad Nationes*, Tertullian again clearly says that it was a hunter in the amphitheatre who held up an anti-Christian picture.[40] This is important as it allows us to link the tablets bearing the imprecations with the accusation against the Christians. The tablets, which date from the end of the second or the beginning of the third century, show above the requests inscribed on them pictures of figures with human bodies and serpents' or asses' heads. This is clearly what the gladiator's tablet is saying: the god of the Christians, the fruit of a union with an ass, half man and half ass, like the demons who were responsible for the fate of a condemned hunter. One may wonder whether this was a form of mockery, but it probably was not. These demons had proved that they existed by showing their powers. Why should someone in the amphitheatre not liken the god of the Christians to one of these demons and consider him as one of them, praying to him to ensure the death of one of the condemned prisoners? The ass was linked with the notion of fertility as it was considered one of the most potent animals in terms of reproduction.[41] Thus the term 'ass's penis', *onobeli*, was applied to those whom Elagabalus sought out for their exceptional sexual abilities.[42]

Like the victims, those condemned to death had to be well fed,[43] especially the day before the combat. Perpetua says to her jailer, 'Does your reputation not depend on producing well fed prisoners in the arena?' The names of the Christians condemned to die at Carthage made them perfect offerings to Saturn: the commonest names among those who engraved the record of an offering to Saturn were Saturus, Saturninus and Felicitas.[44]

Saturninus and Revocatus were 'attacked by a leopard, then, on the platform, they were torn apart by a bear.' Saturn, whom the animals ignored for a long time, was preaching to a soldier by one of the gates, while Felicitas and Perpetua were being attacked by a cow. When a leopard set upon Saturus the people of Carthage, seeing his blood flow, cried 'He is washed, he is saved!'[45] The *Martyrdom* considers this

---

[40] Tertullian says that this hunter was a Jew who had been converted to paganism, which explains the strength of his anti-Christian feeling, his defence of paganism and Tertullian's harsh description of him.

[41] Elagabalus' sexual practices, as described in the *Augustan History*, are to be taken seriously in a religious context.

[42] *Life of Elagabalus*, VIII, 6.

[43] Leglay, *Saturne africain*, p. 345.

[44] Ibid., p. 381.

[45] J.-P. Brisson, *Gloire et misère de l'Afrique chrétienne*, 1948, chapter II; J.-C. Fredouille, *Tertullien et la conversion de la culture antique*, 1972, uses Brisson's translation on p. 149. I prefer and have used France Quéré-Jaulmes' French translation of the Passion of Perpetua and Felicitas, in *La femme*, 1968, pp. 194–210. See also the translation by H. Musurillo, 1972.

exclamation a sacrilegious allusion to baptism, but in the context of human sacrifice it is probably the ritual exclamation during a sacrifice to Saturn. We are told that spilled blood saves, and the first person to be saved is he who is sacrificed.[46] The reference to the beasts devouring the scraps of flesh torn from the victims of the hunt is the only equivalent in the circus of the myth in which Saturn devoured his children, or the devouring of the sacrificed child in the texts by Minicius Felix and Tertullian.[47] The spectators went to great lengths to obtain the meat of these animals which had eaten the condemned prisoners, even the tripe of bears which had died before they had digested human flesh.[48]

The sacrifice was all the more certain, the victims more acceptable to the gods if the condemned prisoners agreed to their fate. Perpetua says, 'We came here willingly so as to defend our freedom. We are sacrificing our lives so as not to have to do such a thing (i.e. putting on the robes of Saturn and Ceres). On this point we have made an agreement with you. Perpetua sang.' After the combat,

> the people demanded that the wounded be brought back to the centre of the arena so that they could enjoy the sight of the sword plunging into their living bodies and thus be witnesses and accomplices to the killing. The martyrs rose and dragged themselves to the spot where the crowd wanted them. They gave one another the kiss of peace, the ritual gesture of martyrdom according to their faith. They all remained still and received the fatal blow in silence . . . Perpetua had time to savour her pain: she uttered a loud cry as she was struck between the ribs, then she seized the inexperienced gladiator's trembling hand and guided the sword to her throat. Such a woman could only die by her own will, so much did the demon fear her.

This was a voluntary and joyful death, as was the death of the children offered to Saturn in the Carthage molks. The parents played with them so that they would die laughing for the salvation of themselves, the city and their family.[49] It is clear that in Roman sacrifice the gods did not tolerate

---

[46] Leglay, *Saturne africain*, p. 331.

[47] On indirect cannibalism via an animal, see Bernadette Bucher, Les fantasmes du conquérant, in C. Lévi-Strauss, *Textes de et sur Lévi-Strauss*, collected by R. Belloun and C. Clément, 1979, p. 327. In this context Bucher analyses Montaigne's texts on the West Indies and South America. In this case it was the Europeans who had the Indians devoured by animals trained to eat human flesh. This subject is further discussed in *La négresse aux seins pendants*, 1977.

[48] Tertullian, *Apology*, 9, 11.

[49] S. Reinach, Le rire rituel, 1911, p. 585; cf. Leglay, *Saturne africain*, p. 329.

any reluctance on the part of the victim,[50] but it seems that in Africa voluntary and joyful human death was for a very long time associated with the idea of religious salvation. We should not think only of the joyful death of the Christians in 203, or even the willing death of the Donatist Circumcellions in the fourth century, but rather of the usefulness of their death in the minds of those who sacrificed them. Claude Lepelley has drawn attention to the episodes which show the Christian Circumcellions interrupting the games held by the young men's associations in Africa with the affirmed purpose of provoking the young people to run them through with the spears intended for the animals.[51] Lepelley analyses the complicity of the Circumcellions and the young people, all sharing the African mentality. It was during the games that the Circumcellions chose to drive the young people to murder, and Lactantius Firmianus, who came from Africa, says at the beginning of the fourth century that the 'hunts, which the municipality was obliged to hold, were offered to Saturn'.[52] One might also remember that the young people, the colleges of *juvenes*, were adorers of Mars and that the African Mars was Hadad, lord of Tellus.

Tertullian reveals one further element of the sacrificial nature of the African games, and that is laughter. It is not mocking laughter, although this was certainly heard in the amphitheatre. Nor was it comic laughter, which Tertullian shows as a response to pantomimes, although this, like all feast-day amusements, can have a religious significance. It is not the laughter which the orator sometimes tries to raise from his audience.[53] It is the ritual laughter or at least gaiety which was supposed to accompany human sacrifices to Saturn. Tertullian's words must be translated bluntly: 'You need a baby which is still tender and which does not know of death and laughs as you raise your knife.'[54] This is a willing and joyful death. Tertullian had been a pagan and he describes the pleasures he has known: 'We too have seen Attis castrated and a man disguised as Hercules burned. We too have laughed in the lunchtime interval to see Mercury testing the bodies with a red-hot sword. And we have seen Jupiter's

---

[50] R. Turcan, Le sacrifice mithriaque: innovations de sens et de modalités, in *Le sacrifice dans l'Antiquité, Entretiens sur l'Antiquité Classique*, 27, 1981, pp. 352–3; A. Rousselle, Paulin de Nole et Sulpice Sévère, hagiographes, 1983.

[51] Lepelley, *Iuvenes* et circoncellions, 1980, pp. 261–71.

[52] Charles-Picard, *Les religions de l'Afrique antique*, p. 134; Leglay, *Saturne africain*, p. 340.

[53] Fredouille, *Tertullien et la conversion*, does not distinguish between these different types of laughter in the amphitheatre.

[54] And not *smiles* as Botte and Glover translate it in their versions of Tertullian, *Apology*, 8, 7.

brother pulling gladiators' bodies out of the arena with his hammer.'[55]
Tertullian promises the Christians sacrificial laughter when the last
judgement comes:

> What a spectacle! What should we admire first? What should we
> laugh at? There is joy, there exultation, at the sight of so many great
> kings who we were told had gone up to heaven, with Jupiter and
> those who believed in him, all groaning in the darkness. There too
> are those who ordered the persecution of the Lord's name, in their
> turn consumed by harsher flames while the Christians hurl insults.
> What else? There are the philosophers who thought they knew
> everything, blushing before their disciples in the same furnace.

This is a terrible kind of laughter, the laughter of those who were willing
to kill children without showing any sense of horror as Saturn demands.
It is this laughter which was heard in the amphitheatre at the death of the
condemned people, made up to show their blood and the character they
were representing. It is the same laughter which rang out when Attis was
castrated, he too condemned to wear this costume. This was the second
part of the fertility cults: if the first part was fertilization the second was
the harvest.

Attis, 'whose genital parts were harvested by a potsherd',[56] was the
perfect symbol of harvest. And yet the texts show us that at the beginning
of the third century, away from the rural world, it was not the fertility of
the earth which was at the centre of the sexual practices implied by the
rites, but individual salvation. Hence this psalm by Valentinus:

Harvest

I see everything held up by the spirit,
I see everything borne by the spirit
Flesh attached to the soul
The soul attached to the air
The air hanging on the ether
Fruits emerging from the abyss
The child emerging from the womb.[57]

[55] Tertullian, *Ad Nationes*, 1, 10, 46, repeats the same text but with *saepe*: 'We have often
seen . . .' Seneca tells us that the midday show, which was an interlude between the bloody
games of the morning and afternoon sessions, generally consisted of games and amusements
which did not involve human death. Seneca thought he could find entertainment without
witnessing any deaths if he went to the theatre at midday: in fact he found these supposedly
comic games in which condemned people were the victims. 'The only outcome of this
combat is death.' (*Letters to Lucilius*, 1, 7, 3.)

[56] Minucius Felix, *Octavius*, 24, 12.

[57] French translation in F.-M. Sagnard, *La gnose valentinienne et le témoignage de saint
Irénée*, 1947, p. 123.

The act of castration has two meanings: the return to childhood, which makes the castrated male the perfect victim for Saturn, and the adult whose *pneuma* can be purely psychic, since there can be no further loss of the vital seed.[58] The practices described in the life of Elagabalus mark the return to a pre-pubertal condition: he had his friends' bodies shaved of 'the positive signs of puberty.'[59] He himself tied up his testicles when celebrating the rites of Cybele and Attis. The doctors made men who wanted a son tie their left testicle, so tying both testicles was a sign that one wished to avoid fertilization. Indeed, one of the methods of castration was twisting a cord around the testicles, which crushed not the glands but the vas deferens. Oribasius quotes two medical techniques given by Paul of Aegina for making men eunuchs, 'since some powerful men often make us, against our will, turn men into eunuchs'.[60] He describes first the method which consists of crushing a young boy's testicles, and then surgical excision of the glands, which he says is more effective. This was not the method used by the Galli, the adorers of Cybele, who practised on themselves ablation of the testicles.[61] But Elagabalus' method should not be thought of as some game, although he was certainly very young as he was only eighteen when he died. The essential point seems to have been the renunciation of transmitting *pneuma* through sperm, the conservation of the vital spirit and its transformation into psychic pneuma. 'The Mother of the Gods mutilated Attis although he was her lover, because the blessed nature of the eternal beings who are superior to the world wishes to make the masculine virtue of the soul rise up to her.'[62] In fact the Galli, who mutilated themselves after adolescence and puberty, after they had acquired the signs of virility, were still able to feel desire and to achieve erection and ejaculation of seminal fluid from the prostate and the seminal vesicles after they had removed their testicles. Thus those who argue that the Archigallus of Tusculum could not have been a eunuch since he was married,[63] and that the priests of Pessinus were not castrated since they had wives, are wrong since the aim of these men was to be able to continue their sexual life but to remain infertile after the removal of their testicles or the cutting of the vas deferens which we know today as vasectomy. The male characteristics

---

[58] In the opinion of J. Frazer, *Adonis, Attis, Osiris*, 1914, p. 283, the castration of Attis is a parallel to that of Uranus by Kronos and then that of Kronos by Zeus according to ancient interpretations. But the castration of Attis, unlike that of Kronos and of Uranus, was not carried out by another man.

[59] *Life of Elagabalus*, 6, 5.

[60] Paul of Aegina, French tr. R. Briau, 1855, pp. 288–91.

[61] H. Graillot, *Le culte de Cybèle, mère des dieux, à Rome et dans l'Empire romain*, 1912, pp. 290–7.

[62] Hippolytus of Rome, *Philosophumena*, V, 7, 13.

[63] Graillot, *Le culte de Cybèle*, p. 232.

already acquired are retained after removal of the testicles, for other male hormones are produced in the body by the suprarenal glands.

The brutal cutting off of the testicles does not seem to have led to death by haemorrhage, except in the mythical case of Cybele's lover. The very fine artery which takes blood to the testicle stopped bleeding very quickly as a result either of the natural process of haemostasis or of some procedure which the Galli learned to use on the Day of Blood, 24 March.

The ancients must have known that removal of the testicles did not prevent sexual activity. It is impossible to believe that Elagabalus, high priest of Emesa, but only eighteen years of age, could have tied his testicles (the tying was done above the testicles in fact, so as to block the vas deferens) if he had not been taught by tradition to do so.[64] This external ligature, blocking both the vas deferens which takes spermatozoa to the ureter and the vessels carrying blood and hormones, must have produced necrosis of the testicles, the bloodless equivalent of ritual ablation. The same effect could be achieved by internal torsion of the vas deferens and the blood vessels. Accidental torsion, which is extremely painful, results in necrosis of the testicle within six or seven hours if no steps are taken to prevent this. The ancients must have had experience of this, affecting one testicle, and must have known that this did not prevent sexual desire or satisfaction. This explains why Basil of Ancyra in the fourth century advised virgins not to frequent eunuchs: 'It is said that those who, having attained virility and the age when the genital member is capable of copulation, have cut off only their testicles, burn with greater and less restrained desire for sexual union, and that not only do they feel this ardour, but they think they can defile any women they meet without risk.'[65]

As Galen had clearly described the epididymis's long course through which, as he thought, male blood was refined into sperm carrying *pneuma*, the vital spirit, it must have been realized that section of the vas deferens prevented the flow of the purest blood towards the penis for the purpose of fertilization. The ancients who practised ritual ablation of the testicles must have appreciated the distinction between fertilization linked with the vas deferens and the testicles, and sexual activity with ejaculation which was independent of fertilization.

How else can one explain the reputation which the Galli had of leading a very active sexual life and of shocking the Romans by their activities. They practised a kind of sacred prostitution. If it is considered that they felt no sexual desire then it is understandable to regard their relations as

[64] *Life of Elagabalus*, 1, 5.

[65] Basil of Ancyra, *De Virginitate*, French tr. A. Vaillant, 1943, p. 77. In ancient times as in our day, there was a tendency to ignore or forget the fact that men who had no testicles still possessed sexual powers.

purely passive homosexuality. Here again, the example of Elagabalus can help to clarify matters.

The *Historia Augusta* relates, as a scandal, the official sexual life and sex-related religious practices of this young man who was Emperor at the age of fourteen in 218 and assassinated at eighteen. As his behaviour was considered in traditional Roman circles as the result of madness it is not considered as shedding light on ritual beliefs and behaviour in general. Elagabalus was Syrian, and he had been brought up to be the priest of a Syrian god, Baal of Emesa.

He tried in vain to introduce in Rome the practice of sacrificing noble children whose parents were still alive.[66] Lucian reports that in the second century AD children were thrown from the top of the propylaea of the temple of Atargatis.[67] The children's parents themselves performed this rite, making jokes as they did so. In Antioch in the second century a young girl was sacrificed either by Trajan or in his presence.[68] So the ancient rites persisted and were still practised in the third century AD in Syria as in Carthage. Elagabalus even tried to romanize the practise of child sacrifice by introducing examination of the victim's entrails.[69] Before banquets he also held animal hunts in the amphitheatre, in which condemned people took part.[70]

Elagabalus, who was destined to be a priest of Baal, had not been castrated as a child. Those who had were the only true eunuchs: their voices did not always break, they did not show the signs of virility in adolescence and some did not feel sexual desire. Elagabalus shaved or had his body depilated when he reached puberty,[71] and made his lovers do the same.[72] His passive homosexual relations were talked about,[73] and shocked the Romans.[74] He was reproached for practising fellatio with his male lovers,[75] as he himself revealed as he talked openly about his sexual life. He spoke with naïvety and conviction in favour of the ritual worship of Baal, and was surprised at the embarrassment of the old senators when

---

[66] *Life of Elagabalus*, VIII, 1.
[67] Lucian, *De Syria dea*, 58.
[68] Graillot, *Le culte de Cybèle*, p. 129, n.3.
[69] *Life of Elagabalus*, VIII, 2.
[70] Ibid., XXV, 7.
[71] Ibid., V, 5, and XXXI, 7.
[72] Ibid., XXXI, 7.
[73] Ibid., V, 1.
[74] Ibid., V, 2; XXVI, 3. The fact that Rome accepted active homosexuality on the part of a citizen, but not passive male homosexuality is pointed out by J. Boswell, *Christianity, Social Tolerance and Homosexuality*, 1980, and by Veyne, La famille et l'amour à Rome, pp. 35–63. I think that this notion of passive behaviour in homosexual as well as heterosexual relationships deserves further attention.
[75] *Life of Elagabalus*, V, 2; VI, 5.

he asked them about their sexual practices during a Dionysian celebration of the wine harvest.[76]

Alongside the passive homosexual activities connected with his religious practices, it is known that he also had active heterosexual relations 'never twice with the same woman, except his own wife',[77] and that at banquets where he entertained his male friends or lovers he ordered his servants to bring in women 'whom they used'.[78] But there was also a religious side to his heterosexual practices, for he sought out Roman female prostitutes to whom he gave, as he did to their male colleagues, gold, respect and sometimes freedom.[79] Sacred prostitution was still at that time one of the essential features of the Syrian temples.[80]

He thus had in him something of both sexes, for he was a woman with men and a man with women. He expressed it thus: 'Nothing is better than to be one's own heir and one's own wife.'[81] He wanted no children,[82] and could not have any as he had ligatured himself.

In the third century AD then, some men deliberately and scientifically renounced fertility by ritually removing their testicles. But this did not mean that they renounced desire or sexual activity. We should bear this in mind when we read the work of Sallustius, a friend of Julian, writing in the fourth century about the castration of Attis: 'But since it was necessary that the process of coming into being should stop and that what was worse should not sink to the worst, the creator who was making these things cast away generative powers into the world of becoming and was again united with the gods.'[83] Like child sacrifice and other types of human sacrifice, the sacrifice of a man's fertility must be voluntary, therefore the man must have reached sexual maturity and must be capable of making his own decisions. The true Galli cut off their testicles in the

---

[76] Ibid., XI, 2.

[77] Ibid., XXIV, 2.

[78] Ibid., XXX, 5.

[79] Ibid., XXV, 5; XXVI, 3.

[80] F. Cumont, *Les religions orientales dans le paganisme romain*, 1963, p. 109. Boswell's only reference to Elagabalus is in relation to his homosexual marriage, which he considers of doubtful authenticity. No scholars choose to see Elagabalus' behaviour as typical of any group, but it should in fact be considered in the context of the Syrian religion, which is not in the least classical, and as far removed from the Romans as the Greeks. But the latter are generally considered the only cultures relevant to rational demonstration. On Elagabalus' religious politics, see R. Turcan, Le culte impérial au IIIe siècle, 1978, pp. 1066–70.

[81] *Life of Elagabalus*, XXXI, 2.

[82] Ibid., XXXI, 4.

[83] Sallustius, *Concerning the gods and the universe*, ed. and tr. Arthur Darby Nock, 1926; French tr. A.-J. Festugière, *Trois dévots païens*, 1944, p. 25.

full knowledge of what they were doing and they retained their sexual potency.[84]

For a man who wishes to escape time and enter into eternity, fertile sexual activity is not a manifestation of potency, and sexual activity is not in itself solely related to fertility. For this reason the documents concerning eunuchism should not be examined only from the point of view of fertility and reproduction. First of all it must be accepted that ablation continued to be practised throughout the Roman Empire, even among Christians (the terms eviration and emasculation, derived from the Latin, are misleading for they imply the loss of masculine characteristics, of desire and satisfaction), and not simply by a few Phrygians who were permitted to carry out the age-old practices demanded by the Great Mother of Pessinus, as Carcopino has suggested. Having shown very clearly that the Emperor Claudius gave Attis a place in the official Roman religion alongside Cybele, Carcopino says that the ban on castration, mentioned in the legal texts, had brought to an end the existence of Galli, the castrated priests of the Great Mother and of other female divinities, among Roman citizens and even those who were not citizens.[85]

First of all we must dismiss the example of a slave deported for having castrated himself in 102 BC. Even though suicide was sometimes glorified among citizens, attempts at suicide by slaves were always punished, for in harming his own body a slave was mutilating another's property.[86] The law says, 'Let no man be made a eunuch',[87] and it lays down the penalties for those, whether or not they are doctors, who castrate a free man or a slave, and for those who have had this operation performed on them of their own will. But the Romans kept to the letter of the law, as is clear from all the subtle interpretations which have come down to us. He who *se abscidit, se eviravit*,[88] in order to serve the Great Mother, did not come into the definition of the law which supposed that there would always be two individuals, the one who performed the castration and the one who was castrated. So this was no malicious rumour unrelated to reality, put

[84] Cumont, *Les religions orientales*, p. 222, n. 13. The opinion of historians on this subject may be summarized as: 'Castration is a radical means of ensuring chastity.' But this is contradicted both by experience and by modern knowledge of hormones and spermatazoa.
[85] The argument that the priests of Cybele at Pessinus were married and that the priesthood was passed down from father to son must be rejected. (Carcopino, *Aspects mystiques*, p. 161, uses this argument.) Of course a man's testicles might be removed after he had produced children. Among the Christian bishops of the fourth and fifth centuries, who were sometimes called to the bishopric after a secular career in secular administration and a fruitful marriage, it was common in Gaul for sons to succeed their fathers. A. Rousselle, Aspects sociaux du recrutement ecclésiastique, 1977, p. 370, n. 175.
[86] P. Veyne, Suicide, fisc, esclavage, capital et droit romain, 1981, pp. 217–68.
[87] *D*, 48, 8, 4, 2, Ulpian.
[88] *Se abscidit*, Hippolytus, *Apostolic Tradition*, 16; *qui exciderit*, *D*, 48, 8, 4, 2; *exsecti*, Claudian, *In Eutropium*, 1, 468. See also Cumont, *Les religions orientales*, p. 223, n. 19.

about by the detractors of the Galli, be they pagan or Christian: the castrated priests really did continue to have a sexual life.

The eunuch is like the child who has not reached puberty. Those being initiated into the cult of Attis drank milk and honey, like a newborn baby,[89] and, along with virgins and children, they were fit to serve the goddess. It is not stated anywhere that a virgin had to be below the age of puberty, and indeed we know that some mature women were priestesses of Cybele and were obliged to abstain from sex. Only those who believed, like Aristotle, that female sperm did not exist, could see these women as fulfilling the same role in the cult as children, the role of the infertile.

The eunuch was more than this, especially the eunuch who had been castrated in adulthood of his own free will. For the seat of the vital spirit was not the genital organs. These transmitted the vital spirit, fertilizing a woman and giving life to a child, or, in the ritual practice of fellatio, to a brother or son of the faith. But this spirit could be retained, and could continue on its journey, becoming a psychic spirit, that of the superior man. This notion is found in the various gnoses and one can only see it as the basis for the pagan practices which existed at the same time as the gnostic sects. Eunuchism has always been a part of gnosticism and there has been no opposition to it.[90] In order to understand the positive aspect of emasculation one must turn to the physiology of the vital spirit, a very physical pneumatology. A.D. Nock saw the practice as entirely negative, representing abstinence.[91] On the contrary, however, it reflects the individual's strict application to himself of the most rigorous logic. Nock considered that emasculation was a radical method used because the Greeks did not trust men to remain continent. But if we admit that ablation of the testicles left sexual activity intact, particularly if ablation was seen by the individual as a positive act, and given the strong motivation that infertile sexual activity was necessary both to the goddess's cult and to the salvation of the initiated, then we must also accept that continence was not the aim of the Galli.

When Saturn called for children to be sacrificed to him he meant those who had not yet reached puberty, whose reproductive powers were still unrealized. Puberty is the point at which the individual's salvation, his eternal life, is assured. Only initiation and, in the cult of Saturn, slaughter can guarantee the eternal life of the child who has not yet reached puberty. Between 252 and 254 the plague raged in Carthage, and it troubled the Empire for twenty years. Human sacrifices were very common during plagues: 'As, on top of all the other ills, the plague raged,

---

[89] Leglay, *Saturne africain*, p. 389.
[90] Noonan, *Contraception*, pp. 83–5.
[91] A. D. Nock, Eunuchs in Ancient Religion, 1925, pp. 25–33.

they turned to murder as a remedy. They sacrificed men as victims, and they brought to their altars adolescents who had not reached puberty as a way of seeking the enemy's mercy.'[92] These sacrifices ensured the child's salvation and also brought hope that the epidemic would end. It was during this plague that the Third Council of Carthage in 253 stated, before any other Christian authority, that children could be baptized at birth.[93] In Africa children were also initiated into the mysteries of Caelestis at birth.[94]

The calm bodies for whom the ancient doctors drew up a daily regimen, a programme of voluntary health care which the individual could observe himself, were those which were preoccupied by notions, closely related to reality, of child sacrifice and voluntary castration. And it is important for us to know whether mutilation and murder were real as well as imagined. The games of the Roman Empire made everyone familiar with the sight of people dying a bloody death, and persecution of the Christians provided a few, rarely very many, people to add to those, originally slaves or those found guilty of serious crimes, who were condemned to die in the arena, sometimes dressed up as gods or other mythological figures.

The spilling of blood and the renunciation of fertility by bloody mutilation bear witness to a tragic view of life, a wondering study of the passing on of life and the permanence of the world, a desire for eternity. Paradoxically, the spilling of blood, whether human or animal, symbolized the respect in which life was held by all. Everyone was insistent on the necessity of spilling blood, as it was the price that had to be paid for the survival of the community and for the salvation of each individual. This necessity was so clear and so much in everyone's minds every day that when Tertullian could think of no further arguments against paganism he cried: 'And if you must have blood, then you have Christ's.'

---

[92] Orosius, *Historiae adversum Paganos*, IV, 6, 3–5. French tr. Leglay, *Saturne africain*, p. 319.
[93] Cyprian, *Letters*, 64.
[94] Salvian, *De gubernatione Dei*, VIII, 2. F. Cumont, *Recherches sur le symbolisme funéraire des Romains*, 1966, epitaphs mentioning the initiation of children, pp. 281–5; sarcophagi, pp. 343–7.

8

Female Virginity and Male Continence: an Introduction to the Christian texts

The practice of child sacrifice which occupied a powerful place in the African imagination in the third century, the human sacrifices carried out in the form of public executions in the amphitheatre, the voluntary castration of Cybele's lovers, all this has taken us away from everyday life into the realm of those fundamental aspects of life which do not need to be talked about or to occur very frequently in order to influence the choices people make in everyday life. There is an obvious link between the ordinary subject matter of family medicine and the permanent prevention of the emission of fertile sperm: the aim is the same whether one is talking about an individual who asks for his doctor's help in curbing his sexual drive or a religious man who removes his own testicles.

Within the framework of the various gnoses those men and women who were concerned with the realm of divine mystery experimented very widely in the sexual field. Their aim was not the simplistic one of separating body and soul so that the soul could ignore the body and the body could take advantage of this to obtain satisfaction in any way it chose. In many cases the body itself was the instrument by which the soul experienced the ecstasy of the eternal. The experience of a body sated with pleasure, of drunken transport, of an orgasm so short that it left one craving for a world in which such wonders might last forever, artificially induced hallucinations, all of these short-lived but common experiences in which the body became the messenger of the spirit, had to be repeated to make the individual aware of the reality which was in store for him.

The fleeting experience might be a taste of eternity, and recalling an experience was the most effective way of forgetting the humdrum human existence which one could not take with one into the world of eternity. But if orgasm and physical delight were the body's link with infinity, heterosexual relations also signified the passing on of the vital spirit and the beginning of something finite, subject to time, through the process of generation. The gnostic doctrines hesitated between the two poles of orgasm and generation. They did not argue against desire, but against the exercise of sexual faculties and the emission of sperm. The clearest exposition of this was in those sects which encouraged all forms of sexual experience providing that they could not result in fertilization.[1]

This led to a profusion of intellectual and physical experiments within a multiplicity of small groups, each with its own inflexible doctrine which excluded all others, led by intellectuals who produced more and more interpretations and clarifications as questions were raised in relation to the here-after and the behaviour to be adopted in preparation for the here-after.

We shall not study this process in detail here, although it is as much a part of the background to the birth and astonishing expansion of the Christian movement which made virginity both an ideal and a way of life as are daily behaviour and the law.

Between the works of Galen and Tertullian, and the expansion of the monastic movement, the chief episodes in the development of a new world, which was to be a Christian world, seem to have been the persecution of the Christians in the third century, the Barbarian invasions and the conversion of Constantine. Like human sacrifice, persecution was neither widespread nor continuous,[2] with the possible exception of the attempt to eradicate Christianity. In pursuit of this goal Diocletian allowed methods of torture which were banned throughout the Mediterranean, even for use on the most miserable of slaves, to be used on the Christians, in a war without rules where the most savage practices were permissible.[3] The small scale of persecution up until Diocletian's time, and the rarity of martyrs did not stop the pagans from worrying about the

[1] Noonan, *Contraception*, gives an account of the various doctrinal positions on this problem.

[2] For the results on the Christian faith of widespread and bloody persecution, see H. Grégoire, *Les persécutions dans l'Empire romain*, 1951; J. Moreau, *La persécution du christianisme*, 1956; in relation to Africa, C. Saumagne, La persécution de Dèce en Afrique d'après la correspondance de saint Cyprien, 1962, pp. 1–29. In La persécution des chrétiens, p. 222–251, I have shown that the persecutions carried out by Septimus Severus and Decius were bloody, even if the number of known deaths was small, and the nature and number of condemnations varies from province to province.

[3] G. E. M. de Sainte-Croix, Aspects of the 'Great' Persecution, 1954, pp. 75–113, has shown the geographical and penal inconsistencies of the persecution of 303–4, pointing out that in the east the number of deaths makes the problem of surrender of holy books and of apostasy a side issue, whereas it is a central issue in subsequent years in the western provinces where there were fewer martyrs. On the atrocities committed upon the Christians in Egypt, see Eusebius, *Ecclesiastical History*, ed. and French tr. G. Bardy, 1958, vol. III, pp. 8–36.

advance of Christianity, nor the Christians from living, even during the periods of calm which sometimes lasted twenty years, in fear of raids, torture and martyrdom.[4]

The ending of this period of fear once the Emperor was converted in the fourth century and Christianity had been established in an unassailable position of power perhaps explains why uncompromising minds sought in individual asceticism the perfection which up until then the dangers of the time had demanded of the Christian,[5] and all the more so since political conversions and the ease with which people could be admitted into the churches had diminished the intensity of the gatherings which a minority certain of power were now allowed to hold.

The changes that took place in the third and fourth centuries are thus generally considered as explaining the birth of the ascetic movement in Egypt which in turn, following the Gospel and the Christian mission, provided the inspiration for the Christian era. The most surprising aspect of asceticism is, of course, the decision to remain chaste. While asceticism in general may be explained by the aim of recapturing the heroism of martyrdom, virginity can be traced back to Jesus' words[6] and to Saint Paul's development of these.[7] Yet the most interesting question is not so much the origin of the command to remain chaste as the way in which this was observed and the reasons for the popularity of this way of life. In this context, the pagan experiments with sexual abstinence and the social conditions which prevented women from giving free expression to their sexuality prepared the way for Christian asceticism and even in a sense led to its emergence as an alternative to hysteria.

The first Christian writings on sexuality were addressed to women.[8] Tertullian wrote *On the veiling of virgins* at the beginning of the third century, and Cyprian, also in Africa, wrote *Virgins and their Apparel*. These works reflect the fact that there already existed women who had

---

[4] Pierre Vidal-Naquet, *Les Juifs, la mémoire et le présent*, 1981, pp. 197–8, led me to reconsider my research into the number of martyrs, even though I had previously considered that deaths, and bloody deaths, had indeed occurred among the Christians, at least in certain parts of the Empire and in certain periods. Whatever the number of deaths, the threat of persecution remained, and the whole community lived in fear. This fear, sometimes unfounded, remains one of the essential elements in the establishment of the community and of contemporary doctrinal development.

[5] This explanation was given by the ancients themselves. See H. Delehaye, *Sanctus, Essai sur le culte des saints*, 1927, p. 109 et seq. Pachomius' master sought to rival the martyrs through illness: *Life of Pachomius*, 13.

[6] Matthew, 19, 12.

[7] I Corinthians, 7. On this point, see M. Aubineau's introduction to Gregory of Nyssa's *Treatise on virginity*, 1966.

[8] A list of treatises on virginity is to be found in T. Camelot, *Les traités de virginitate* au IVe siècle, 1952. One might add Augustine's letter, number 150, to the grandmother and mother of Demetrias who had just renounced marriage in order to take the virgin's veil.

been brought up to remain virgins or who had chosen virginity. We also have two epistles from the third century, perhaps written in Syria, addressed to virgins, which show that there were experiments within the Church, as there had been among the Gnostics, which entailed men and women who had taken vows of chastity living together as if in families in individual houses. In this way followers of the faith could live in entirely Christian cells but adopt the pattern of family life with the traditional division of tasks between men and women. The main advantage of this was that a man could have a woman at his disposal: 'So that she can take care of my possessions, my coat, whatever is left to me in my poverty; so that she can lay the table, spread out my bedding, light the fire, wash my feet and provide other comforts'.[9] Experiments were made with this way of life in Africa and Cyprian ordered investigations into those who lived this way and prescribed penance.[10] This lifestyle was so common that Athanasius accused Leontius, Bishop of Antioch, of adopting it.[11] The experiments continued, and we find them discussed by John Chrysostom in Antioch at the end of the fourth century. All the works so far mentioned treat virginity as a condition which already existed and attempt to regulate the way of life followed by virgins, but none of them deals with virginity itself.

It was Methodius of Olympus, who died in 311, who in a work which took the form of a banquet debate (symposium),[12] began the series of works genuinely devoted to virginity. Male sexuality was certainly discussed: 'the marrow-like generative part of the blood, which is liquid bone, gathers from all parts of the body, curdled and worked into a foam, and then rushes through the generative organs into the living soil of the woman.'[13] But the main emphasis is on ten women debating the relative merits of marriage and virginity.

Discussions on virginity became something of a fashion during the fourth century.[14] They were defences of this way of life, and even when the speaker appears to be addressing a male reader as well as a female reader, the subject is always a female virgin. Gregory of Nyssa seems to

[9] John Chrysostom, Les cohabitations suspectes, 9.

[10] Cyprian, Letters, IV.

[11] Cyprian, Letters; on Bishop Leontius, Athanasius, De fuga sua, 26, in PG, XXV, col. 677 B; Historia Arianorum ad monachos, 28, in PG, XXV, col. 725 A.

[12] On the banquet as a real event and as a literary genre, see Florence Dupont, Le plaisir et la loi, 1977, which deals with earlier periods; Methodius of Olympus, The Symposium – A Treatise on Chastity, ed. and tr. H. Musurillo, 1958; French tr. and notes V.-H. Debidour, 1963.

[13] Methodius, The Symposium, II, 2, tr. Musurillo.

[14] According to Gregory of Nyssa in the introduction to his treatise De Virginitate, 1, 1. The number of treatises which have survived to our day is in any case proof of this.

be the only exception to this.[15] Most of the works are expressly addressed to women, and deal with the type of upbringing which prepares women for virginity or expose the errors which have led virgins to fall from grace, in other words to practise the sexual act either within or outside marriage. The subject matter was thus above all female virginity, and most of the works laid down rules for virgins. The bishops described to their female audience the harsh realities of conjugal life, the pain of childbirth, the bad temper of husbands, the sorrow of losing a child, compared with the abstract beauty of the ideal of virginity, depicted in platonic terms.

When addressing girls who have to choose between marriage and remaining virgins, John Chrysostom never mentions the difficulty of remaining chaste: the problem never seems to arise.[16] But when he is writing for widows, he feels that the fact that they have known sexual pleasure and can remember it is a serious obstacle to the abstinence they are now being called on to observe.[17] So sure is he that the knowledge of pleasure is a form of slavery that he shows women unable to repudiate their unfaithful husbands, women who have been maltreated and beaten prevented from leaving their husbands simply because they could not have sexual relations with another man after leaving their husband if they wished to remain within the Christian Church.[18] He thus agrees with the medical school of thought which considered that abstinence was easy for those women who had never tasted the pleasures of love.[19]

About the real problems encountered by women who took vows of celibacy and the solutions found for them, the treatises tell us almost nothing. Basil of Ancyra, who was both a bishop and a doctor, deals with this more fully than other writers.[20]

The bishops use other rhetorical genres when addressing themselves to men, and one can tell from their sermons when the audience for whom they were intended was male. When a bishop was working on a treatise intended for female readers he would compare marriage with virginity.[21]

[15] John Chrysostom probably wrote his treatise for women. See B. Grillet's edition and French tr. of John Chrysostom, *De Virginitate*, 1966, p. 25, n. 2.

[16] On John Chrysostom, see C. Baur, *Johannes Chrysostomus*, 1930; on his family and his education, see A. H. M. Jones, St John Chrysostom's Parentage, 1953, pp. 171–3.

[17] John Chrysostom, *De Virginitate*, 39, 2–3.

[18] Ibid., 40, 2.

[19] *Gyn.*, 1, 30.

[20] This is why I believe that it is wrong to study these treatises on virginity when one is dealing with continence.

[21] The following lines dealing with the treatises on virginity and the homilies are based on analysis according to the model put forward by R. Robin, *Histoire et linguistique*, 1973, and on the first application of this method to ancient history: Texte, Politique, Idéologie: Cicéron, Histoire ancienne, 20, *Annales littéraires de l'Université de Besançon*, vol. 187. By analysing the vocabulary used in texts for men and those for women, and then grouping together the terms for marriage and those used in opposition to this notion and to that of virginity, it has been possible to conclude that the word marriage has many meanings and that its value is relative.

But when John Chrysostom was preparing a homily for an essentially male audience,[22] he would begin by comparing marriage with the different types of fornication: visits to prostitutes,[23] affairs with a servant, married men having affairs with a servant,[24] and erotic fellatio, presumably within a homosexual relationship.[25] And when he describes the hardships of marriage, turning them into spiritual training, a kind of 'domestic gymnastics', useful for the purpose of helping the sufferer win the prize of eternal life, he evokes the insults hurled by a wife at her husband, female gossip,[26] all the things which men find unbearable and which make marriage an ordeal.

In general, John Chrysostom did not preach virginity to an entire congregation – it was probably too late for that anyway – and he advised single fornicators to marry, and those who were already committed to marriage he advised to remain within that estate and behave soberly.[27]

Neither the homilies nor the works on virginity by Christian authors deal with a man's sexual life. Two very different sorts of work are devoted to this subject. There are treatises which show how to supervise the virginity of little boys so as to guide them towards monastic vows, and there are Rules which examine the ways in which adults can adopt an ascetic lifestyle and remain chaste virgins. It is these treatises which reveal the sexual experiences of the men of Asia Minor and Roman Syria, where John Chrysostom was writing at the end of the fourth century. Although the legal age at which a boy became a man was fourteen, a boy received his sexual initiation, which would be homosexual, at the age of ten, sometimes even before.[28] Ten was also the age at which John Chrysostom advocated, if this had not already been done much earlier, placing a boy in the care of monks who would take care of his education up to the age of

---

[22] This has been pointed out by J. Bernardi, *La prédication des Pères cappadociens*, 1968, in relation to Basil, Gregory of Nazianzus and Gregory of Nyssa. A. Natali also considers that John Chrysostom had an essentially male audience in the church at Antioch. I am grateful to him for having passed on to me this result of the research he is still carrying out.

[23] John Chrysostom, *passim* and *Homilies*, XI, 4.

[24] Ibid., XII, 5.

[25] Ibid., XVI, 4.

[26] Ibid., XV.

[27] Bernardi's study shows the insurmountable difficulty of trying to define the audience using the text of the homilies. On p. 335 et seq. Bernardi shows that those who lived in the countryside, the majority of the population in the fourth century, did not attend these sermons. See p. 337, 'the lower classes of town-dwellers were represented by only a few people'. There is nothing about the slaves. Is this because these categories of people were not present, or because the bishop was primarily addressing the noble men and their servants and a few craftsmen?

[28] See A.-J. Festugière's fine book, *Antioche païenne et chrétienne, Libanius, Chrysostome et les moines de Syrie*, 1959. In particular, Libanius, *On Invitations*, Festugière, pp. 202–6.

twenty.[29] John Chrysostom reveals that these boys had usually been violated, while Libanius describes the touching that went on under the blankets at banquets during winter celebrations, and the insidious escalation of these practices which led as far as fellatio. Christian children, taken to these official banquets by their fathers, were not safe from these assaults.[30]

One may well ask whether this is rhetorical exaggeration in the full flow of a sermon, but no apologetic or polemical speech systematically uses arguments which have no connection with reality and which have therefore no power to impress the audience. Besides, neither the pagan Libanius nor the Christian John Chrysostom draws his images from anything other than homosexual relations. Libanius, in a discourse on man's enslavement to passion, says, 'There is no request, however impossible, that the boy he loves can make which the man wounded by love does not regard it as an absolute necessity to fulfil.'[31] When John Chrysostom sets out to dissuade men who wish to remain virgins and who are nevertheless living with a woman who has agreed to a kind of unconsummated marriage and intends to remain chaste also, he gives the example of the passion aroused when two men embrace one another. 'A philosopher, seeing one of his disciples covering a handsome young man with kisses, cried in surprise: "That bold young man who with his kisses is lighting a furnace in the other's breast could easily do a cartwheel right into the fire." '[32]

How then can one explain the thinking behind John Chrysostom's advice not to live with a woman but rather to live in the same way in a private house with another man?

> In the first place, if she takes a bath or if she feels unwell, the brother can not help her, however low he has chosen to sink, and she can not manage on her own. But if two brothers live together they can help one another in this way. Besides, when it comes to night time, if one of the parties is a woman, it is necessary to have two beds, two sets of rugs and blankets, and really two separate rooms. If two brothers live together, their needs are more similar

---

[29] John Chrysostom, *Against the Detractors of the Monastic Life*, in Festugière, *Antioche*, p. 188.

[30] John Chrysostom, *Against Detractors*, in Festugière, *Antioche*, p. 206. A. Natali has shown that the Christians in Antioch did not withdraw from social life and their duties as citizens which included banquets: Christianisme et cité à la fin du IVe siècle d'après Jean Chrysostome, in *Jean Chrysostome et Augustin*, 1975.

[31] Libanius, *Moral Discourses*, Intro., text and French tr. B. Schouler, 1973, p. 189; *Orations*, 25, 27, with references in note 26 to the same motif in the work of Libanius.

[32] John Chrysostom, *Cohab. susp.*, 2. Boswell, *Christianity, Social Tolerance and Homosexuality*, devotes a page to homosexuality in Antioch as described by Festugière. More useful is Marrou's chapter on this in *Histoire de l'éducation*, and the bibliography. For earlier periods, K. J. Dover, *Greek Homosexuality*, 1978.

and they can manage with less, for a single room, a single cushion, one bed and the same blankets will suffice for two.[33]

On the one hand, John Chrysostom shows 'males in the centre of town practising their base acts on other males, as if they were in the middle of the desert', and on the other he advises fathers to send their young sons to the Syrian desert to be educated by monks. The problems encountered by the monks who did discover how difficult it was to remain chaste in the desert are never mentioned in these works intended to persuade a lay audience to join those who lived a solitary and chaste life.

These problems are dealt with in a quite different set of works, the *Lives* of the first monks, the accounts of monastic life and the recorded words of those holy men who lived in solitude. We must remember that the treaties on virginity do not deal with the difficulties of abstinence but rather describe the mediocrity of marriage compared with the ideal and eternal beauty of the virgin. Moreover, the texts on virginity say little about married sex, which they neglect in favour of a variety of arguments based on the difficulties of daily life. All these commonplace arguments are turned on their head in a different rhetorical context, namely the discourses aimed at persuading men to marry if for no other reason than to fulfil their civic duty,[34] in a society where homosexuality and male and female prostitution made marriage a social duty unrelated to desire. In this we see the force of Christian argumentation: it takes a line of argument which is firmly established in male minds and changes the terms slightly when applying it to women so that the opposition prostitution or homosexuality versus marriage becomes marriage versus virginity.

The only descriptions of reality one is likely to find in the treatises on virginity, then, are perhaps in the passages on marriage, and then one must compare these with other documents in order to temper the negative exaggeration of rhetorical fervour. We can summarize the Christian Fathers' views of marriage, as expressed in their works intended to convince women to remain chaste, by these words of John Chrysostom: 'The Apostle said, "Endure this servitude; only when he dies will you be free." '[35] The most outspoken of the Fathers on this point was Basil of Ancyra, who as we have seen was a doctor, and who wrote before 364: 'With her dowry a woman buys herself a master.'[36]

But female virginity, which was not always the result of personal

---

[33] John Chrysostom, *Cohab. susp.*, 9.

[34] On the treatises *On Marriage*, see Festugière, *Antioche*, p. 184, n. 1.

[35] John Chrysostom, *De Virginitate*, 40, 1.

[36] Basil of Ancyra wrote a treatise, *De Virginitate*, which has come down to us in the works of Basil of Caesarea, see *PG*, XXX, col. 669–809, and in the form of fragments in Old Slavonic, see A. Vaillant, *De Virginitate de S. Basile, Texte vieux slave*, 1943. This quotation from *De Virginitate*, 23, *PG*, XXX, col. 718.

choice, can not be considered as a social model, particularly since the very existence of female sperm was the object of scientific and philosophical debate. It was only because men chose this path that a whole civilization was affected by their action and the philosophical and moral, in other words ideological, arguments behind it.

Scholars have often said that in the Roman world not everyone had the chance to remain celibate.[37] In fact it was possible for anyone to do so, provided he gave up the right to receive most of his heritage. This obstacle was removed by Constantine,[38] who revoked the laws disqualifying unmarried people from receiving their inheritance, and gave them the same rights as those who were married. In any case, for someone who wanted to choose a life of chaste celibacy before this date the renunciation of his inheritance must have been of small consequence. The main obstacle in the fourth century lay elsewhere, although it does not seem to have been insurmountable: this was the obligation which gradually evolved during the fourth century for each individual to remain in his social function, his profession, whether he was a producer of goods, a land-owner, a soldier or a servant of the state.[39]

As long as the individual could carry on his life of chastity without making any noticeable changes to his lifestyle or the place where he lived, as the experiences of those who lived a life of domestic asceticism show, the question did not arise. It was the monastic movement which brought the problem to public notice when in the fourth century more and more men were tempted by the prospect of the solitary life.

The desire to live one's life in solitude, away from the world seems to have sprung up towards the middle of the third century. Antony chose the solitary life in around 270, but before any written records were made of the lives, rules and sayings of the hermits the experiences of the solitary monks in Egypt were passed down orally for about a century.

While the bishops were preaching the virtues of virginity to young girls of aristocratic birth to dissuade them from accepting a husband, many men were setting off for the Egyptian desert to undertake a life of abstinence which they hoped to practise till the end of their days. The first monks, all of whom were Egyptian, were from more modest social backgrounds, but they were a source of extraordinary interest first to the Greek nobles of Egypt's large cities, then to those of the Greek world and finally to those of the whole Roman world, both east and west. One of the questions which is essential to an understanding of the changes which

---

[37] Gaudemet, *L'Eglise dans l'Empire romain*, pp. 198–9, shows that Constantine's law was probably not Christian in inspiration.

[38] *Codex Theodosianus*, 8, 16, 31 January 320.

[39] On this obstacle, see Rousselle, Aspects sociaux du recrutement ecclésiastique, pp. 336–70.

affected the civilization of the Empire is not the reason why peasants eager to discover the Christian god set off for the desert, but why this action on the part of humble fellahin had so great an impact when reported by the learned men and aristocrats of east and west.[40]

It was soon clear that the aristocrats and the Egyptian monks had arrived at the same question: was it possible to observe total and permanent abstinence, and if so how. The nobles of the west, who sought their physicians' advice so keenly on ways of reducing their sexual activity, travelled to the east or sought reports of the Christians' experiences in the desert. Men and women called for information on the monks' experiences and relayed their aims and methods throughout the western world.[41]

The *Life of Antony*[42] became popular among these educated people. It was the first account of the life of a holy monk, and was written soon after 356 by Athanasius, bishop of Alexandria, who had probably taken refuge in the region of the Thebaid where the monks looked after him. The same aristocratic milieux eagerly greeted the *Life of Paul of Thebes*, an Egyptian monk, writen by Jerome, and later the *Life of Saint Martin*, written in Gaul by Sulpicius Severus. One might expect these works to be austere, but they are not. They convey very evocatively the passionate experiences of the monks and the strength of their questioning. These humble men from modest backgrounds seemed to be finding an answer to the fundamental problems with which everyone was concerned. To the anxious pilgrims who came to see them the monks replied that they were seeking and had not yet found the answer, but that that they could pass on some of the things they had learned. To the astonished ears of their listeners they would then impart little stories, all very down to earth, and all leading to some other adventure. They were not mere anecdotes, and the listener who laughs at the old monk running as fast as his legs could

---

[40] P. Resch, *La doctrine ascétique des premiers maîtres égyptiens du quatrième siècle*, 1931, pp. xxxi–xxxviii, gives a useful résumé of the learned works which have sought to find in Egyptian paganism the origin of monastic practice and in the lives of pagans (*Life of Pythagoras, Life of Apollonius of Tyana*) the pagan models used by the first hagiographers. This line of research has not been abandoned and remains very worthwhile.

[41] See for example the public audience of the *Vita Martini* and the *Dialogues* of Sulpicius Severus: Rousselle, Paulin de Nole et Sulpice Sévère. The bishops of the monasteries of southern Gaul were aristocrats from senatorial families, Rousselle, Aspects sociaux du recrutement ecclésiastique, pp. 362–8.

[42] On the *Life of Antony*, see *Vita di Antonio*, critical text and commentary G. J. M. Bartelink, Italian tr. P. Citati and S. Lilla, ed. Christine Mohrmann, 1974. This work includes an introduction to the origins of asceticism and to the text of the *Life of St Antony*. The text which is edited and tr. into Italian in this work is that of the oldest Latin tr. The *Life of Antony* was tr. twice shortly after it had first been written in Greek. One of these trs. is ed. by Bartelink, the other, by Evagrius of Antioch, is to be found in *PG*, col. 835–976. See Bibliography for details of English tr.

carry him in the direction of the prostitutes of Alexandria learns that this old man once mocked a novice who showed the same desires.[43] These men went off to apply their whole bodies to the search for the meaning of existence.

Their experiences are passed on with the same earnestness. Palladius, who came from Galatia, spent seventeen years with them (from 388 to 399 and then from 406 to 412), before becoming a bishop in Bithynia. He dedicated his account to the Emperor's chamberlain, Lausus, in 419–20, whence the title *Lausiac History*.

The *Historia Monachorum in Aegypto* recounts a visit paid by six young monks in 394–5 and John Cassian reports, after 411, what he saw and heard in the desert between 385 and 399. These texts are the works of authors who took trouble over their composition, to varying degrees, but their authors had also tried as hard as they could and for many years to live the lives about which they were writing.

Alongside these lives of the first monks and the accounts of their experiences in the desert, there exists a very different body of work which consists of collections of the deeds and actions of the monks, which were sometimes taken up in learned writings. They formed separate collections such as the *Sayings of the Fathers*, although their actions were often more eloquent than their words. They were collected together and translated in ancient times into seven languages. Nothing seemed more useful to readers of the time than this summary of the Egyptian experience.[44]

Jerome and Cassian both wrote in Latin, and it was in southern Gaul that Cassian, at the request of the Gallic anchorites, wrote his *Institutions* and his *Conferences* of the Desert Fathers. The aristocrats of the west often read Greek[45] but Jerome and Rufinus translated the *Rule of Pachomius* and other Pachomian texts[46] as well as the *Historia Monachorum in Aegypto*. The *Life of Antony* had been translated almost

---

[43] *PJ*, V, 4 = *Coll.*, II, 13.

[44] J.-Cl. Guy, *Recherches sur la tradition grecque des 'Apophtegmata Patrum'*, 1962. The *Apophtegmata* exist in two forms: an alphabetical series listing the sayings attributed to each of the Fathers, (*PG*, 65, 71–440), to which must be added the anonymous sayings, some of which have been ed. by F. Nau, 1907–13, and a systematic collection, in about twenty chapters, which was tr. into Latin by Pelagius and John, (*PL*, 73, 851–1022). For details of English trs. see Bibliography.

[45] P. Courcelle, *Les lettres grecques en Occident de Macrobe à Cassiodore*, 1943, 2nd edition, 1948; P. Riché, *Education et culture dans l'Occident barbare*, 1962, pp. 83–4.

[46] The *Life of Pachomius* has come down to us in Coptic in several versions, and the first written account was certainly in Coptic. The Latin tr. by Dionysius Exiguus, in the first half of the sixth century, used a Greek text which was a tr. from the Coptic: *La vie latine de saint Pachôme*, a critical ed. by J. Van Cranenburgh, 1969. The most complete account of the Life and the version nearest to the original Coptic text is contained in a Greek manuscript: Festugière, *Les moines d'Orient, IV²*, *La première vie grecque de saint Pachôme*, 1965. For the benefit of the monks in the Pachomian monasteries who did not

as soon as Athanasius wrote it in 357. Rufinus produced another version of the ascetic writings of Basil of Caesarea, which constitute in effect a Rule. At the beginning of the sixth century the *Life of Pachomius* was translated into Latin, and the *Sayings of the Fathers* and the *Lausiac History* at the end of the sixth century, while a second Latin translation was made of the *Historia Monachorum*.

Other documents, Greek rules of uncertain origin, initially intended for the use of Egyptian solitaries, had the same success in the west through their Latin translations.[47]

It may seem strange to choose to study these translated documents rather than to seek the original flavour of eastern monachism in documents which are closer to the wishes of the founders of the ascetic movement. But this choice is deliberate and allows us to appreciate the choice made in the west between the eastern texts, which were not directly accessible to all since Greek was no longer widely studied. Almost all the treatises on virginity had already been written when the experiences of the desert monks were noted down. None of the treatises on virginity was translated: they were of no use whatever in solving the very real problems which arose for those following the solitary life, even in the area of abstinence.

A considerable body of work has come down to us in the west through these Latin translations. Short, practical works, dealing with the concrete problems of daily life, these little books were extremely popular and have remained the inspiration of monasticism in the east and in the west. It seems to me that one might even regard them as one of the chief sources of inspiration, perhaps in a less conscious fashion, of European civilization since the fourth century. Monasteries do not remain in existence through hereditary renewal, but need a constant flow of recruits from the outside world. Thus if the secular world had not remained convinced of the value of the examples and the thoughts of the founders of monasticism, this flow of new members would not have continued as it did and as it does to this day.[48]

read Coptic, Greek trs. were made of the *Rule of Pachomius*, his *Letters* and the *Rule* of his successor Theodorus, and the *Teachings* of the third leader of the community, Horsiesios, who died around 380. This is the collection which Jerome tr. into Latin; critical ed. by A. Boon, *Pachomiana latina*, 1932. For English and French trs. see Bibliography.

[47] They were collected by Benedict of Aniane, *Codex Regularum* and *Concordia Regularum*, PL, 103. French tr. of the *Trois Règles des Pères*, the *Règle orientale*, and the *Règles de Macaire*, in *Règles monastiques d'Occident d'Augustin à Ferréol* tr., introduction and note by Father Vincent Desprez.

[48] There is a considerable body of literature on monasticism and its origins, but it does not, as a rule, deal with the problems discussed here. General histories of Christianity may serve as an introduction to the subject for those who wish to have a better understanding of Egyptian monasticism. The best introduction in my opinion is Derwas Chitty, *The Desert a city*, 1977.

9

The Strength of Desire

'Was freedom of thought not enough for me in the desert?'
Alph., Sisoes, 26

The *Lives* of the first monks and the words of the desert Fathers which were passed on to people in the west provide a vivid record of the experiences which led the hermits to impose the Rule of silence and the Rule which counsels the monk to keep his eyes lowered. 'A monk met some nuns as he walked along. He moved off the path when he saw them, but their superior said to him: "If you were a perfect monk you would not have looked at us and you would not have seen that we were women." '[1] And this account of a monk who did succeed in following the advice:

> One day the priest of Scetis went to visit the bishop of Alexandria. On his return, the brothers asked him for news of the town, and he replied: 'Believe me, brothers, I saw no-one but the bishop there.' This reply made them worried and they said: 'Has the whole population been destroyed, Father?' But the priest replied: 'It is not that, but I did not succumb to the temptation to look at men.'[2]

The texts depict the solitary life as something that has to be worked out through successive experiences rather than as an end result. These experiences were quite new, and the discoveries they led to were also new, even though the ancient writers, trained in philosophy, borrowed

---

[1] *PJ*, IV, 62. In the remainder of the book, quotations from the Pelagius and John collection of the *Apophtegmata Patrum* (indicated by the abbreviation *PJ*) are given in F.P.'s translation of the version used by the author, namely that from *Les Sentences des Pères du désert*, tr. Dion and Oury. Quotations from the alphabetical (*Alph.*) series are from Benedicta Ward's *Sayings of the Desert Fathers*, 1975.

[2] *PJ*, IV, 55.

from pagan doctrinal texts in order to express them. But this process of continuous refinement in response to events is more apparent in the *Apophtegmata Patrum* and the accounts of the monks' lives than in the writings which set out to translate the results into theories, especially as regards what the monks' experiences teach us about human nature. The texts are generally studied as roads to holiness, which they are if one accepts the definition of holiness which they give or which is given today. But this is not the way in which I wish to examine them. The first Fathers of the Church did not go to the desert armed with a set of precepts on solitude, abstinence or fasting. They simply set off, and they discovered the rest little by little as they began to have a clearer picture of the men they really were, which had not been apparent to them while they lived in towns and villages.

What made Antony leave the village community was Christ's words, which he received in his village church 'as if the lesson had been addressed to him': 'If you wish to go the whole way, go sell your possessions, and give to the poor, and then you will have riches in heaven; and come, follow me.'[3] It was easy to understand the command to sell one's possessions, and Antony gave his to the Curia, that is the municipal senate. But how did one follow a Christ who had been dead for more than two hundred years? Antony interpreted this as a call to seek personal knowledge of Christ through the Scriptures and through prayer. But how could he be alone in an Egyptian village when the flooding of the Nile made everyone settle on small hillocks which rose out of the flood water?

> The inhabitants of Egypt have adopted the following custom as a result of the flooding of the Nile. For a large part of every year, the country is entirely covered by flood water, and it looks like an enormous sea. People can only travel in boats. Consequently, after they have been embalmed with the strongest aromatics, the dead are placed in small cells which are built above ground level.[4]

Antony followed the example of an old man in a neighbouring village and at first went to live a little way from everyone else. In order to avoid the contacts with others which village agricultural life imposed, he chose a craft which he could practise alone. He soon discovered that solitude and silence were filled with the amplified voice of man's desires. And yet his biographer does not present this discovery in these terms, but rather as a series of assaults from demons outside man, outside Antony. How could

---

[3] Matthew 19, 21, New English Bible. *Life of Antony*, 2.

[4] *Coll.*, XV, 3. On the seasonal changes in the Egyptian countryside, see D. Bonneau, *La crue du Nil, divinité egyptienne à travers mille ans d'histoire*, (332 BC–AD 641), 1964.

the first men who were determined to live by the Word of God have understood that these assaults came from within them? But Antony tells his disciples: 'The demons' traps are evil thoughts'.[5]

It was only the fact that so many monks underwent the same experiences that made them realize that there was a whole series of facets to human nature, even if they persisted in seeing them as called up by demons. Antony's first discovery was the overwhelming force of sexual desire. He fought this desire to the point of exhausting himself, and he was determined to overcome his body by all means possible, depriving it of sleep, of comfort and of food. He used the money he made from making and selling objects to buy bread and gave what he did not need to the poor. To weaken his body he ate only once a day and sometimes only once every two or four days; all he ate was bread and salt, and he drank water.

But his struggle continued and Antony wished to avoid the contacts with people which selling his objects and buying bread necessitated. He shut himself in a tomb, away from the village, and conducted the trade on which his subsistence depended through a friend who came occasionally to bring him provisions. He maintained this way of life for fifteen to seventeen years. He learned that total absence of human contact did not eradicate desire, but on the contrary it turned it into a torturing obsession. 'He who wishes to live in solitude in the desert is delivered from three conflicts: hearing, speech and sight; there is only one conflict for him and that is with fornication.'[6]

Others too shut themselves in tombs: there was a young man who wept for his past faults[7] and a servant woman named Alexandra who died in the sepulchre where she had lived as a recluse for ten years.[8] This was also a pagan practice in Egypt, but we are not told if the pagans who lived in tombs for twenty-three years confined themselves completely to their tombs as did the Christian recluses.[9]

Shutting oneself away in this manner at first seemed the only way to avoid contact with other people, which was considered, in the beginning, to be the source of temptation. The monk John of Lycopolis taught that the most perfect failed in their endeavours if they remained close to villages.[10] He who wished to isolate himself must first solve the problem

---

[5] *Life of Antony*, 23.

[6] *Alph.*, Antony, 11. J.-C. Guy, *Paroles des anciens*, Antony, 10, p. 16, and Ward translate correctly *fornication*; L. Regnault, *Alph.*, Antony, 11, and J. Dion and G. Oury, *PJ*, II, 2, translate 'celui du coeur, (that of the heart)'.

[7] *HM*, I, 37.

[8] *LH*, 5.

[9] Festugière, *Les moines d'Orient*, p. 19, n. 242.

[10] *HM*, I, 31.

of food. We are used to the idea of the ascetics' fasting, in other words restricting their intake of food,[11] but the monks' first problem was to find a means of obtaining food, not of restricting its consumption. Near to a village, shut up in a tomb, a hermit who wished to reduce the number of contacts he had with other people had to eat food which was easy to keep, and in Egypt as elsewhere bread seemed the most suitable. It would be kept dry and dipped in water before being eaten. The monks had to work in order to buy bread, and the work they chose was basketry, so they produced baskets and mats. They could store the raw materials easily, for they were dried stems, and each evening they would put to soak the quantity of straw they would need the following day. Some managed to live like this for years. Alexandra wove cloth every morning,[12] Dorotheus the Theban[13] and Pambo[14] plaited palms. Pachomius himself in the early years spun and wove bags of hair,[15] and then later, with his brother, cut rushes and made mats.[16]

But following Antony's example, those who aspired to solitude moved further away from the valley. Antony took this economy of the recluse with him to the desert. He wove baskets and exchanged them for produce which his visitors brought with them.[17] He and his disciples did, however, travel to inhabited areas from time to time, taking with them on a camel the objects they had made to exchange them for bread, and renewing their supply of water.[18] Thus contacts with the outside world remained unavoidable. But each time the hermit went down into the valley and passed through villages he received a dazzling reminder of the joys he had left behind and it was here that he would weaken. The *Apophtegmata* tell how some of the monks yielded to the desire to have intercourse with a woman.[19] They took a young girl along the river and made love to her among the reeds.[20] They found that age and the time they had spent in the desert did not remove this temptation. A sick old man, who did not want to be a burden to the brothers in the desert,

[11] See H. Musurillo's remarkable discussion of this question, The problem of ascetical fasting in the Greek patristic writers,, 1956, pp. 1–64, with a bibliography, which looks at contemporary medical research, and research into fasting and into the asceticism of the first Christians, with regard to both theory and practice.

[12] *LH*, 5.

[13] Ibid., 2.

[14] Ibid., 10.

[15] *Life of Pachomius*, 6.

[16] Ibid., 23 and 51.

[17] *Life of Antony*, 53.

[18] Ibid., 54.

[19] *PJ*, 27; *Alph.*, anon., 43. See J.-C. Guy, *Les Apophtegmes des Pères du désert*, anon., 43. *Les sentences des Pères du désert*, 1977, N. 49 and N. 50 with women who washed their clothes in the desert.

[20] *PJ*, V, 41.

decided to take himself off to the village where a family took him in and where he was cared for by his host's young daughter. One of the Fathers had advised him not to go, but he had assured him that 'his body was dead'. But when the young girl became pregnant he confessed to being the father, and took the child back to the desert with him.[21] This was such a common occurrence that pregnant girls who did not want to betray their real lovers falsely accused the anchorites. Hence this episode of Macarius' life which he himself recounts:

> Now it happened that a virgin in the village, under the weight of temptation, committed sin. When she became pregnant, they asked her who was to blame. She said, 'The anchorite.' Then they came to seize me, led me to the village and hung pots black with soot and various other things round my neck and led me through the village in all directions, beating me and saying, 'This monk has defiled our virgin, catch him, catch him.'[22]

Abba Nicon had a similar experience in the middle of the Sinai, where a nomad's daughter, on the advice of her lover, accused the holy man of corrupting her. Her father believed her and went off to strike the monk with his sword.[23] These accounts were not included in the Latin collections, perhaps because the trade between craftsman monks and peasant labourers was abandoned to a large extent after these experiences.

The first solution that occurred to the monks was to do without bread and to live as far as possible from what they could gather from around them. This was not so difficult in Egypt where gathering wild plants was one of the usual ways of collecting food, as it was throughout the Mediterranean,[24] particularly in times of famine.[25] This was doubtless what made a number of hermits move towards the swamps, for even though they had given up eating meat, it was easier to find food here than in the desert. Some of them cultivated the delta swamps,[26] but soon these areas attracted so many people that Macarius came to consider this as a sign that the monastic experience was finished: 'When you see a cell built close to the marsh, know that the devastation of Scetis is near. When you

[21] Ibid., V, 25.
[22] *Alph.*, Mac., 1.
[23] Ibid., Nicon, 1.
[24] R.J. Forbes, *Studies in ancient technology*, vol. III, 1950, p. 50 et seq., and J. André, *L'alimentation et la cuisine à Rome*, 1961. On Egypt, A. C. Johnson, *Roman Egypt to the Reign of Diocletian*, in Tenney Frank, *An Economic Survey of Ancient Rome*, vol. V, 1936, p. 2; F. Hartmann, *L'agriculture dans l'ancienne Égypte*, 1923, mentions natural products and gathering wild plants, pp. 26–9, 42–7, 152.
[25] J. Vandier, *La famine dans l'Égypte ancienne*, 1936, p. 5.
[26] *HM*, II, 2.

see trees, know that it is at the doors.'[27] Abba Zeno used to leave his cell by night to go to the swamp and look for provisions without being in danger of meeting anyone.[28]

So the hermits needed to choose a deserted spot where it was nevertheless possible to find water and pick plants. It was even possible to survive in the middle of the desert, as did Abba Or, who lived on grasses and roots.[29] Some monks still found the watering places too crowded, and they settled some distance away, depending on how far they could walk carrying jars of water. The Ethiopian monk Moses, who was a penitent thief and probably murderer,[30] spent his nights going to the watering place and filling the other monks' water jars which he left at their cell doors.[31] The cells were between 740 metres and 7½ kilometres away from the watering place. Chaeremon lived alone more than 17 kilometers from the nearest well or swamp, where he used to go to fill his two amphorae.[32] One hermit settled more than 26 kilometers from a well and tried to fill his clay pots with dew collected in December and January so that he would not have to travel to the wells, but he could not entirely avoid making the journey. He lived this way for fifteen years.[33]

Finding fuel to make a fire might have been another problem,[34] but most of the hermits, wishing to devote all their time to meditation, decided to eat their plants and roots raw.[35] But they were not completely without firewood: Pachomius went to collect thorns at the foot of a mountain.[36] Some hermits thus managed to live without seeing anyone and without bread, as did Saint Posidonius, who spent forty years in the desert without eating bread.[37] Living off plants and water was so much a part of the solitary life in the desert that a former hermit, who had retired to a monastery in the valley, went back to this diet when he wanted to assure himself that he was capable of leaving.[38] The hermits adopted the primitive methods of collecting food, gathering plants, bulbs, roots, rhizomes and berries. They rediscovered the techniques of preserving

[27] *Alph.*, Macarius the Egyptian, 5.
[28] *PJ*, XVIII, 7. *Life of Pachomius*, 23 and 51: he cuts rushes; *Alph.*, Macarius, 10 and 33, gathering leaves from the swamp and palm leaves. *Alph.*, Macarius the city-dweller, 1, cuts rushes.
[29] *HM*, II, 4.
[30] *LH*, 19, 1–3; *Coll.*, III, 5.
[31] *LH*, 19.
[32] *Alph.*, Chaeremon, 1. Six kilometers, *Coll.*, XXIV, 2; four and a half kilometers, *Inst.*, V, 36. Seven days' walk, Abba Paul, *Inst.*, X, 24.
[33] *LH*, 27.
[34] *Inst.*, IV, 21; *Alph.*, Longinus.
[35] *LH*, 11; 18; *HM*, 6; 13.
[36] *Life of Pachomius*, 11.
[37] *LH*, 36.
[38] *Alph.*, Gelasios, 6.

food by drying it,[39] and preparing food without cooking, using infusions or decoctions in water which was often only tepid, which they had warmed using stones heated in the sun and placed in a ceramic pot.[40]

But this life seemed too harsh. The only solution was to live near watering places where irrigation made it possible to cultivate a garden. Antony, in his first desert retreat on Mount Colzin, procured a mattock, an axe and a little wheat which he sowed. He managed to grow enough to make his own bread, and he grew a few vegetables for his visitors.[41] The hermits who lived in the Nitria desert, and the monks in the monasteries founded by Pachomius did the same,[42] and the virgins who joined convents also had gardens. The monks planted date palms, fruit trees and olives.[43] So it was the need for food which brought the hermits back towards the swamps where the men and women of the villages also came to find papyrus, game and edible plants, and to the watering places in the desert which were on the routes of the nomads and merchants.

Thus the question of human contact and the sexual temptation represented by encounters with others arose again and in new ways. We hear of the desert Fathers' sexual relations not from malicious pagans, but from the hermits themselves, who were tempted to abandon their lives of solitude as soon as the first woman they had seen for twenty years destroyed their hopes of one day loving only God.[44] Some women did travel through the desert: nomads' daughters,[45] families who were on the run because they were in debt and who took refuge in uninhabited areas, groups of mothers, sisters and other female relations who wanted to see the men who had left them to go and seek God,[46] wives who had agreed to the separation and who brought to their husbands sons they could not feed,[47] and even courtesans who had come to win a bet that they could not seduce one of the hermits.[48] The texts make it clear that the monks could not always resist them.

Even more than women, who were so rare in the desert, young boys

[39] *HM*, II, 8; *Inst.*, IV, 21 and 22.

[40] Forbes, *Studies in ancient technology*, vol. III, pp. 50–51.

[41] *Life of Antony*, 49.

[42] *LH*, 7.

[43] *HM*, XII; *Alph.*, Tithoes, and Gelasios, 1.

[44] F. Dolto, *La difficulté de vivre*, 1981, in a chapter entitled 'Continence et développement de la personnalité', regrets the fact that we do not possess any detailed accounts of the problems caused by voluntary abstinence, or any analyses of those who remain continent. But in order to achieve useful results, one would need to make 'detailed daily observations of monks and nuns', 'free association, and non-systematized data, collected by an observer who was subject to the same sociological conditioning'.

[45] *Alph.*, Nicon, 1.

[46] *PJ*, V, 23.

[47] *Alph.*, Poemen, 76. And Guy, *Apophtegmes des Pères du désert*, anon., 44 and 29.

[48] *Alph.*, Serapion, 1; anon., 57.

aroused the desires of the monks who were unable to resist the need for sexual satisfaction.

Some of these young boys had come to the desert with their fathers,[49] like the son of the anchorite who had been cared for in the village. Some of the boys had never seen a woman,[50] and the father of one told him, when he saw women for the first time, that they were monks. One young boy was brought to the desert by his mother when there was a famine so that his monk father might feed him.[51] Other children were given to the monks at a very young age to be brought up by them. John of Lycopolis, when asked by an officer for advice, told him to bring up his son himself until he was seven, and then take him to the desert.[52] He felt it appropriate that the child should receive the care which was generally bestowed by the women of a family and then be sent to the desert at the age where a male child entered the male world of school. The monks make it clear that these children did represent a temptation and that sexual acts did take place. One example of this was a sick child whose father took him to the desert to ask an old monk to cure him. One of the young disciples of this holy man abused the boy outside the cell.[53] This is why a great many of the *Sayings* warn against living with a child.[54] Brothers who did this always aroused the suspicions of the other monks. Abba Paphnutius refused to keep near him a young man whose face he found feminine.[55] Carion, who brought up his own son, was suspected of succumbing to temptation once the boy had grown up, and the son was so mortified by the accusation that he bathed in a saltpetre lake so as to make his body hideous to look at.[56] Macarius had doubtless seen so many sexual relationships develop with children in the desert that he strongly advised monks not to take them in and educate them. 'When you see young children [in Scetis], take up your sheep-skins, and go away.'[57]

Finally, affinities developed between the hermits themselves and desires rose to the surface.[58] Some were obsessed by the friendships between other brothers; one of them denounced two brothers whom he thought he had caught in the act, and when the monks went up to them

---

[49] *Inst.*, IV, 27; *Coll.*, II, 7 and 11; *PJ*, V, 21. And also *Sentences des Pères*, new collection, 1977, Apophtegmata translated from the Greek into French, N. 456, 457 and 458.

[50] *PJ*, V, 21.

[51] *Alph.*, Carion, 2.

[52] *HM*, I, 10.

[53] *Alph.*, John the Persian, 1.

[54] *Alph.*, John Colobos; Matoes, 11; Poemen, 190.

[55] *Alph.*, Eudemon, 1.

[56] *Alph.*, Carion, 2.

[57] *Alph.*, Macarius the Egyptian, 5.

[58] *Alph.*, Macarius, 21.

they found nothing but two sheaves of corn.[59] One old monk, to whom one of the brothers took a false accusation, made the denouncer live by himself in a cell, saying: 'He himself has the vice of which he accuses others,' thus identifying the phenomenon of projection.

One must not imagine that performing the sexual act usually meant the end of a hermit's solitary life. It is rare to find in the texts accounts of monks leaving for good after succumbing to temptation. It is more usual to find a brother stunned by his fault, ready to despair, and turning to one of the older monks for advice. Now the old monks had discovered that the sexual act was generally the result of a lack of caution when the opportunity to sin presented itself, and they called this pride and presumption. They considered that nothing, and particularly not the commission of a sin, should turn the monk away from his goal, which was a life of solitude with God. So, after reminding their readers that it was wrong to judge the brothers who had sinned,[60] even those who were homosexual,[61] they described the experiences of those who had made a new start on the life of solitude and chastity. In general, like Antony, although he did not have to attone for a sexual act, they tried to subdue their bodies through fasting. Lot shut himself in a cave and ate only every two days for three weeks.[62] Sisoes said that a year, or six months of penitence was too harsh a punishment, and that three days of sincere prayer would satisfy God.[63]

The examples given in the texts concentrate on the monk's development, so that apart from those cases where a girl's family demanded that the hermit support the girl and her child, or those cases where a monk undertook to bring up his son, there is no reference to any compensation for the sexual partner, and no mention either of whether or not he or she had consented to the act, which can by no means be taken for granted.

The monks discovered in the desert that progress was only possible through freedom and personal commitment. They made this discovery in relation to hunger: Serapion, who was passing through Athens, was gnawed by hunger after four days of unsuccessful begging, for 'hunger, if it is not voluntary, is terrible, especially if it is accompanied by uncertainty.'[64] As far as sexual matters were concerned, the Fathers

---

[59] *Alph.*, Poemen, 114.

[60] *PJ*, IX, 1 and 7; *Alph.*, Ammonas, 8, Theodotus, 2.

[61] *Alph.*, Macarius, 21.

[62] *Alph.*, Lot, 2.

[63] *Alph.*, Sisoes, 21.

[64] *LH*, 37, 5. In fact the text says, as Meyer translates it, 'for hunger, if it is not voluntary, is terrible, especially it is accompanied by misbelief.' The Greek word translated as misbelief indicates lack of faith, of trust, which I prefer to translate by a word which expresses the psychological state more clearly: he who has faith knows that God will feed him. He who lacks faith is uncertain.

considered that denunciation was of little help to the denounced and very harmful to the denunciator. An account concerning the bishop Ammonas, a former hermit, gives an example of this. A monk used frequently to receive a woman. One day, knowing that she was in his cell, a crowd dragged Ammonas there to take them by surprise. The monk hid his woman under a cask before opening the door to the bishop, who guessed what had happened and, sitting on the cask, reprimanded the denunciators and told them to search the cell. Then he rose and as he left said, 'Brother, be on your guard.'[65]

With experience, the conditions in which the monks pursued their solitary life were perfected and opportunities for meetings and sexual acts became rarer. Then the insurmountable nature of sexual hunger became apparent, and the monks found themselves avidly recalling any memories they had of women.

> Abba Cyrus of Alexandria was asked about the temptation of fornication, and he replied, 'If you do not think about it, you have no hope, for if you are not thinking about it, you are doing it. I mean, he who does not fight against the sin and resist it in his spirit will commit the sin physically. It is very true that he who is fornicating in fact is not worried with thinking about it.' The old man questioned the brother, saying, 'Do you not usually talk to women?' The brother said, 'No; my thoughts are about old and new representations of them: it is their remembrance which overcomes me.' The old man said to him, 'Do not fear the dead, but flee from the living, and before all things persist in prayer.'[66]

When he was first in the desert, Palladius confided in an old monk that desire filled his thoughts night and day, and that he was increasingly tormented by visions of women to the point where he was close to leaving the desert. Pachon reassured him, which was the customary function of old monks in the accounts of temptation, and revealed that after forty years in the desert he still suffered the same intolerable urges. He said that between the ages of fifty and seventy he had not spent a single night or day without desiring a woman.[67] Father Apollo, too, although old, each day experienced 'the same feelings of revolt and the same storms'.[68]

By day, the conscious mind found that when it wanted to concentrate on prayer it was besieged by thoughts and visions of women.[69] At night,

[65] *Alph.*, Ammonas, 10.
[66] *Alph.*, Cyrus.
[67] *LH*, 23.
[68] *Coll.*, II, 13.
[69] *Alph.*, Gerontios, 1, Olympios, 2, Paphnutius, 5.

dreams would wake the hermits.[70] It is difficult to distinguish between waking dreams and dreams that took place in sleep in these monastic tales. They were neither visions nor dreams, in truth, but fantasies which rose to the surface. When he was almost dying of thirst in the desert, Macarius saw a girl dressed in white linen carrying an urn of sparkling water in her hands.[71] Pachon, in his cell, saw a young Ethiopian girl whom he had watched gleaning in his youth. She sat on his knees and he was devastated.[72] One brother proclaimed that it would take ten women to satisfy his desire.[73] John Cassian explains that the mind moves imperceptibly from the image of one's mother or sister to that of some other female relative, and then to a pious women met some time ago, and then on to other women.[74] Widowers or those who had left a wife to come to the desert would think of their spouse.[75] The hermits took these visions of women as so many faces of the devil.[76]

These dreams are generally heterosexual in our texts, but John Cassian gives an example of an obsessive homosexual fantasy.[77] The greatest of these founding Fathers were continually tested, and they would tell this to their disciples or their visitors to encourage them in their pursuit of the religious experience. Some begged God to calm their desire, and dreamed of castration. Abba Elias fled from a convent which he had founded for women: 'Three angels . . . took hold of him, one by the hands and one by the feet, and the third took a razor and castrated him – not actually, but in the dream.'[78] And for forty years he felt no more desire. Abba Serenus, who prayed to God to make him a eunuch, saw an angel open his body and remove a tumour. A voice told him that God had granted him perfect chastity.[79] This radical cure through a dream must have been extremely rare, for examples of the incessant struggle against sexual desire seem to have been the norm. Before they developed a coherent system for dealing with this problem, the hermits adopted harsh measures to repress the flesh which troubled them so sorely. Ammonius used to burn his body with a red-hot iron every time.[80] Pachon shut himself in a hyena's den, hoping to die sooner than yield, and then he held an asp against his genital

---

[70] *LH*, 19.
[71] Ibid., 18.
[72] Ibid., 23.
[73] *Alph.*, Paphnutius, 5.
[74] *Coll.*, VI, 13.
[75] *Alph.*, anon., 42.
[76] *Life of Antony*, 23; *LH*, 23; *Alph.* anon., 56.
[77] *Inst.*, XII, 20.
[78] *LH*, 29, tr. Meyer.
[79] *Coll.*, VII, 1.
[80] *LH*, 11.

organs.[81] Evagrius spent many nights in a frozen well.[82] Philoromus wore irons.[83] One hermit agreed one night to take in a woman who was lost in the desert. He left his light burning all night and burned his fingers on it to remind himself of eternal punishment.[84] A monk who had treasured the memory of a very beautiful woman, when he heard that she was dead, went and dippled his coat in her decomposed body and lived with this smell to help him fight his constant thoughts of beauty.[85]

Some hermits who adopted these harsh measures against their bodies but who had come to know their physical nature, achieved a peace which made them renowned by all who trod this path. Some took refuge in lies, taking credit for chastity but fornicating in secret. Their guilt came to the surface in the form of illnesses like that of the village priest who developed a sore which made him lose his hair at the back of his head and whose hair started growing again when he confessed his sin and returned to the secular life.[86] Evagrius was drained by the love he bore for a noble woman at court, and remained feverish and ill until he returned to the desert where his health remained fragile.[87] One Father claimed he had given up seeing women altogether.[38] A number of stories tell us with admiration that other brothers had done this.[89] But Abba Paul, who was walking to an old monk's cell, retraced his steps so as to avoid passing a woman, 'running towards his monastery faster than if he had seen a lion or a monstrous dragon.' And there he was struck by paralysis which made him unable to move at all, so he was cared for by the gentle hands of nuns who looked after him until he died four years later.[90]

The examples which are furnished by these monastic tales are not intended to be followed. They show first of all that why men suffered in living a life of abstinence, and further that they tried various means to free

---

[81] Ibid., 23. The main point of this story is probably the discomfort of life in the cave rather than the danger represented by the hyena. The Egyptians used to tame hyenas and use them for hunting; Hartmann, *L'agriculture dans l'ancienne Egypte*, p. 202; the story of the asp is incredible unless it is taken as a reference to the Egyptian tradition of Guardian serpents.

[82] *LH*, 38.

[83] *LH*, 45.

[84] *Alph.*, anon., 57.

[85] Ibid., 40.

[86] *LH*, 18.

[87] *LH*, 38.

[88] *Coll.*, VII, 26.

[89] *LH*, 35.

[90] *Coll.*, VII, 26. One might say that his real wish was thus granted. These stories are ambiguous, as is that of the man who lived with the smell of the decomposed body of the woman he could not forget. I have reproduced them here as they have been passed down, without interpreting the part played by the unconscious. This shows the significance of the ancients' discoveries and places them in their historical context.

themselves from the obsessive sexual urge. There is no reference to masturbation in these tales of the lives of hermits who came from the Egyptian countryside and who were generally of Egyptian culture. By ancient tradition masturbation was repressed in Egypt. Those who had practised masturbation or sodomy were denied access to the hereafter.[91] John Cassian, a Latin writer from near the mouth of the Danube, does mention it in a study of types of lust in a work which takes the form of a series of conversations between the Fathers in which they replied to questions put to them by young monks. Here is his typology, which may owe a great deal to John Cassian himself, but which is based on the monks' experience in the desert as it is described in the other texts.:

> There are three types of fornication. The first consists of union between the two sexes. The second does not involve contact with a woman. It said that the Lord punished Onan, the son of the patriarch Judas, for committing this act, which the Holy Scriptures call impurity . . . The third is committed through desire and thought. It is this to which the Lord refers in the Gospel when He says: 'He who looks at a woman and desires her has committed adultery with her in his heart.'[92]

Masturbation was a form of sexual satisfaction which was invisible to other people. These men who had resolved to forget their bodies were obsessed by their memories of female bodies. And the old monks helped those who yielded in the presence of a man or a woman, but they did not consider those cases where hermits had founded their devotion to God on an invisible but constant weakness. And yet one must not believe that masturbation did not matter, and that it was not talked about because it was of no consequence. The main concern of the texts we have been considering is not occasional encounters and lapses, but obsessions, thoughts and mental images, the physical manifestations of desire, namely involuntary erections and ejaculation. These men whose faith forbade mutilation, which was not always effective in suppressing these sexual manifestations,[93] were certain that the path to perfection required the suppression of all sexual expressions.

[91] There are scarcely any references to female homosexuality in Pharaonic Egypt. Male homosexuality, which was not uncommon, was forbidden in Memphis. Masturbation and sodomy were condemned by the divine court which decided whether or not people could proceed to the hereafter; see A. P. Leca, *La médecine égyptienne au temps des Pharaons*, 1971, p. 423; see also C. Maistre, *Les déclarations d'innocence, Livre des Morts*, chapter 125, 1937.

[92] *Coll.*, XII, 3; John Cassian is recalling St Paul, Ephesians 5, 5 and Corinthians 6, 9–10: 'No fornicator or idolator, none who are guilty either of adultery or of homosexual perversion . . .' (New English Bible).

[93] *Coll.*, XII, 1.

Nourishing themselves scantily on a few vegetables or a little bread, dehydrated because they eked out their supplies of water, praying late into the night, rising before daybreak, the monks were reminded of their human condition by emissions of sperm which took place while they were asleep. Troubled and anxious, they would confide in an old monk, one of the masters who had gathered a store of experience through similar confessions by other hermits. They would begin by examining their state of mind when they went to sleep, trying to find out if some sensual image was occupying them at that stage. They thus became convinced that the hermit who indulged in thoughts of women before going to bed was responsible for his nocturnal ejaculation,[94] and even that he must abstain from communion until he had done penance.[95] They learned to avoid anything which might bring such images into their minds, even the reading of holy books which mentioned women. These texts were omitted from those read to young monks.[96] Before he went to sleep, Evagrius used to think about the tortures of hell: 'Remember also what happens in hell and think about the state of the souls down there, their painful silence, their most bitter groanings, their fear, their strife, their waiting. Think of their grief without end and the tears their souls shed eternally . . . The eternal fire, worms that rest not, the darkness, gnashing of teeth, fear and supplications.'[97] But he also thought of the joys of the just to chase out thoughts of desire.

These discoveries took place in the desert, in total isolation. The experiences which the monks confided in their older brothers were passed on to those who were alarmed by the call of their own body. It was in response to this accumulation of anchorite experience that a new, organized form of solitary life was established. When the aspiration to a life of contemplation of God to the exclusion of all else had attracted so many converts, the whole process of the villagers moving to the desert had to be considered afresh. Disciples had gathered in great numbers all around the hermitage where Antony ended his days at the age of 113, served by two brothers. During the fourth century, thousands of men from all over Egypt joined the first hermits and begged them to guide them. In the desert of Nitria, around five thousand monks lived alone or in small groups.[98] Around Antinoë in the Thebaid there were one thousand two hundred monks, and the neighbouring caves sheltered any number of anchorites.[99] The *Historia Monachorum* tells us that Abba

[94] *HM*, 20.
[95] *HM*, 16 and 20.
[96] *Coll.*, XIX, 16.
[97] *Alph.*, Evagrius, 1.
[98] *LH*, 7.
[99] *LH*, 58.

Apollo had around him five hundred disciples living the solitary life near a village called Hermopolis.[100]

It was for groups of between one thousand two hundred and one thousand six hundred monks that Pachomius devised the system of organization first put into practice at Tabennisi. He formed a monastery which consisted of thirty to forty houses each containing around forty brothers. This community, in which the silence of the individual was respected, solved the problem of trading with the villagers, because the monks could share tasks, cultivate gardens and make most of the objects they needed. When it was necessary to go outside the monastery this was not a matter for individual discretion, and monks never went alone to a town or village.

These new living conditions gave rise to carnal relationships. But we only know of this from the mechanisms which were put in place at a very early stage in order to prevent such things. Where we see in the rules a repressive command, in reality it was something which all the monks wished to see imposed, in the same way as the precepts arrived at in the desert, to help them live the life they had chosen. Pachomius' *Precepts*,[101] as they have come down to us in the western world, are quite clear on this point. Monks must avoid tempting their brother monks, and must cover their knees when sitting together.[102] They must not tuck their tunics up too high when washing clothes together.[103] Monks must avoid looking at others, whether it be at work[104] or at mealtimes.[105] Two monks should not speak to one another direct, but should go through the monk who was in charge that particular week. They must not lend or borrow from one another,[106] and must not do one another favours; they must not even remove a thorn from another monk's foot,[107] and must certainly not bathe and apply ointments to a brother.[108] Monks had no opportunity to be alone in pairs, either in a cell,[109] or when they lay down to sleep on the same mat on the terraces,[110] and in a boat[111] everyone must take his rest up on deck. Two monks might not ride a donkey together.[112] They might

[100] *HM*, VIII.
[101] See C. de Clercq, L'influence de la règle de saint Pachôme en Occident, 1951.
[102] Pachomius, *Precepts*, 2.
[103] Ibid., 69.
[104] Ibid., 7.
[105] Ibid., 30.
[106] Ibid., 106; 113.
[107] Ibid., 96.
[108] Ibid., 93.
[109] Ibid., 89; 112.
[110] Ibid., 95.
[111] Ibid., 118.
[112] Ibid., 109.

not talk to one another in the dark,[113] nor hold hands,[114] and must always keep an arm's length apart.

Children and young boys who lived in the monastery were reprimanded for playing and neglecting their work[115] just as the older brothers were reprimanded for sharing in their laughter and their games.[116] John Cassian set down these same rules, inspired by experience, for the monks of southern Gaul.[117] But although all opportunities for physical contact were removed by the organization of the monasteries, the monk still had to contend with his own body, without any direct external stimulation, and he thus relived the experiences of the pioneers who had tried to resist desire in total isolation in the desert.

If monks were forbidden to lock their cell doors in an attempt to prevent masturbation,[118] although one was supposed to knock before entering into another monk's cell,[119] and if we assume that the monks came with the sincere intention of living a life of abstinence, the only genital manifestation left these men was ejaculation during sleep.

We have seen how the doctors replied to those who were worried by the fact that they ejaculated. There the concern was above all the man's health. In the desert the question was entirely different. We must first of all turn back to the texts. The question was raised and debated.[120] John Cassian is the most explicit on this point which is clearly related to his

[113] Ibid., 94.

[114] Ibid., 95.

[115] Ibid., 172.

[116] Ibid., 166.

[117] *Inst.*, II, 15; IV, 16.

[118] Pachomius, *Precepts*, 107.

[119] Ibid., 89.

[120] Once the issue was permanent abstinence, it was inevitable that the question should be raised, and a theological solution had to be found if those who had committed themselves to seeking God through the monastic life were not to be discouraged for ever. Here is the solution put forward by Jean de La Croix in *La montée du Carmel*, 1942, p. 98 and p. 107: 'The natural appetites present little or no obstacle to the union of the soul if they do not receive the agreement of the individual's will and do not go beyond the first movements (which are all those in which the conscious will has had no part either before or after) for it is impossible to avoid them and to mortify the body completely in this life. They do not prevent the individual from achieving divine union, even though they have not been totally mortified, because while they may remain in the individual's nature, his soul and that part of his spirit which reason can control may remain free. For sometimes the soul may be in a deep state of quiet prayer and yet these natural appetites may still remain in a man's senses, although the superior part of him which is at prayer has had no part in them.' (I, XI) And I, XII: 'For although the confusion and passion which they arouse make the individual feel that they are defiling and blinding him, nevertheless this is not so; on the contrary, they bring benefits, because in resisting them the individual acquires strength, purity, light, consolation and several other compensations.' Thus the genital manifestations of desire are detached from the conscious will. Conscious desire is an evil thought which must be resisted, and conscious life is narrowed down to voluntary life.

theology of man's merit which opposed the theology of grace which Augustine imposed on the Church. Cassian devotes one entire dialogue[121] in a collection of twenty-four 'Conferences' to 'illusions of the night', and he deals with ejaculation in sleep in his dialogue on concupiscence and chastity, and in relation to other questions.[122] We also have a saying by Antony on this subject,[123] and a discourse by Dioscorus.[124] In order to define and elucidate the problem, the monks must have compared experiences. The frequency with which some of the older monks ejaculated was known and presented in order to show that they had won the struggle. Thus of Abba Serenus it was said: 'He was very privileged to receive the gift of chastity to such a high degree that he was no longer disturbed, even during sleep, by the natural arousal of the flesh.'[125] Evagrius died at the age of fifty-four, stating that he had known no lust for three years.[126] The Fathers concluded that if one observed a truly ascetic lifestyle one should not ejaculate in one's sleep more than once every two months[127] or even every four months.[128] In this period of seeking one's goal, visible signs of sexual activity were not seen as bad in themselves, but as harmful to the goal one had set oneself. John Cassian distinguishes six degrees of chastity.[129] The first consists of not succumbing to the assaults of the flesh while conscious and awake. In the second degree, the monk rejects voluptuous thoughts. In the third, the sight of a woman does not move him any more. In the fourth, he no longer has erections while awake; in the fifth, no reference to the sexual act in the holy texts affects him 'any more than if he was thinking about the process of making bricks', and in the sixth and final degree of chastity 'the seduction of female fantasies does not delude him while he sleeps. Even though we do not believe this fantasy to be a sin,' says Cassian, 'it is nevertheless an indication that lust is still hiding in the marrow'.

Thus these genital manifestations were considered as signs of the stage the individual had reached in his pursuit of a life directed constantly towards God.

In affirming that the monk is responsible for his thoughts and his dreams and even for the 'natural movements of his body', Cassian, who is

---

[121] Coll., XXII.
[122] Inst., III, 5; VI, 10 and 22; Coll., II, 23; IV, 15–16; V, 11; VII, 1; X, 10; XII, 7. On John Cassian, see O. Chadwick, John Cassian, a Study in primitive Monasticism, 1950.
[123] Alph., Antony, 22.
[124] HM, XX.
[125] Coll., VII, 1.
[126] LH, 38, 13.
[127] Inst., VI, 20.
[128] Coll., II, 23.
[129] Ibid., XII, 7.

here doubtless reproducing the conviction held by numerous Fathers of the desert, is proclaiming the unity of the body and the mind:

> Indeed, the quality of one's thoughts, which requires less care during the day because one has many distractions, is tested when one rests at night. So when an illusion of this sort occurs to one, one must not blame sleep but one's own negligence in the time before sleep. This is the sign of evil hiding within, to which night has not given birth, but which, buried deep in the soul, has risen to the surface in sleep, revealing the hidden fever of the passions with which we have been infected by thinking unhealthy thoughts all day long.[130]

The hunger which gripped the solitary monks gave rise to no theological reflections on this subject, and did not make them question how far they were responsible for this sensation, because stomach cramps were not enjoyable. But the sexual impulse seemed to pursue its search for pleasure despite all the mortifications devised to combat it and without the conscious agreement of the will. Some monks ended by attributing these nocturnal ejaculations to nature, which was beyond their control and outside the individual's responsibility. John Cassian has Abba Chaeremon, in a dialogue on chastity,[131] criticize this theological position. According to Chaeremon, one must not

> commit the error of those who claim that stains which go beyond the necessities of nature are a result of their natural condition and not due to their negligence. While it is clear that it is they who are doing violence to nature and multiplying abominations which she would not produce, they attribute their intemperance to the needs of the flesh, and even to the creator himself, laying their own faults at nature's door.

Some monks, like Antony[132] or Theonas,[133] blamed the Devil for ejaculations which occurred during sleep, in the absence of dreams or pleasure, and particularly on days when they had experienced great fervour, for the demon thus prevented them from taking communion the following day.

Nevertheless, determining how far these ejaculations could be blamed on the demon and how far they were the monk's responsibility could lead

---

[130] *Inst.*, VI, 11.
[131] *Coll.*, XII, 8.
[132] *Alph.*, Antony, 22.
[133] *Coll.*, XXII, 3.

to hours spent in reflection which were thus lost to God. So the Egyptian solitaries had tried, like Antony, to weaken their bodies and had tackled their difficulties alone in the desert. When disciples flocked to them a norm had to be established, and it was the Greek notions on the production of sperm which furnished the elements of the theory which regulated the monks' physical life.

10

From Abstinence to Impotence

'Venus, without Liber and Ceres, is a-cold.'
Latin proverb quoted by Minucius Felix, *Oct.*, XXI,2 and Jerome, *Letters*, LIV,11

'Often, when (Pachomius) sat down to table and said grace, (the demons) would appear before him, each one in the form of a very beautiful woman; they would attract his attention with their provocative and indecent nudity, and would seem to sit near him and try to touch his plate.'[1] Pachomius ate very little, as did the other solitary monks, and yet he did not dream of bread as the contemporary Coptic proverb suggests[2] – bread, the dream of the starving – but of women. As we have seen, the hermits first had to solve the problem of establishing food supplies before they could fight the demands of the body through fasting. This is why, before dealing with the problems of feeding and fasting, they had to have experienced hunger. Cérès Wissa-Wassef has shown that the diet of the Copts in the twentieth century is based on abstinence and periods of fasting. These are voluntary practices, linked to ancient Christian rites. But the expressions and proverbs on the subject of hunger and satiety which she has collected all refer to bread and to hunger due to penury. Hunger was no stranger either to the peasants of the Egyptian countryside in antiquity. Satiety and dearth depended on the corn harvest, in other words on the flooding of the Nile.[3] It was relatively easy to predict the date of the flood,[4] but it was much more dificult to know how extensive it would be. When the area covered by the flood water from June to August was too small, the area of land which could be sown after the waters had retreated, at the end of September, was also too small.

---

[1] *Vie latine de saint Pachôme*, ed. Van Cranenburgh, 17; *Vie grecque*, ed. Lefort and French tr. Festugière, 19; this quotation tr. A. R. and F. P.

[2] Cérès Wissa-Wassef, *Pratiques rituelles alimentaires des Coptes*, 1979.

[3] Vandier, *La famine dans l'Egypte ancienne*.

[4] Bonneau, *La crue du Nil*, p. 29 et seq.

If the flooding was too extensive the length of time it took for the waters to retreat delayed the sowing and left less time for the next crop to grow before it was necessary to harvest it.[5] The chief request made of those who specialized in divination was to predict the extent of the floods each year. One of Antony's temptations was to make such a prediction on the basis of what the demons whispered to him.[6] But John of Lycopolis, born fifty years after Antony, around 305,[7] did not hesitate to predict what the flood would be like and how fertile the following year would be.[8]

The Ptolemaic period saw the development of a system of royal taxation on the production of corn, which Rome retained after the annexation of Egypt. So during its Greek and its Roman periods Egypt, like India and China in former times, suffered rural famines despite the fact, indeed because of the fact that it was exporting grain. The monastic texts make frequent reference to the hunger experienced by the Egyptian peasants, and they mention famines, without giving dates, as frequent natural phenomena. 'For example, there had been a famine in the Thebaid not long before.'[9] This was not the Year of the Famine, but a famine during which the villagers came to ask the monks for bread as they had a supply of it. It was famine which drove one woman to take to his father in the desert the son whom she had up until then fed herself in the valley so that her husband could live alone.[10]

Thefts, which already existed as a result of the hunger that was a fact of life even in normal times, increased greatly when there was a famine. As a child, Macarius had picked wild berries and stolen figs.[11] The hermits' bread supplies were not safe from the men who roamed the desert in search of food. Their supplies were large, even though they only consumed a small quantity each day, for when he went to the village Antony bought enough bread to last six months, in other words around sixty kilogrammes. Athanasius writes that the Thebans made bread which kept a whole year.[12] One hermit had two snakes to guard his cell as he had had bread and other food stolen from it.[13] Another monk had been a

[5] Vandier, La famine, pp. 47–8.

[6] Life of Antony, 39.

[7] G.J.M. Bartelink, commentary on Palladius, Lausiac History, p. 364.

[8] LH, 35, and HM, I, 1 and 11.

[9] HM, VIII, 41.

[10] Alph., Carion, 2.

[11] Alph., Macarius the Egyptian, 37.

[12] Life of Antony, 12.

[13] HM, IX, 5. This example is quoted by P. de Labriolle, in L'Histoire de l'Eglise, directed by A. Fliche and V. Martin, vol. III, De la Paix Constantinienne à la mort de Théodose, by J. R. Palanque, G. Bardy, Labriolle P. de, 1950, p. 304, under the title Orgie de surnaturel. But on the contrary, it refers to a literary tradition, that of the guardian serpent, which is in turn based on the custom, observed to this day, of keeping a cobra to kill dangerous animals in the Egyptian household. I owe these details to Nicolas Grimal.

thief himself and had repented after stealing from a recluse's storeroom.[14] Once Macarius helped a thief load onto a beast of burden the contents of his own cell, without telling him that he was the legitimate occupant of the place.[15] Vegetables were even taken from the monks' gardens.[16] But the solitaries also gave bread to those who came begging.[17]

In good years, the corn was stored to provide for the bad years that might come,[18] so the poor, whether voluntarily or involuntarily, always had to make do with a restricted supply of food, because they had to be provident. A Coptic proverb says: 'Save your breakfast and you will find your dinner.'[19] A rich Roman who had retired to the desert with a slave, and whose poverty seemed luxurious to an Egyptian monk, questioned him thus:

> 'What country are you from?' 'I am Egyptian.' And he asked: 'From what town?' 'I am not from a town; I have never lived in one.' 'What did you do in the area where you used to live before you were a monk?' 'I used to watch over the fields.' 'Where did you sleep?' 'In the fields.' 'And you had a bed?' 'How could I have had a bed if I was sleeping in the fields?' 'How did you sleep?' 'On the bare earth.' And the Roman continued: 'What did you eat in the fields, and what wine did you drink?' 'What do you think one finds to eat and drink in the fields?' replied the monk. 'So how did you live?' 'I ate dry bread, a little salted meat if I could find any, and I drank water.' 'It must have been a hard life,' said the old man.[20]

Antony, like the other founding fathers, had not been one of the poor who had no land after the waters retreated. They came from fairly well-to-do village families, but they had lived in villages where the poor ate a little soaked bread as late as possible so that they could go to sleep with full bellies. Abandoning his heritage of farm land, Antony had deliberately adopted this poverty and this dependence. He, however, had no wife and no children to feed. Monks who burned with the desire to return to the valley and take a wife were given the example of a monk who was so tormented by desire that he said ten women would not be able to satisfy him. No one could stop him. Passing through the village one day, Paphnutius heard his name called by a thin and ragged man whom he did not at first recognize. ' "No doubt you have taken ten wives?" And

[14] *HM*, X, 3.
[15] *PJ*, XVI, 6.
[16] *HM*, X, 34.
[17] *PJ*, XIII, 15.
[18] Vandier, *La famine*, p. 2.
[19] Wissa-Wassef, *Pratiques rituelles*, p. 257.
[20] *PJ*, X, 76.

groaning, he said, "Truly I have only taken one, and I have a great deal of trouble satisfying her with food." '[21]

To cure himself of wanting to go and take a wife in the village, one solitary had made himself a woman out of clay and he would work as if he had to feed her. Then he made a daughter, and worked even harder to feed her. His exhaustion cured him of wanting to leave the desert.[22] Although Egyptian wives certainly earned their living, these were the conditions in which the half-starved day workers who possessed nothing of their own lived. The monastic texts give a few figures which make it possible to assess the poverty of the fellahin of the rich Nile valley in the fourth century. The land registers of Hermopolis and Theadelphia give an idea of the distribution of land. At Hermopolis the register deals with a quarter of the city and lists the land-owners who lived in the town: 5.8 per cent of the land-owners owned three-quarters of the land between them, each one having more than 250 *arurae* (one *arura* = two acres). The poorest land-owners (27.5 per cent) owned less than ten *arurae* each. The Theadelphia register shows peasant land-owners who also owned less than ten *arurae*, the poorest having one and a quarter *arurae*.[23] The monastic texts tell us that the monks would hire themselves out as seasonal workers at harvest time.[24] The *Historia Monachorum* says that each monk earned something like twelve *artabae* of corn (about 348 kg) at harvest time.[25] The monks' daily ration was two loaves of bread weighing in total about one Roman pound, in other words 327 grammes. If we estimate that this bread was one third water, each monk brought back from the harvest enough to feed about four people for a year if each ate 327 grammes of bread a day. The text tells us that the monks kept what they needed and sent the surplus by boat from Arsinoe to feed the poor of Alexandria.[26] As Arsinoe was not far from Theadelphia, we can put together the figures given in the documents of these two nomes. The land-owner in Theadelphia who owned one and a quarter *arurae* sowed one *artaba* per *arura*, which the harvest increased tenfold. He would obtain 3.6 daily rations of 327 grammes of bread if he kept enough to sow, and less still if we take account of the tax in kind.[27] So, after a whole

---

[21] *Alph.*, Paphnutius, 4.

[22] *Alph.*, Olympios, 2.

[23] A.H.M. Jones, *The Later Roman Empire*, vol. II, 1964, pp. 772–3.

[24] *PJ*, XIV, 14; XVII, 20; XIX, 8; *HM*, XVIII, 1.

[25] The Latin translator gives the equivalent in *modii*, thus 40 *modii* = 348 litres of corn.

[26] *HM*, XVIII, 1.

[27] By comparison, the consumption of corn in Athens in the fifth to the fourth century BC is estimated at 6 *medimnes* a year per head, in other words 311 litres, which is three or four times more than this Egyptian ration. Claire Préaux, *L'économie royale des Lagides*, 1939, calculates that between two and fifteen *arurae* were needed to feed an average family, given that rent and taxes in the Ptolemaic period absorbed half of the harvest of a royal farmer.

year's work, he could feed a family of three or four on monk's rations, that is if he did not also work as a day-worker for a large land-owner. It is quite clear, from the monks' texts and other sources, that these small land-owners depended entirely on their employers. One of the latter was considered a saint because he did not sow his field first, which would have ensured that his crops ripened well before the floods, and at harvest time he let the small farmers harvest their crops before coming to provide the labour on which he depended, so that if the flood was early the small farms would be harvested in time.[28] Thus we see that the daily ration of bread adopted by the monks was entirely comparable with what the day-labourers and small land-owners in the valley might hope to obtain after a year of agricultural work if they shared their produce with a small family.

But although their diet was based on that of the fellahin, the monks, who had no dependents except sometimes one of their number who was ill or unable to work, did not have to devote all of their time to work in order to eat, and if they did they produced a surplus which they could distribute to others.[29] Their diet should be examined in this context. I have indicated how much this diet owed to the circumstances of their departure for the solitary life, but from the start they excluded from their meals certain foods which nature offered them. Antony gave up meat,[30] as did Evagrius some time later.[31] One solitary who set off for the heart of the desert refused to hunt birds or other animals.[32] The monks often came across hyenas, and in times of famine as a last resort they would eat them[33] – hence the expression 'a hyena year' – but the monks did not as a rule hunt this animal. Even when a hyena brought Macarius the skin of a sheep it had devoured he did not use the animal to hunt for him as was the custom, but preached vegetarianism to it.[34]

There were different views as to the consumption of wine. Antony did not drink it,[35] and some of the fathers banned its use,[36] but monastic groups grew vines in the desert of Nitria and sold wine.[37] They would

[28] HM, XIV, 14.
[29] A. Rousselle, Le modèle économique transmis par les règles orientales dans les oeuvres de saint Benoît d'Aniane, 1975, pp. 5–23.
[30] Life of Antony, 7.
[31] LH, 38.
[32] HM, I, 46. On abstaining from meat, see J. Bidez and F. Cumont, Les mages hellénisés, 1938 (second printing, 1973), vol. I, p. 26, on Porphyry's De Abstinencia; and J. Haussleiter, Der Vegetarismus in der Antike, 1935.
[33] LH, 18; Alph., James.
[34] On the Egyptian hyena, see Hartmann, L'agriculture dans l'ancienne Egypte, p. 202 and 214; L. Stözk, s.v. Hyäne, in Lexikon der Aegyptologie, vol. III, 1980, col. 91–2.
[35] Life of Antony, 7.
[36] PJ, 26, 31, 36, 37, 53, 54.
[37] LH, 7.

give old men who were ill wine to drink,[38] although some resisted this pleasure which they had given up years before. The solitaries did not eat preserved fish, or rather fish sauce.[39] The brothers of Scetis who worked at harvest time, after giving a part of the corn they earned to the poor, would receive a pint of oil each, which they kept in their cells for use in the coming year.[40] Before they set off for the following harvest most of them would bring their container of oil intact to the church where they met each week.[41] But Evagrius consumed a pint of oil per quarter during fourteen years in which he observed a strict diet.[42] This was the quantity of oil set aside each year for any guests who might pass through.[43] The oil in question was that generally used in Egypt, either colocynth or sesame oil. The monks ate the olives they were given and regarded them as a delicacy.[44]

Once we set aside the foods which all the monks gave up, it is not easy to determine a universal diet followed by all.[45] But we can, and the monks did, define two tendencies, based on the distinction between cooked and raw food. A Coptic proverb says, 'Better raw food at my house than cooked food at some one else's'.[46] The problems of the length of time needed to cook food, keeping a fire going and finding fuel were very real. The raw diet included bread.[47] This was the diet of Moses[48] and the solitary monks of Galatia[49] who also denied themselves raw fruits, and that of Macarius when he lived at Tabennisi in Pachomius' monastery.[50] It should thus be understood that a text which indicates that a solitary ate no cooked food meant that his diet was based on bread accompanied by fruits, usually figs,[51] raw cabbage leaves as at Tabennisi,[52] and other vegetables eaten raw or simply soaked in water.[53] Antony offered Paul

---

[38] *PJ*, 35.
[39] *Greek Life of Pachomius*, 64, not reproduced in the Latin version by Dionysius Exiguus.
[40] *Alph.*, Benjamin, 1.
[41] Ibid., 1 and 2.
[42] *LH*, 38.
[43] *Coll.*, XIX, 6.
[44] *HM*, VII.
[45] On this point and the rest of the chapter, see A. Rousselle, Abstinence et continence dans les monastères de Gaule méridionale à la fin de l'Antiquité et au début du Moyen Age; Etude d'un régime alimentaire et de sa fonction, 1974, pp. 239–54.
[46] Wissa-Wassef, *Pratiques rituelles*, p. 236.
[47] *LH*, 11; *PJ*, VIII, 21.
[48] *LH*, 19.
[49] *LH*, 45.
[50] *LH*, 18.
[51] *PJ*, X, 30.
[52] *LH*, 18.
[53] *LH*, 18.

bread and honey when he came to visit.[54] John Cassian taught that the best diet was soaked bread seasoned with a drop of oil.[55] The second, cooked diet, did not include bread, but was based on boiled cereals: lentils,[56] chick-peas,[57] wheat flour[58] or other dried vegetables.[59] Sometimes this porridge would be sweetened with honey[60] or cooked with prunes.[61] Apollonius of Tyana, a pagan miracle-worker who ate no meat, also lived off dried fruits and vegetables.[62]

These were the basic diets of which there were various ascetic variants. Some mixed the two diets: barley bread and lentil flour,[63] lentils and soaked bread,[64] or bread and chick-pea flour alternately.[65] By eating both cereals and leguminous plants they were increasing their protein intake and compensating for the absence of animal protein from their diet. But it was more usual for the monks to make a point of adopting one or other of the diets and to restrict the foods they would eat even within one type of diet. The bread diet, which was really a diet of bread plus raw vegetables or fruit, would become a diet of bread without vegetables or without fruit. Arsenius would taste the first fruits when they ripened each year and would then not eat them again,[65] but would stick to a diet of bread and salt, without either fruit or vegetables.[67] When the texts say that a solitary consumed no bread for forty years, like Posidonius,[68] or fifty years,[69] this probably means that he followed a strict diet of boiled cereals. This was one of the favourite customs observed by the men and women who had consecrated their lives to Cybele, and a virgin devoted to the god Hadran had inscribed on her funerary stela that she had abstained from eating bread for twenty years.[70] It was perhaps this ritual pagan abstinence which made the monks abandon the diet without bread and prompted them to say 'that none of those who set aside this rule (two

---

[54] *LH*, 22.
[55] *Coll.*, VIII, 1 and XIX, 6.
[56] *PJ*, IV, 57.
[57] *PJ*, VIII, 22.
[58] *HM*, XV, 4.
[59] *HM*, XIV, 20.
[60] *PJ*, IV, 59.
[61] *PJ*, IV, 65.
[62] Philostratus, *Life of Apollonius of Tyana*, I, 8.
[63] *PJ*, IV, 3.
[64] *PJ*, IV, 56.
[65] *PJ*, VIII, 7.
[66] *PJ*, IV, 6.
[67] *PJ*, VIII, 21; XIV, 2 etc.
[68] *LH*, 36.
[69] *PJ*, X, 15.
[70] *CIL*, III, 13608. Graillot, *Le culte de Cybèle*, pp. 119–20. Also Cumont, *Les religions orientales*, p. 217, n. 39.

loaves a day), and abandoned the use of bread in order to eat dried or fresh vegetables and fruit, was ever counted among those who were truly tested and indeed none obtained the grace of discernment or knowledge'.[71] Dried vegetables were kept in the form of grain, and so this made it necessary to go to the mill every few days to collect enough flour for the next few days.[72] This gave an opportunity for meeting other people and talking, which represented a danger that was avoided by those who ate bread which could be kept for six months. Very rarely a solitary would deny himself bread and eat not nourishing porridges but the raw vegetables which normally accompanied bread. Thus some of the monks in Nitria ate wild chicory[73] and Apollo, after forty years in the desert, only ate on Sundays and abstained from eating bread, leguminous plants, fruits and cooked food, which is impossible to believe, but is nevertheless put forward as a model.

The term fasting referred to the practice of imposing restrictions within a diet and not generally to abstaining from food altogether. These restrictions might affect the frequency with which the monks ate as much as the nature of the food taken. Thus a young monk said: 'Father, I fast for two consecutive days and only eat two little loaves of bread,'[74] and another brother fasted for the whole of the Easter week, taking only a little grass pickled in brine but no bread.[75] So the text of the *Sayings* uses the term 'fast' for a restriction applied to the quality and quantity of foods which might still be taken every day. In general, fasting affected the time at which one ate: 'The sun has never seen me eat,' boasted one solitary.[76] What else could be meant by the text which states that Pachomius fasted every day during the summer?[77] When monks offered a meal as a mark of honour to solitaries who were passing through, the visiting brothers would accept the offer in order to celebrate their meeting, but would deny themselves drink during the afternoon in order to respect the fast they had broken,[78] for fasting also meant depriving oneself of water.[79]

Those who received visitors also broke their fast to celebrate the occasion: this was one of the strictest rules of the desert, and is mentioned in all the texts.[80] They would make up for this the following day, as Macarius did when he drank no water for a whole day because he had

---

[71] *Inst.*, XXIII, 2, and *Coll.*, II, 19.
[72] *PJ*, VIII, 7.
[73] *HM*, XX.
[74] *PJ*, X, 65.
[75] *PJ*, IV, 69.
[76] *PJ*, IV, 20.
[77] *Life of Pachomius*, 6.
[78] *PJ*, IV, 40.
[79] *PJ*, IV, 67.
[80] *PJ*, XIII, for example.

accepted a drop of wine at the meal he had shared.[81] The daily fast, which consisted of not eating until the sun had gone down, is rarely referred to, for it was taken for granted. When Pastor was asked about the best way to fast, he replied that one should 'eat regularly every day, but deny oneself a little and not eat one's fill'.[82] John Cassian, writing for the solitaries of southern Gaul, said that one should eat once a day, after sunset, except during the period between Easter and Whitsun,[83] and Saturdays, Sundays and holy days.[84] This was asking a great deal, and some found it impossible to observe this rule.

> One monk was hungry in the morning. He fought against the temptation to eat before the third hour. At the third hour he forced himself to wait until the sixth hour. He soaked his bread and sat down to eat, but rose immediately saying to himself: 'I can wait till the ninth hour.' At the ninth hour, he prayed and then saw the diabolic temptation rise out of him like smoke; and he stopped feeling hungry.[85]

Those who could not manage to fast were allowed to divide their daily ration into two meals, one taken at the ninth hour (between 2 and 3 in the afternoon), the other at sunset.[86] The evening ration, which made it possible to sleep without excessive stomach cramps, was intended chiefly to allow the monks to eat with any visitors they might have, without going beyond the normal daily limit. At feast times, the first meal of the day was taken at the sixth hour (between 11 and 12), but the daily ration remained unchanged.[87]

When greater restrictions were imposed, the term used was no longer fasting but eating: thus Pachomius fasted every day during the summer, but he ate every three days during the winter.[88] In order to be saved, advises Ares,[89] one must begin by eating only bread and salt every evening for a year. The following year one should eat only every two days. This is what Antony did.[90] But the practice of eating only every two days is not mentioned very often, as it was very common. The texts

[81] *PJ*, IV, 26.
[82] *PJ*, X, 44.
[83] *Inst.*, II, 8.
[84] *Inst.*, III, 12.
[85] *PJ*, IV, 58.
[86] *Inst.*, V, 5, 2; *Coll.*, I, 25–6.
[87] *Coll.*, XXI, 23.
[88] *Life of Pachomius*, 6.
[89] *PJ*, XIV, 2.
[90] *Life of Antony*, 7.

admire those who ate twice a week[91] or once a week,[92] but do not really hold them up as models. On the other hand, long fasts, undertaken as an exceptional measure, to help a monk resist in a period of violent temptation, are described as a possible medication. Copres, at the start of his monastic life, went without food for forty days. This number was chosen to recall Christ's fast, but it is probably accurate. Helle, like Macarius, fasted for three weeks.[93] This is not impossible, and in fact the body, particularly the brain, suffers less from a total fast than from excessive restriction of the daily rations.[94]

It is very difficult to say why the Egyptian monks reduced their intake of food in this way. Their poverty was not such that they were unable to feed themselves in a reasonable manner. Megethios managed to buy enough food by making three little baskets a day.[95] It is true that we are told that Dorotheus had to make baskets all night to achieve the same result.[96] He ate half a pound of bread (163 g) a day, and a bunch of vegetables. But one ascetic, who kept a little garden, used to make objects so as to keep his hands busy, and would burn them every year.[97] As they had no families to support, the monks could make a better living than the fellahin in the valley from the same amount of work. The reason for the strict ascetic diets which some monks imposed on themselves and which were later imposed by the rules in the large monastic communities was thus not the poverty which they had adopted. We have always known this, but through the Greeks, whose reasons, as we shall see, were quite different from those of the first Coptic solitaries. Even the accounts of the lives of the Egyptian monks, written by Greeks or passed down in Greek, are not reliable. Here is an example: Moses the Ethiopian, a repentant thief and murderer, is known through the *Sayings* and the *Lausiac History* as a man racked with sexual desire.[98] The text of the *Lausiac History* shows him overwhelmed by his struggle, confiding in Father Isidore the sensual thoughts which assail him. The latter advises him not to eat any cooked food, so as to drive away the demon of *porneia*. Sozomen, who includes this passage of the *Lausiac History* in his *Ecclesiastica Historia*,

---

[91] *HM*, XV, 4.

[92] *HM*, VII.

[93] *HM*, XII and XXI.

[94] I am drawing on Dr Escoffier-Lambiotte's article, La résistance au jeûne, *Le Monde*, 20 May, 1981, pp. 17–18, which says that 'medical literature contains very little information on these subjects'. I am grateful to Dr Escoffier-Lambiotte for referring me to V. R. Young and N. S. Scrimshaw, The physiology of starvation, 1971, pp. 14–21. My article, Abstinence et continence, includes a short bibliography on this question.

[95] *Alph.*, Megethios, 1.

[96] *LH*, 2.

[97] *Inst.*, X, 24.

[98] *PJ*, XVIII, 12; *LH*, 19.

alters it, saying that Moses had to abandon his first diet which overheated the body,[99] in other words he introduces into Isidore's advice dietary notions of his own time. In doing this, he is simply adding to the alterations already introduced by the Greek editors of the monastic texts to assimilate them to their own culture.

The texts tell us that all those who suffered sexual temptations fought them by restricting their diets. Denying oneself sleep[100] and tiring the body by hard work[101] were also recommended. And following the example of the men who fought in the amphitheatre, who would refrain from sexual intercourse and were afraid of ejaculating in their sleep the night before a show, they would be advised to wear pieces of metal attached to their testicles to keep them cool, as the fighters did.[102] But dietary privation remained the principal weapon in the fight against sexual desire. 'When one wants to take a town, one cuts off the supply of water and food. The same applies to the passions of the flesh. If a man lives a life of fasting and hunger, the enemies of his soul are weakened', said John the Dwarf.[103] The *Apophtegmata* quote a letter written by Antony[104] on the subject of erections.

> I think there are three types of motion of the body. There is that which is implanted in the body by nature, compacted with it in its first creation; but this is not operative if the soul does not will it, save only that it signifies its presence through a passionless movement of the body. And there is another motion, when a man stuffs his body with food and drink, and the heat of the blood from the abundance of nourishment rouses up warfare in the body.

The monks in the Egyptian desert thus made the link between food and sexuality, but our texts express this in terms of Greek physiology. The clearest passage in this context is one from the *Historia Monachorum* in which Dioscorus, abba of some hundred monks in Thebaid, warns them against dietary excess:

---

[99] Sozomen, *Ecclesiastica Historia*, VI, 29, 16, ed. J. Bidez, Die griechischen christlichen Schrifsteller der ersten Jahrhunderte, 1960, p. 281. The text of the *Lausiac History* was later contaminated by Sozomen's text and the notion of foods overheating the body thus found its way into the Greek manuscripts and the Latin translation, as indicated by Butler, *The Lausiac History of Palladius*.

[100] *Inst.*, II, 13.

[101] *Coll.*, VI, 1.

[102] *Inst.*, VI, 7.

[103] *PJ*, IV, 19.

[104] *PJ*, V, 1 = *Alph.*, Antony, 22; this tr. from D. Chitty, *The Letters of St Antony the Great*, 1975. Although the authorship of Antony's letters is disputed, they certainly date from the fourth century and were written first in Coptic, and translated into Greek in which language Jerome came to know them. They were translated into Georgian and Arabic.

He used to say to those who were intending to approach the grace of God, 'Take care that no one who has pondered on the image of a woman during the night dare to approach the sacred Mysteries, in case any of you has had a dream while entertaining such an image.

'For seminal emissions do take place unconsciously without the stimulus of imagined forms, occurring not from deliberate choice but involuntarily. They arise naturally and flow forth from an excess of matter. They are therefore not to be classed as sinful. But imaginings are the result of deliberate choice and are a sign of an evil disposition.

'Now a monk,' he said, 'must even transcend the law of nature and must certainly not fall into the slightest pollution of the flesh. On the contrary, he must mortify the flesh and not allow an excess of seminal fluid to accumulate. We should therefore try to keep the fluid depleted by the prolongation of fasting. Otherwise, it arouses our sensual appetites.

'A monk must have nothing whatever to do with the sensual appetites. Otherwise how would he differ from men living in the world? We often see laymen abstaining from pleasures for the sake of their health or for some other rational motive. How much more should the monk take care of the health of his soul and his mind and his spirit.'[105]

It is extremely difficult to determine the influence of Egyptian culture in ascetic theory since the texts which predate the Ptolemaic period, written between 500 and 485 BC, in other words before Greek domination was established in Egypt, prove that Egyptian medicine had a theory which linked bone marrow, especially that of the spine, with male sperm which produces the child's bones.[106] The first Greek texts which put forward this link are by Hippo in the fifth century BC. The only writer who remained resolutely opposed to this theory was Alcmaeon who weighed an animal before and after copulation and discovered when he dissected the animal that it had suffered no loss of marrow.[107] Of course, reflections on the origin of the child and reproduction are closely interwoven with questions on the origin of life and the creation of man which preoccupied everyone in the second and third centuries AD. Religion popularized what was essentially the domain of the educated man. Those who have studied gnoticism have shown that the *Timaeus*

[105] *HM*, 20, tr. Norman Russell, 1980.
[106] J. Yoyotte, Les os et la semence masculine, à propos d'une théorie physiologique, 1962, pp. 139–46, which also refers to S. Sauneron, Le germe dans les os, 1960, pp. 19–27.
[107] Rey, *La science dans l'Antiquité*, p. 490.

was bedside reading for all educated men during this time of anxiety.[108] Galen's philosophy teacher, Albinus, wrote an *Epitome*, a manual of philosophy, which was used by Tertullian and later by Iamblichus and Proclus and even Eusebius of Caesarea. This philosopher, who was trained in Platonic philosophy, taught in Smyrna in 151–152, and popularized the ideas contained within the *Timaeus*, which thus influenced both philosophy and medicine: 'The gods made man with a quantity of earth, fire, air and water which they borrowed and which they will one day return. They assembled men using invisible pins and made a unified body . . . With the smooth and regular triangles of which the elements were formed, they produced marrow which was to give birth to seed.'[109]

When the Barbelognostics whom Epiphanius frequented in Alexandria, and who were Gnostics integrated into the Christian community until Epiphanius denounced them to the bishop, smeared their bodies with sperm and prayed naked, they were carrying to its extreme the logic of the Platonic deductions of their time. Like the worshippers of Attis, they renounced reproduction, not through castration but sodomy. Their aim was to produce as much sperm as possible and they proscribed fasting altogether.[110] It is essential to examine in this philosophical and religious context, and in the context of the ideas popularized by medicine, as Dioscorus indicates, the link made by the Coptic monks and theorized by the Greeks between diet and sexuality.

If, as both doctors and ascetics[111] say, sperm consists of the excess of humours which results from absorbing too much food, then the ascetic must follow a diet which will dry his body out: 'The monk raises his soul from the depths by drying out his body. Fasting dries up the source of pleasure.'[112] 'The drier the body, the more the soul flourishes.'[113] Evagrius advised monks to deprive themselves of water, for 'the demons frequently light on well-watered places.'[114] John Cassian referred directly to medical theory when setting out and justifying his diet for monks. If there is an excess of liquid concentrated in the marrow, nature must expel it. These humours are most easily eliminated at night for 'the quantity of

---

[108] G. Quispel, La conception de l'homme dans la gnose valentinienne, 1947, p. 273; also U. Bianchi, Le 'gnosticisme syrien', carrefour de fois, 1978, pp. 75–90.

[109] Albinus, *Epitome*, tr. P. Louis, 1945.

[110] Epiphanius of Salamis, *Panarion, (On Heresies)*, XXVI, 4–5; French translation of Epiphanius' chapters in H. Leisegang, *La gnose*, 1951, chapter V.

[111] *Coll.*, II, 23; XXII, 3.

[112] *PJ*, IV, 47.

[113] *PJ*, X, 17.

[114] *HM*, XX, 15, tr. Russell.

urine which gathers constantly while we are asleep, overfilling the bladder, arouses the relaxed members of eunuchs and children as well as grown men . . . One must eradicate this excess even to the point of drinking less water, so that as less fluid passes through the increasingly idle and parched members every day, this physical movement which you consider inevitable becomes rarer and also weaker.'[115] The foods on which the monks' diet were based form part of the drying diet recommended by doctors as we see from the relevant books of Oribasius' *Medical Collection*.[116] Doctors advised firstly abstinence[117] and staying awake, for sleep moistens the body.[118] This was what the solitaries did, for whether standing or sitting, they would either pray all night long or rest without ever lying down.[119] Foods which relax the stomach, such as lentils, salted olives, figs, grapes and prunes, were considered drying. Salt, particularly grilled (*sal frictum*), was thought to make the body sweat, and salted fish[120], brine and vinegar were all part of the monks' diet. The only green vegetable recommended by John Cassian, the leek,[121] was considered by the doctors to be drying. Chick-peas, which doctors held to have flatulent and aphrodisiac properties, were roasted and eaten as part of the monks' diet with bread. Oribasius says that they lose their aphrodisiac properties if roasted. One only has to compare this list with the diet Oribasius gives for those suffering from sexual impotence to see the rationale behind it: sleep,[122] plentiful food, wine, bread made without bran (for it was noted that bran made food pass through the intestines more quickly and therefore dried the body out), meat and flatulent dried vegetables.[123]

This theoretic basis for the ascetic life was so common that it made a good subject for jokes in the desert. A group of young novice monks who had come from their monastery to visit the solitaries were welcomed by an old monk who broke his fast in their honour. He heard them joking about this diet which they thought was normal for the solitaries. To teach them a lesson, the solitary asked them to give the following message to the monk who received them at their next port of call: 'Do not water the vegetables.' They did so, and the old monk who received them next

[115] *Coll.*, XII, 7, 9 and 11.
[116] *Med. Coll.*, I, II, XIV.
[117] Ibid., VI, 3.
[118] Ibid., VI, 4.
[119] *HM*, XX, 17.
[120] *Inst.*, IV, 2.
[121] *Inst.*, IV, 22.
[122] *Med. Coll.*, VI, 4.
[123] Ibid., VI, 38.

realized that he was to make them fast and work as he usually did. On one point, however, the Greek and Egyptian doctrines did not agree. The Greeks held that lettuce produced impotence because it was cold, and thus considered it anaphrodisiac.[124] But the Egyptians considered that the lettuce's white sap gave rise to its name 'that which makes one protrude' and to its reputation as an aphrodisiac.[125] Evagrius, who never ate lettuce in the Egyptian desert, which Palladius considered noteworthy,[126] had thus accepted the Egyptian view. The notions of the dry and the wet were familiar to all. Everyone based his diet and his lifestyle on these opposing tendencies once he had carried out his daily examination of his state of health. Thus the lawyer Minucius Felix talked with two friends as he walked along the beach at Ostia where he had gone 'as a course of sea baths seemed an agreeable and apt treatment as a corrective for the humours of my body'.[127] John Cassian based the monastic lifestyle chiefly on the medical opposition between the dry and the wet, but the monks also made use of the second opposition, that between the hot and the cold, which was more difficult to follow since some schools held that heat helped the union of the soul with the creator, provided it was dry. This was one of the reasons why both doctors and philosophers hesitated to say that woman was warmer than man.[128] Nevertheless, the advice was to eat raw, cold food. Here is the explanation given by Jerome at the end of the fourth century in a letter to one of the women he was directing towards the ascetic life: 'The doctors and physiologists who have written about the human body – particularly Galen in his books on hygiene – say that in children, young people and adults of both sexes, the body burns with innate heat; and that at these ages foods which might increase this heat are harmful, it being healthier to eat all foods cold'.[129] Jerome thus aimed to avoid all foods which warmed the body: no wine, except when one was ill, no meats or flatulent and heavy vegetables. He recommended fresh or dried vegetables to Paulinus of Nola, and also suggested going to bed with an empty stomach.[130] To a young western man who asked him to provide a rule by which he could live, he wrote that he must 'extinguish the heat of his body by the cold process of fasting'.[131] He recommended that this young lawyer and orator should take up

[124] M. Détienne, *Dionysos mis à mort*, 1977. This notion exists in Oribasius and therefore was clearly part of the whole medical tradition.
[125] Yoyotte, Les os et la semence masculine, p. 141, n. 1.
[126] *LH*, 38.
[127] Minucius Felix, *Octavius*, II, 3, tr. Rendall.
[128] Rey, *La jeunesse de la science grecque*, p. 493, on the theories of Empedocles who was a doctor.
[129] Jerome, *Letters*, LIV, 9.
[130] Ibid., LVIII.
[131] Ibid., CXXV.

gardening and grow vegetables and fruit, as well as keep bees.[132]

John Cassian provides enough details concerning the time, the number and the quality of meals, which confirm the sparse information contained in the other texts but which he conveys in a more organized fashion, for us to be able to attempt to calculate the calories contained in the daily diet of the ascetics living in the desert. He describes a meal held to celebrate a meeting with other solitaries, which consisted for each person of two loaves of bread weighing in total one Roman pound (327 g), a drop of oil, five roasted chick-peas, three olives, two prunes and a dried fig. Those who ate this meal would have absorbed about 1,000 calories each – and this was an exceptionally rich meal for them. It is easy to see that this daily ration is not adequate for a man of 65 kg leading a fairly sedentary life. And yet the average daily calorie intake of a black African before 1957 was 1,800 calories, and of an Indian 1,850, which meant that, given the great discrepancies between a well-fed minority and an ill-fed majority, the poorest members of the population must have been receiving less than 1,500 calories a day. This was probably the level at which the ascetics lived in the Egyptian desert for years. It was probably also the amount on which the poorest Egyptian peasants survived, since the shepherd to whom Arsenius described the conditions to which he had reduced himself as a former senator converted to the ascetic way of life, considered that the solitaries enjoyed a quality and quantity of food that he had so far never come across.[133] He was not alone in this, and so many people shared this view that the first attempts at organized life in communities of ascetics provided for a trial period to ensure that candidates had not come to the institution because of hardship.[134] The monks mocked an old man who had come to Tabennisi asking to be admitted, and accused him of seeking shelter for his old age and hoping above all to be fed.[135]

For the poor, the anchorite life or life in a monastery brought a lifestyle similar to that they had known since childhood, sometimes better. For those who possessed some worldly goods, and particularly those who had

[132] These dietary theories, which make up a quarter or more of Oribasius' work, and which were considered as one aspect of medicine, have not been picked up by scholars collecting 'medical allusions' in the works of the Fathers. The first and finest work in this area of medicine is that by A. Harnack, Medicinisches aus der ältesten Kirchengeschichte, 1892, pp. 37–152; A. S. Pease, Medical allusions in the work of St Jerome, 1914, pp. 73–86, examines illness, the doctor and the patient, but not health. Nor is there anything on this in G. Bardy, Saint Augustin et les médecins, 1953, pp. 327–46; a few notions in P. Antin, La vieillesse chez saint Jérôme, pp. 43–54. But chapter V in M. Spanneut, Le stoïcisme des Pères de l'Eglise, is full of information.

[133] Alph., Arsenius, 36; PJ, X, 76.

[134] Inst., IV, 3. Or to escape the law, Pachomius, Precepts, 49.

[135] Coll., XX, 1.

abandoned high social position like the senator Arsenius, Evagrius Ponticus, and later the great Cappadocians or Paulinus of Nola, the diet of the monastery, even if they supplemented it slightly as did Arsenius, was a diet of undernutrition, and deliberately brutal at first.

To the young men who sought to become perfect, Ares recommended a year of confinement on a diet of 327 g of bread per day seasoned with salt, in other words around 1,000 calories.[136] Let us suppose that the monks' stale bread contained more calories and that the novice supplemented his daily ration with a few roots or wild plants. All we know is that he remained alive and often strong, for the ascetics lived well into old age. What we need to consider here is not the dietary deprivations, or the question of how their bodies survived such restrictions, but the sexual effects of undernutrition.[137] These effects have most commonly been studied in relation to women[138] rather than men, chiefly because in times of famine, including those brought about among the civil population by the Second World War, large numbers of anxious women went to their doctors to complain of amenorrhoea. The effect of famine on reproduction, with reference only to women, is known in history as one of the certain causes of demographic decline. In 1944 the effects of undernutrition on male sexuality were revealed by experiments carried out in the United States. Thirty-two men in good physical condition and of heterosexual or homosexual tendencies agreed, under medical supervision, gradually to reduce their daily rations while maintaining their sexual activities with their usual partners. Once their calorie intake dropped to 1,700–1,400 calories a day, this level was maintained for nearly six months, during which time all sexual manifestations ceased: desire, dreams, aggression and ejaculations in their sleep. A return to a normal diet did not lead to an immediate and trouble-free resumption of their initial sexual activity. Thus famine can produce male impotence, and not simply infertility, which probably explains why it is only the female complaint of amenorrhoea – which leads women to believe at first that they are pregnant – which has attracted the historians' attention.

John Cassian says that by depriving himself of sleep, drinking little and

---

[136] *PJ*, XIV, 2.

[137] The following lines are based on my reading of P. Desclaux and C. Ramon, Famine et vie sexuelle de l'homme civilisé, in *Nutrition et fonctions de reproduction*, 1952, 1953, pp. 137–150, and of C. Richet and F. Delbarre, *L'insuffisance alimentaire*, 1950, p. 241. One must not forget Josué de Castro's *Géopolitique de la faim*, 1952.

[138] 'Why did married women, who were normally fertile, suddenly become infertile during the worst weeks or months of hunger.' This is how E. Le Roy Ladurie sums up the frequently asked question in L'aménorrhéee de famine (XVIIe-XXe siècle), 1969, reproduced in *Le territoire de l'historien*, 1973, pp. 331–48.

living on two loaves of bread a day, the novice could achieve almost perfect chastity in six months.[139] It is therefore likely that the Egyptian ascetics, by means of a brutal diet of undernutrition and a strictly controlled lifestyle, succeeded in reducing their sexual impulses and even their ejaculations during sleep, which most of them, like everyone else of that period, considered necessary to the pursuit of union with God.

Whereas undernutrition could bring about a truce in the struggle against insistent sexual desire in monks who came from a well supplied table, the malnutrition experienced since childhood by the poorest converts made this method of reducing suffering quite ineffective. Moses the Ethiopian, who had been forced to steal in his youth because of his poverty, and who had come to the desert to expiate his faults and find the road to salvation, exhausted his body in all ways possible in order to conquer his throbbing sexual needs.[140] He began by depriving himself of food, but his desire and dreams only increased. He went without sleep, praying all night standing in the middle of his cell. But still the need persisted. So he spent his nights fetching water for his brothers. But this did not work either. All this time he was denied communion by Isidore, a wealthy man whom asceticism does not seem to have made any thinner. After Moses had been attacked near the well to which he went at night, and had been greatly weakened by a long illness, Isidore allowed him to take communion, saying that Moses' *phantasia* had been attacks by the demon and that the Ethiopian was not responsible for them. John Cassian also says that sexual fantasies and desire increase during the first phase of undernutrition,[141] which has been confirmed in studies on hunger.[142] They were known as 'intensified attacks by the demon' as soon as a monk began to fast, in other words to limit both the quantity and the quality of his food.

It is probable that the sexual effects of famine were known in Egypt, as they were doubtless known in Hesiod's Greece, and when the shortage of land made the poor emigrate towards the Black Sea, Cyrene and Sicily. They were also expounded by the doctors who were writing for an aristocratic clientele. It is the first phase of undernutrition which prompted the remark passed on by Aetius,[143] 'Parmenides, Empedocles: depriving oneself of food provokes desire'.

The knowledge acquired by the poorest people in times of famine was widely tested by men from all social classes in the Egyptian desert. But from the beginning of the fourth century, the Christian texts are full of

[139] *Coll.*, XII, 15.
[140] *LH*, 19.
[141] *Coll.*, XXI, 35; XXII, 2 and 3.
[142] de Castro, *Géopolitique de la faim*, p. 101.
[143] Aetius, V, 9, 14, Dox. 398.

these notions of physiology linked with dietetics. They appealed to the whole Graeco-Roman world. Control of sexuality through a lifestyle based on physiology and a carefully chosen diet was an everyday concern. It was on these notions and not simply on the praise of virginity that the call to live a life of abstinence and the new enthusiasm for the solitary way could be based.

11

From Virginity to Frigidity

Female asceticism is linked to the whole history of the spread of Christianity. But perhaps the texts place more emphasis on the fulfilment found by women in the service of Christ than on the sacrifices this service demanded of them. Y. Nehlig has studied the role of Greek and particularly Roman women in the spread of Christianity.[1] It was their freedom of movement and their freedom to manage their own property which made the women who were subject to Roman law so useful to the preachers of the new religion. And yet we have almost no texts written by women in those centuries in which they contributed so much to the advance of Christianity, as indeed they had done in the past for other religions.

Through the letters of their male correspondents we can, nevertheless, come to know at least in part the contents of their own letters. These men wrote them discourses on asceticism to encourage them, despite the distance separating them, in the life of abstinence to which the men had converted them. But the women's letters to their menfolk did not consist solely of laments on this subject. Here are two examples of letters sent from exile by two men to the two women who were closest to them; the first writer was an early fourth-century pagan, the second an early fifth-century Christian.

The philosopher Porphyry was advanced in years when he met Marcella, a mother of seven children and a widow, who seemed virtuously inclined. He married her to save her from marrying some other husband who might prove to be a despot. He recalls this at the start of a letter written to her when they were separated as a result of a period of exile, doubtless political, ten months after their marriage. The whole letter is a response to the sadness, presumably Marcella's, caused by their separation, and to the deprivation of sexual love imposed by Porphyry's exile and his wife's duty to remain with her daughters. He is sure of being

[1] Y. Nehlig, *Le rôle des femmes dans l'Eglise du Ier au IIIe siècle*, 1981.

loved and sure that she cannot do without him: 'Your spiritual teacher, in whom is concentrated all the affection one holds for a father, a husband, a master, one's family, even, if you like, one's country.' Having described the sadness he is sure she feels as she loves him so much, Porphyry summarizes for her the practical side of his philosophy, and ends by advising her not to ask her servants to do what she can do herself. He has essentially given her the philosophical basis of the sexual asceticism which their separation imposes on her if she wishes to remain faithful – although Porphyry does not make this last qualification as he takes it for granted.

In AD 403 John Chrysostom, bishop of Constantinople, was deposed by a synod which succeeded in its request that the Emperor exile this indomitable preacher. We possess seventeen of his letters addressed to an aristocratic woman in Constantinople named Olympias. He was then sixty-six and she thirty-six. Like Porphyry's letter to Marcella, some of these are short treatises on separation and suffering. Letter VIII is a treatise on virginity. We know of this woman from other sources: she came from an important family and had been orphaned at a very early age. Her guardian had given her in marriage at the age of eighteen and when she was widowed before she was nineteen she decided to live a life of chastity and not remarry. She was deaconess of Constantinople before the age of thirty. While the literary prose John Chrysostom wrote her seeks mainly to console her for their separation and expresses his certainty of being loved and of being, by his absence, the cause of infinite sadness to her,[2] the letters he received from her mainly give the news of the Church in Constantinople and Olympias' attempts to have John's place of exile moved to somewhere by the sea instead of in the middle of Anatolia where there was a constant risk of being attacked by the Isaurians. He quotes her: 'Perhaps you will be angry with us because we have neglected ourself' while trying to have him moved. She tells him of the whereabouts of a bishop of Mesopotamia with whom John wishes to remain in contact, she passes on the letters he sends for the members of the Constantinople clergy, she seeks advice with regard to the attempt to make the bishop of Ephesus resign, and she has to play for time when the Goths are demanding that a new bishop be appointed.[3] When he replies to news of Olympias' misfortunes when she was exiled and ill, we learn that she has been tried by the prefect of Constantinople after being called as a witness in the investigation of a fire in the cathedral and at the Senate, and condemned because of her support for John. So she must have described the trial in her letter and given a certain amount of political information.

She thus appears as a key agent in John Chrysostom's political

[2] John Chrysostom, *Letters to Olympias*, VII.
[3] Ibid., IX.

manoeuvring while in exile (403–407). While he reproaches her for her anxiety and the sadness which prompted him to write his 'Consolations' in the pure rhetorical tradition, John Chrysostom in each of his letters gives alarming accounts of his own health, describing his symptoms and conveying the concern caused him by brigands' attacks when he was being moved or the threats of barbarian incursions. He had felt sick when he was being moved on one occasion: 'You can imagine the result, with no doctor, no bath, none of the necessary things.' The bath was necessary for treatment, as the medical tradition shows,[4] for after vomiting one must moisten the body. John Chrysostom seems to have had a liking for this treatment, for during the trial which led to his exile he had been accused by the clerks of his church of having baths prepared for his sole use. The clerks added: 'When he had washed, Serapion shut the door, so that no one else could wash.'[5] When we read his letters to Olympias and his complaints about his health this seems quite plausible.

The relationship between John Chrysostom and Olympias is similar to that between a Christian woman from Egypt, one of whose papyrus letters we have, and her son who had gone to live some distance away.

> Greetings to you, my son Theodulus, from your mother Kophaena and from Zenon.
>
> Firstly, I pray to Almighty God to grant you health and prosperity. I wish you to know, as the merchant told you, that your mother Kophaena has been ill for thirteen months, and yet you have not written me even one letter although you know that I treated you better than my other children, and you did not think to send even a word to me when you learned that I was ill. But take care to send me ten pounds of flax and I will make you some clothes if I can, for I have no more to use for you. Also send me a little stock of grain and I will send you . . . Greetings to you from your mother Kophaena, your son Zenon, your sister Cyrilla and her children. If you could, Theodulus my son, buy me five pounds of black wool to make me a coat, I will send you the amount you pay for it. I wish you good health for years to come.[6]

Olympias' political news was rather different from Kophaena's weaving for her son, but the aristocratic woman at the court of Constantinople shows the same concern and the same generosity for the

---

[4] A. Rousselle, Du sanctuaire au thaumaturge: la guérison en Gaule au IVe siècle, 1976.

[5] See A.-M. Malingrey's introduction to his ed. and French tr. of the Lettres à Olympias, 1968, p. 24. These accusations were passed on by Photius.

[6] Naldini, Il cristianesimo in Egitto. Lettere private nei papiri dei secoli II–IV, 1968, no. 93.

old bishop, fearing that he will be cold[7] and worrying about his health. But whereas the sands preserved Kophaena's letter, and those of Porphyry and John were copied often enough for them to have come down to us, Marcella's and Olympias' letters have been lost.

Of course many of the letters which have survived the centuries were preserved by those who sent them. We know that the orator Libanius, 1,600 of whose letters survive, kept copies of his own letters in a notebook which was later used to produce an edition of his collected works. The letters of the Emperor Julian were kept by his correspondents and as soon as anti-pagan feeling died down after his death, his friends began to collect his writings. His correspondents were willing to provide them, sometimes making available copies of their own letters which were included in the collection.[8] So it is either the author's action of keeping his letters along with his other works, whether they were treatises in the form of letters or more personal letters, or else it was the friendship and honour felt by those who received letters which saved them from disappearing. Among other less extensive correspondences, we possess that of John Chrysostom, Basil of Caesarea, Jerome and Augustine. Augustine's correspondence, consisting of 270 letters, contains 47 letters received by him and six letters provided by his correspondents: not one letter from a woman.[9] And yet these Christian writers corresponded very frequently with women, but they lost the originals of these letters and the women did not keep copies. Jerome, who exchanged letters with educated women who were as committed as he was to the ascetic life and who read Latin and Greek,[10] kept his own letters sent from Bethlehem to the women he had known in Rome, but disposed of those he received from them.

Thus even if men did not keep copies of their own letters women did and have passed them down. The letters received by men and collected after the author's death were sometimes published in antiquity accompanied by the letters written in reply to them or to which they were replying. But letters by women were neither kept by their correspondents

---

[7] John Chrysostom, *Letters to Olympias*, IX.

[8] Emperor Julian, *Oeuvres complètes*, ed. and French tr. J. Bidez, vol. I, 2nd part, *Lettres et fragments*, 2nd edition, 1960, p. VIII et seq., and J. Bidez, *Recherches sur la tradition manuscrite des lettres de l'empereur Julien*, 1898.

[9] There are three letters to women in Julian's correspondence; John Chrysostom's correspondence: 53 letters to women; Basil: 13 letters to women; Jerome: 34 letters to women, including one to a couple (a man and a woman); Augustine: 14 letters to women, 9 to a man and his wife; the collection includes 6 letters received by Augustine from Paulinus of Nola and his wife Therasia, but which were almost certainly written by Paulinus. The letter from Paula and Eustochium, included in the collection of Jerome's letters, is generally thought to have been an exercise in style, here feminine style, by Jerome.

[10] Melania, *LH*, 55.

nor annexed to the letters the women received and which they released for publication.[11]

Evagrius had left Constantinople passionately in love with a married woman who was also desperately in love with him. As soon as he recovered from this, in Palestine, he resumed a worldly life which Melania besought him to give up. He could not free himself from desire. The following anecdote recounted by John Cassian is probably about him.[12]

> When after fifteen years he was brought a number of letters from his father, his mother and several friends from his province of Pontus, he took the bundle of letters and, reflecting for some time, said: 'How many thoughts will reading them stir in me which will arouse either boundless joy or sterile sadness?' . . . He decided that he would not only not open them, but that he would not even untie the bundle lest, recalling the names of those who had written them or remembering their faces, he should distract his mind from the path he had undertaken. So he threw the parcel into the fire, still tied as he had received it.[13]

But the greatest Christian letter writers did not have the same excuse of asceticism for allowing the fond letters which they had received from their female friends to be lost.

Only Jerome kept among his letters one written by women, that which his friends Paula and Eustochium sent from the east to a friend who had remained in Rome.[14] They describe the east enthusiastically, and their description has been compared with the only female work we possess from this period of the Roman Empire, Etheria's *Pilgrimage*, the account of a journey to the east.[15] So we know that these women did write. Were their letters destroyed because they lacked the rhetorical form which men strove to observe? Certainly not. The same men kept copies, or their female correspondents kept the originals, of the shortest note written in haste, the simplest letter of recommendation, and even letters of insult,[16]

---

[11] I therefore disagree with the sentence in Malingrey's introduction to the *Lettres à Olympias*, p. 5: 'There remains a large number of letters which can be considered as true exchanges of thought and friendship.' Besides, John Chrysostom prepared his letter-treatises in advance, *ep.* IX, 4.

[12] As indicated by J.-C. Guy, in his edition of John Cassian's *De Institutis coenoborium*, p. 242, n. 1.

[13] *Inst.*, V, 32.

[14] Jerome, *Letter*, 46.

[15] Etheria, *Journal de voyage*, ed. and French tr. H. Pétré, 1964, compared with Paula's letter and with one from Jerome to Eustochium, p. 19.

[16] Basil, *Letter* 115.

although sometimes we do not know to whom they were addressed or about whom they were written.

So it was no small merit for the collectors of the *Sayings* to have kept and copied, and taught the wisdom of those women who, in Egypt, adopted the ascetic life and sometimes led large groups of nuns: Amma Sarah and Amma Syncletica.

Female sexual desire was recognized just as much as male desire by the Greek medical texts, and also by the Egyptian monastic texts. Amma Sarah struggled for thirteen years to repress sexual desire.[17] Egyptian women seem to have been much freer to move about, to meet whom they liked and to do as they pleased with their bodies than Greek or Roman women,[18] as is shown by the stories of young girls from the valley made pregnant by anchorites. It is clear that the women of the Egyptian khôra even those who were slaves, were freer than the Greek women of classical times, and that the Greek women of Alexandria were the first to be able to use a form of marriage contract which mentioned their name and their personal wish to give themselves in marriage.[19] In the same way, an Egyptian woman could make the personal decision to become a nun, as we see from the accounts of Potamiena, Alexandra,[20] Amma Sarah and Syncletica,[21] and from accounts of a few women who dressed as men and lived the anchorite life in the desert. But we are told that Amma Talis was so much loved by the women of one of her twelve convents that it had no key, for, unlike those in other convents, the nuns here did not try to escape.[22] This indicates that some girls from the towns and villages who wanted to leave the monastic life were shut up in convents without their express consent. Antony had a sister for whom he was responsible and he entrusted her to a convent before he could take up the solitary life of an anchorite.[23] Well before Melania adopted this practice on her African properties, Egyptian masters had offered their dependents the choice of taking up the monastic life.[24] Just like their male counterparts, the women who were shut in together suspected one another of carrying on secret sexual liaisons,[25] and falsely accused one another. The *Lausiac History* recounts that convents were the scenes of constant quarrels which were

---

[17] *PJ*, V. 10.

[18] *PJ*, XIV, 16.

[19] Vatin, *Recherches sur le mariage*, chapter IV.

[20] *LH*, 33 and 5.

[21] *Alph*.

[22] *LH*, 59.

[23] *Life of Antony*, 3.

[24] *LH*, 61; *HM*, XXII, 1. *Life of Saint Melania*, 22, Greek text with introduction and notes by D. Gorce, 1962; it is the *Latin life* which describes the conversion of houses into monasteries.

[25] *LH*, 33.

repressed by means of corporal punishment by the monk who had founded the convent,[26] or watched over by an abbot who would shut himself away high up in a separate building whose doors he had bricked up.[27] The nuns were capable of persecuting a holy girl who pretended to be an idiot so that she would be given the most tedious work to do.[28] They mocked her and beat her. So alongside those women who, like Amma Sarah, could say to men who sought to humiliate her: 'According to nature I am a woman, but not according to my thoughts,'[29] there were many who found themselves shut away in nunneries without any clear aim. It is not that there were no arguments between the men in the monasteries – the Rules make it clear that there were – but the reports of their conduct are not as disparaging as the reports we have of the goings on in the women's convents.

It is rather strange to see these Egyptian men preaching continence to their own wives. Amoun, an orphan, who was married at the age of twenty-two by his guardian, locked the bridal chamber, read Saint Paul to his young bride, and tried to persuade her to remain a virgin. She begged him to stay with her and accepted continence on this condition. For eighteen years they remained together, both virgins, and then she suggested that he should go and live in the desert so that all would see his virtue.[30] For her part, she converted her house into a convent for the women of her household.[31] John of Lycopolis himself had left his wife to go and live in the desert.[32] Abba Paul, after years of marriage, found his wife with a lover and left her and their children to go and join Antony in the desert, preferring 'to herd scorpions rather than to live with an adulteress'.[33] Abba Theonas finally left his wife since she refused to accept a life of continence as he had.[34] She argued that 'in the flower of her youth she could not do without her husband. If, as a result of his abandoning her, she fell into bad ways, it would be his fault for breaking his marriage vows.' He then considered her a seductress and left her.

When the anchorites asked God to show them a man who had attained a higher degree of perfection than they, God directed them towards men in the valley, who were married, land-owners with municipal responsibilities, and who lived secretly in complete chastity. Such was the case of a well-known man in a village who, after having three children in three

[26] LH, 29.
[27] LH, 30.
[28] LH, 34.
[29] Alph., Sarah, 4.
[30] LH, 8.
[31] HM, XXII, 1.
[32] LH, 35.
[33] LH, 22; HM, XXIV.
[34] Coll., XXI, 8–9.

years of marriage, resolved not to touch his wife again.[35] When Paphnutius went to see him he had been living this way for thirty years without anyone knowing. One of these chaste laymen was so perfect that he was able to perform miracles. An Egyptian shepherd and his wife wore hair-shirts at night: no one knew that she was a virgin and he was totally continent.[36]

In the third and fourth centuries an individual might arrive at the decision not to marry for various reasons. Christ's words were always at the heart of the decision: 'Alas for women with child in those days, and for those who have children at the breast!'[37] or when he spoke of the woman who had had seven husbands: 'Those who have been judged worthy of a place in the other world and of the resurrection from the dead, do not marry, for they are not subject to death any longer. They are like angels; they are sons of God, because they share in the resurrection.'[38] But these words became associated with a number of different views and social practices which were consistent with them and developed them still further. Like some of the Gnostics, Eustathius of Sebaste rejected marriage: he was condemned by the Synod of Gangra in 340. The same synod forbade women to dress like men and cut their hair. The ascetic movement had to clarify its position with regard to marriage since the synods were affirming that marriage was a path to salvation.

In order to do that the movement had to clarify its view of women. One theory which was held by the Gnostic Theodotus in Anatolia was that the first woman was born from Adam's sperm. But Eve was born not from the true and good 'virile seed, the overflowing of angelic seed', poured into the body of the first man by the Word, but from the female element which came out of this seed and was emitted while Adam slept.[39] This doctrine reveals very clearly the concerns of the Gnostics and the arguments they used to solve the problem of the creation. But it is also found in the works of orthodox authors. Methodius of Olympus takes up this theory which makes woman an emission during sleep as Soranus expresses it, an illusion of the night as John Cassian has it, or a fantasy as Basil writes.

> This was perhaps the symbolism of that ecstatic sleep into which God put the first man, that it was to be a type of man's enchantment in love, when in his thirst for children he falls into a trance, lulled

---

[35] *HM*, XIV, 13 = *Coll.*, XIV, 7.
[36] *PJ*, XX, 3.
[37] Matthew 24, 19; Mark 13, 17; Luke 21, 23, New English Bible.
[38] Luke 20, 34, New English Bible.
[39] S. Reinach, La naissance d'Eve, 1918, p. 185 et seq. Extracts from Theodotus, in Clement of Alexandria, *Stromates*, VIII, 2.

into sleep by the pleasure of procreation, in order that a new person, as I have said, might be formed in turn from the material that is drawn from his flesh and bone.[40]

What then was a woman? Eternity and the here-after were not closed to her. This was the view not only of the Christians, but also of the philosophy which had accepted the creation in these terms, which set the soul on the road to its true home. The pagan philosopher Porphyry (232–305), author of a treatise against the Christians, encouraged his wife Marcella to remain continent with these words:

> Thus the presence of my shadow, that visible phantom, will profit you not, and its absence will not pain you if you earnestly try to leave the body far behind. The surest way of reaching me purely, of keeping me with you night and day by all that is purest and finest in our union, and so that I can never be separated from you, is to try to gather within yourself all the parts of your spirit which are dispersed and reduced to a multitude of small pieces scattered throughout an entity which up till now has enjoyed the full force of its strength.[41]

The gathering together of dispersed parts, a common image in gnosis, found here in the writings of Porphyry, a disciple of Plotinus, is possible and necessary for women as for men,[42] but only if a woman becomes like a man. 'Do not consider yourself as a woman: I am not attached to you as to a woman. Flee all that is effeminate in the soul as if you had taken on a man's body. It is when the soul is virginal and when the intellect is still a virgin that they produce the finest offspring.'[43] Virginity, and failing that continence, allows a woman to arrive at the stage where there are no women and no men.[44]

Only Basil of Ancyra, probably because he was a doctor, wrote a treatise on virginity for women which does not sidestep the difficulties of continence and describes the state accurately and in female terms.[45] He teaches women that all the senses are gateways to genital desire: touch,

---

[40] Methodius, *Symposium*, II, 2, tr. Musurillo.

[41] Porphyry, *Letter to Marcella*.

[42] In hommage to the work of H.-C. Puech on 'le rassemblement de soi sur soi et en soi', J. Magne, Klasma, Sperma, Poimnion, Le voeu pour le rassemblement de Didaché, IX, 4, 1974, pp. 197–208; H.-C. Puech, *Sur le manichéisme et autres essais*, 1979; H. Jonas, *The Gnostic Religion*, 1958, 1963, 1970.

[43] Porphyry, *Letter to Marcella*, 33.

[44] On the original androgyne, see Marie Delcourt, Utrumque neutrum, 1976, pp. 117–23.

[45] Basil of Ancyra, *De Virginitate*, Greek text, *PG*, XXX, col. 669–809; A Vaillant, *De Virginitate de saint Basile, Texte vieux slave*, 1943.

taste, sight, which he studies in turn, aware above all of the images provided by sight, which are retained in the memory and are more seductive than touch but which without fail lead the woman who has not refused to look to seek physical contact. He describes very precisely female masturbation in order the better to fight it: he says it accompanies summer nights spent out on a terrace. Basil shows the virgin the way of attaining absolute purity. She must deny herself the right to touch, to look and above all must deny herself certain foods. In this context he recalls the notions of the dry and the moist, the hot and the cold, and sets out his diet according to these principles, describing the genital sensation of desire which the foods he prescribes are supposed to prevent.

Basil of Ancyra writes for a woman who has decided to remain continent while living in her own home. He tells her what to avoid in order to remain faithful to her goal. Towards the middle of the fourth century it was quite common to find mothers and daughters living secretly in their homes an ascetic life which was quite as demanding as that of the solitaries in the desert. A virgin who was too sure that she could resist temptation and revealed her perfection to others, allowed one or other of her servants to tempt her: she shut the door but opened her window.[46] Basil sets aside the objections against restricting contacts with others which arouse desire: women living alone can and must send away soldiers who arrive with a billet.[47] They must not visit others, even through charity, and must accept no invitations to weddings.[48]

In this society where girls were married off by their fathers, which women could really choose virginity? It seems that few were able to resist the will of a father, mother or guardian who wished to marry them. Indeed, boys were in exactly the same position. Perhaps we should not forget that Antony was an orphan and that Pachomius, a convert to Christianity, had fled his pagan family. Even in Egypt, a prospective monk was married against his wishes by an uncle who had paternal authority over him.[49] So virginity was only possible for a woman who had been orphaned before puberty or who was of marriageable age and able to resist all the pressure put on her. Olympias, married at eighteen and widowed at nineteen,[50] was persecuted by the Emperor Theodosius who, as a gift to one of his relations, wanted to make her marry him.[51] Unless they had been set aside for a life of virginity by their parents,

---

[46] *LH*, 28.
[47] Chapter 15.
[48] Chapter 20–21.
[49] *LH*, 8.
[50] *LH*, 56.
[51] Malingrey, introduction to John Chrysostom's *Lettres à Olympias*, 1947 edition, pp. 12–13.

sometimes from birth, like the daughter of Melania the Younger,[52] women were not in a position to understand the discourses on virginity which were written for them. As we have seen, these were discourses on marriage which based their arguments on the misfortunes of married women. If they had any appeal it was to mothers and not to young girls. It was the mothers who encouraged their daughters to take up a life of continence.

Thus we find the daughter of a military leader preaching virginity to her own daughter while she herself strove to remain continent,[53] and Paula, a woman of the senatorial aristocracy in Rome, persuading her daughter Eustochium to follow the same path,[54] and Avita, converted to asceticism by Melania the Older, keeping her daughter Eunomia a virgin.[55] They left their only sons to take on the family dignity and fulfil the family's obligations: Paula left Rome for Palestine with her daughter, leaving her son Toxotius in Rome; Melania, a consul's daughter, appointed a guardian for Publicola before leaving Rome for Jerusalem.[56] In this way he was prepared for a political career in which a good marriage would play a part.

Mothers who brought up their daughters to remain virgins or encouraged them to follow this path chose themselves to lead a life of continence if they were widows and tried to persuade their husbands to do the same if they were still alive. Melania the Older, once she was a widow, left Rome to go to the Holy Land. While she was away, her son grew up and married. He had a daughter, Melania the Younger, whom he married at the age of thirteen to Pinianus, a Roman noble of seventeen. The young Melania, despite the fact that she was married, wished to follow her grandmother's example. Her husband did not agree to this but suggested that they should wait until they had two children and then give up sexual relations together. Before she was twenty she had had two children, both of whom died. So the husband became convinced that this was God's will and together the couple defied his family and the law which refused them, until they were twenty-five, the right to give up the property which they wanted to distribute to others. Learning of their decision, Melania the Older, then sixty, returned to Rome to help them and to convert to continence her son and her daughter-in-law, the parents of Melania the Younger.[57]

Not all mothers, however, were so pleased to see their sons or

---

[52] *Life of Melania*, I, ed. D. Gorce, p. 133.
[53] *LH*, 57.
[54] *LH*, 41.
[55] *LH*, 41 and 54.
[56] *LH*, 46.
[57] *LH*, 61 and *Life of Melania*.

daughters mortifying their bodies. Albina, mother of Melania the Younger, would sometimes go into her daughter's cell crying: 'I have faith that I too am sharing in your suffering, my daughter, for if the mother of the seven Maccabees shared eternal happiness with them because she witnessed the torments of her sons in one hour, will it not be granted to me all the more since every day I suffer more torments than she as I see you wasting away.' She was referring to the example, which had become a model in the second century AD in hellenized Jewish milieux, of a mother who encouraged her seven sons to suffer death by torture rather than break the Law of Moses. The text shows the mother and her seven sons following the true philosophy which led to immortality, the mastery of passions.[58] In Palestine the tombs which were thought to be those of the Maccabees were revered, and there were relics in Antioch. The philosophical account of the martyrdom of the seven brothers and their mother was used as an argument in the preaching of Gregory of Nazianzus.[59] John Chrysostom delivered three or four homilies before the remains of the Jewish martyrs,[60] in which he pointed to the opposition between maternal feelings and the true philosophy which lay in piety. He was essentially preaching about the mother of the seven brothers. In the west, the fourth book of Maccabees continued to provide the theme of constancy in the face of persecution, and that of strength in the face of others' suffering.[61] We see from the example of Albina that this model helped to calm the worries of parents whose children gave themselves to God and inflicted extraordinary mortifications upon themselves, and, what is more, refused to give their parents any hope of posterity.

One Roman woman who had taken refuge in Bethlehem wrote to her husband who had stayed behind in Rome, exhorting him to abandon everything and follow her in the ascetic life as he had promised.[62]

Thus we have many examples of couples who, by their own example and by other pressures they could bring to bear, induced their own children to follow the way of continence. Asceticism was chosen by whole families.[63] In the western examples we know of, it was generally the wife who took the initiative. Paulinus of Nola, one the richest senators in the west, also waited to have a son before devoting himself to

---

[58] Maccabees IV, Greek text in the LXX. French tr. in A. Dupont-Sommer, *Le IVe Livre des Maccabées*, Intro., tr. and notes, 1939.

[59] Gregory of Nazianzus, *In Mac.*, PG, XXXV, col. 912–33; P. Galley, *La vie de Grégoire de Nazianze*, 1943, pp. 76–7, gives the date of the sermon as 362–375.

[60] A. Dupont-Sommer, *Le IVe Livre des Maccabées*, pp. 68–70.

[61] Prudentius, *Peristephanon*, X, 776, in *Oeuvres*, IV. Text and French tr. M. Lavarenne, 1963, p. 146.

[62] Jerome, *Letter*, 122.

[63] *LH*, 41, father, mother and daughter.

asceticism. He only decided to sell his possessions after his child had died.[64] His wife Therasia followed him in the ascetic life and went with him to his retreat in Nola. He had been forty when he married her. Was it she who converted him to poverty and continence? Paulinus' correspondents called her Tanaquil,[65] as a reference to Tarquin's wife who persuaded her husband to leave his native town and take Rome.[66] The couple then became continent. The bishops advised people at least to abstain from conjugal relations for long periods,[67] to make it easier to pray as the state of marriage made it almost impossible to do so.[68] Continence made it easier for couples to pray.[69] In a treatise on marriage Augustine introduces chapters on the importance of continence.[70] It is here that he explains, doubtless for the benefit of continent husbands, that ejaculation during sleep is not a sin.[71] The forms that a couple's sexual life might take were strictly controlled. Some sexual relations were inappropriate even within marriage.[72] The aristocratic Roman wives were keenest in their search for the right way to lead an ascetic life. So many of them travelled to the east to visit the places where Christ had lived and to speak to the solitaries that Abba Arsenius exclaimed: 'They will turn the sea into a thoroughfare with women coming to see me!'[73]

But wives did not always succeed in persuading their husbands to follow their example. Some husbands were loath to undertake what they saw as a life of frustration,[74] and the bishops were obliged to preach the theme of conjugal duty to those wives who were considered 'responsible for their husbands' misdemeanours'.[75] They reproved spouses who adopted continence without the agreement of their partner: 'The result of this is adultery, fornication and domestic strife', and yet 'many women do

---

[64] On Paulinus of Nola, see P. Fabre, *Saint Paulin de Nole et l'amitié chrétienne*, 1946; W. H. C. Frend, Paulinus of Nola and the last century of the Western Empire, 1969, pp. 1–11.

[65] Paulinus, *Carm.*, X, V. 192.

[66] Livy, I, 34, 4.

[67] I shall not dwell here on the well known theories which consider fertilization the only valid reason for conjugal relations. The Roman practice of limiting sexual relations to fertilization of the legitimate wife, during the first part of the menstrual cycle, was thus held up as the norm, but without the compensation which men were offered of more satisfying relations outside marriage.

[68] John Chrysostom, *De Virginitate*, 29 to 32, 38.

[69] John Chrysostom, *Hom.*, XIX.

[70] Augustine, *De bono conjugali*, XXI, 25.

[71] Ibid., XX, 23.

[72] Ambrose, *Exhort. virg.*, IV, 21, in *PL*, XVI, col. 346.

[73] *Alph.*, Arsenius, 28.

[74] Gregory of Nyssa, *De Virginitate*, III, 1, ed. M. Aubineau, 1966, pp. 273–7.

[75] John Chrysostom, *Hom.*, XIX.

this'.[76] It must have happened fairly frequently among the Christians that a wife who was married, according to the Roman custom, well before the age of twelve, found in asceticism a reason for rejecting sexual relations. But a Christian husband could not seek consolation in concubinage as could the pagans. Some referred to Saint Paul and the Gospel of Matthew in order to have their marriage dissolved. Augustine replied to Pollentius' thesis which held that 'the separation of spouses is admissible not only when there has been adultery on the part of one of the partners, but also where there is incompatibility or if rejection of the conjugal act makes it too difficult for them to live together'.[77]

Women who were attracted by continence, but had been married against their wishes could, if their husbands refused to follow the ascetic life, turn to Basil of Ancyra's treatise, which sets out quite bluntly what the other texts imply: the way to satisfy their husbands without corrupting their own flesh:

> In the time of the persecutions virgins who had been pursued because they remained faithful to the Husband and were given to impious men managed to preserve their bodies from being defiled for He for whom they had suffered paralyzed and struck with impotence the violence those impious men tried to use on their bodies, and He preserved their very bodies, I tell you, completely free of corruption by an astonishing miracle, or else if they had been taken by violence, as their soul took no part in the fleshly pleasures, they seemed to mock their dead bodies and they gave their soul, which had refused to give in to the sensual pleasure of the one who had outraged them, to their true Husband, pure and more shining in its fidelity and virginity. I believe that the Lord wished to show that they held the honour of worshipping him to be far greater than the superficial honour of the body. They had neither their souls corrupted by their denial, nor their bodies soiled by those whose pleasure they refused to share. If a man, in criminal folly, wishes to outrage a murdered virgin and tries to defile her dead body, he can only do her physical violence, he can not corrupt her. He himself is corrupt and defiled, but the virgin, whose soul has left her, remains without stain. It is the same with those who, during the persecutions and all the tribulations, were mistreated by men: having obtained the death of the flesh, whatever they suffered they remained without corruption.[78]

[76] John Chrysostom, ibid., XIX, and *De Virginitate*, XLVIII.
[77] Augustine, *De adulterinis conjugiis*.
[78] See A. Vaillant's French translation from the Old Slavic, pp. 59–61.

Did they really need this advice? The enthusiasm with which they took to the ascetic life, their repugnance for sexual relations within a marriage which had been forced on them, and the chance to be recognized in a way of life in which they could be men's equals made the women of the Empire one of the principal forces in the transformation of the ancient world.

Conclusion

The secular moralists of the late nineteenth and early twentieth centuries accused the Egyptian solitaries of licentiousness which was incompatible with their calling.[1] The defenders of monasticism thus had to come to grips with the descriptions of outbursts of sensualism given in the texts with which they were confronted.[2] But the detractors of the monastic life were also the detractors of free love, and were just as shocked by what they saw as a life of hypocrisy as by the licentiousness revealed in their view by the first solitaries' accounts of their attempts to resist desire. More recently, and in a civilization in which relations between men and women are in some respects different from those in past eras, another accusation has been made against the monks of the ancient world. This takes up one of the elements of the generally western reaction against the ascetic movement. M. I. Finley[3] summarizes the questions relating to the depopulation of the Roman Empire from the end of the second century onwards, and sheds further light on the issue by examining the notion of technical stagnation. One of the causes of this depopulation, according to A. H. M. Jones[4] and later Evelyne Patlagean,[5] is the fact that men and women renounced marriage and fertility, and practised virginity and continence with the encouragement of the Christian Church in the monasteries and convents. Ambrose of Milan replied to this argument at the end of the fourth century by pointing out that the areas from which

[1] The most famous text is Anatole France's *Thaïs*, 1889. But the viewpoint is the same in the criticisms formulated by Amélineau, Histoire de S. Pakhôme et de ses communautés, 1889; Histoire des monastères de Basse-Egypte, 1894.

[2] P. Ladeuze, *Etudes sur le cénobitisme pakhomien*, 1898, p. 327 (reprinted 1961).

[3] M.I. Finley, Manpower and the Fall of Rome, *Aspects of Antiquity, Discoveries and Controversies*, 1968, pp. 153–61.

[4] Jones, *The Later Roman Empire*, vol. II, p. 933, after showing that the monks worked in all sorts of economic spheres, concludes that they were a burden on the limited resources of the Empire.

[5] Evelyne Patlagean, La limitation de la fécondité dans la Haute-Epoque byzantine, 1969, pp. 1353–69.

most people came to the monasteries were those where large families flourished.[6] This is not impossible if we accept that contraception or infanticide were essentially ways to avoid having to divide inheritances and not means of improving women's lives.

In the two areas of historical unease about a movement which has lasted twenty centuries – immorality and demographic decline – its genesis and the years in which it was consolidated have perhaps not been given enough weight. In the case of Egypt, the division of inherited land, the considerable difference that existed between large and small properties, and a civilization which was known to 'accept all the children who were born'[7] might be enough to explain the control achieved by the departure of many men for the solitary life, who left their land to the community or who, taking their property with them to the monastic community, enabled people other than their own families, the poor of Egypt or Alexandria, to benefit from their harvest.[8] The monks worked and as the monastic experiment evolved, work came to be considered as the main safety mechanism in the life of solitude, the anchor of their calling.[9] This work, which was always more profitable than that of married men and fathers, constituted the means of looking after people who were exposed to a famine whose demographic effects must have been well known, namely famine-induced impotence and amenorrhoea. The main problem is thus not the reason why the Egyptian monks went off to the desert, except as regards a deeper analysis of the mystic solitude surrounding their departure, but the reason why this phenomenon met with such a response among the troubled Greek and Roman aristocracy which spread the word of these solitaries and imposed their example on the whole Graeco-Roman world.[10]

This was not easy, even if anchoritism, virginity and asceticism might seem to provide solutions to the various aspirations held in the Graeco-Roman world of the late Empire. As witness this exchange between

[6] Ambrose of Milan, De Virginitate, VII, 37.

[7] Strabo, XVII, 2, 5.

[8] On the trade between the khôra and the monks, see Annik Martin, L'Eglise et la khôra égyptienne au IVe siècle, 1979, pp. 18–25.

[9] A. Rousselle, Le modèle économique transmis par les régles orientales dans les oeuvres de saint Benoît d'Aniane, Etudes sur Pézenas et sa région, IV, pp. 5–23. Work emerges as of value in itself, and money and the object of work are of little significance. Inactivity is considered very dangerous: this is not a modern discovery. Michel Foucault, Histoire de la sexualité, vol. I, 1976, p. 12, challenges the notion that there is a historical link between sexual repression and the rise of capitalism, showing that there is an increase in discussions about sexuality. This is what we find among the monks in the desert who talked about it more and more as they repressed their sexual urges.

[10] On the conversion of the aristocracy, see P. R. L. Brown, Aspects of the Christianisation of the Roman Aristocracy, 1961, pp. 1–11; A. Chastagnol, Le sénateur Volusien et la conversion d'une famille de l'aristocratie romaine, 1965, p. 246 et seq.

Evagrius, who had come to the desert from the court of Constantinople, and Arsenius, the Roman senator who was a convert: ' "Wise and learned as we are, we have no virtue. How do these Egyptian peasants have so much?" Abba Arsenius replied: "We have nothing, for we have applied ourselves to the disciplines and knowledge of this world; but these peasants have achieved virtue through their own efforts." '[11] These educated nobles, trained in the art of discourse or philosophy, had first to free themselves from passions, whereas the Copts had only to free themselves from poverty. They knew that the desire to eat, the desire to clothe oneself, envy of another's property weighed heavily on a man's life. The rich Greeks and Romans of the Empire knew nothing of their bodies, and thought they had to free themselves from the affections and movements of the mind. They found in the desert that these were inextricably linked with the body. In this world of the late Empire, under the influence of Christian Emperors, the presence of the State made itself felt in daily life. A Christian minority outlawed pagan sacrifices and divination on pain of death.[12] Emperors of two Christian denominations successively repressed the supporters of the other sect, by exile and, for those who resisted, by torture or execution. The costs of war, whether civil or foreign, increased the annual tax on harvests and brought the scourge of the law down on insolvent land-owners. The citizen was no longer safe from corporal punishment or infamous execution. Freedom to sell, to buy, to move about was gradually restricted by the duty imposed on young men to succeed their fathers in their professions and in their honours which became a burden for them. Even though many agreed that this was the price of security, the restriction of civil liberties could open the way to the heady experience of internal freedom.

What the experience of solitude in Egypt taught these educated men who were struggling to live by their principles was the body's capacity for resisting all forms of isolation. Genital sexual desire, which was the most obvious form of the body's resistance, and which was sometimes defeated through fasting, was seen as the strongest sign of belonging to the world. Antony said that the solitary could cure himself of hearing and seeing. But in the end the monks had to admit that the desire to hear and to talk, to see and be seen remained as strong as the desire for sexual union. They hunted out all the reasons that each individual might find for satisfying this unquenchable need for communication: eating boiled cereals so as to have a reason to meet others at the mill, hiring oneself out at harvest time

[11] *PJ*, X, 5.
[12] Clémence Dupont, *Le droit criminel dans les Constitutions de Constantin*, I, 1954; II, 1955; Denise Grodzynski, Par la bouche de l'Empereur, in *Divination et rationalité*, introduced by J.-P. Vernant, 1974, pp. 267–95.

when one had already earned enough to live on for a year,[13] taking care of the sick, or helping pious women.[14] This is why this desire to see and be seen, to hear and to talk, to love, was channelled as far as possible into the monks' contact with God, a God above all whom they 'pictured'. Convinced that God was speaking to them through the magnificent words of the Gospel or Hosea, responding to this love with the splendid phrases of the Canticle or the naive and tender words of Peter, they added the face, the body, the hands which their hearts created for their God. When an old anthropomorphite was told that his God had no physical image, and that all his life he had been speaking to an image which did not exist, he went mad: 'Woe is me! They have taken away my God! I have nothing to hold on to! Who can I adore? Who can I talk to? I don't know any more'.[15]

Once this opportunity for contact with God had been lost, the solitary suffered in his cell, his only guide being the advice not to leave his cell again. He lay in wait for the least pleasure and rejected it. Abba Pior would eat what little food he had as he walked along.[16] The Fathers would sleep standing or sitting. To fight sleep Sisoes hung himself up above the precipice of Petra.[17] Pachomius slept leaning against a wall.[18] Work, the only activity possible, became a necessity. They limited the individual's choice of work, fixed the timetable for work, and when a disciple was called he had to stop in the middle of the letter he was tracing.[19]

The desert made it possible to examine the resources man draws on to fulfil his need for communication, a need which always involves the senses, revealing desire, the complement of the powers of attraction of other people and other things. But once the monks had recognized desire they quickly repressed it and then denied it, pushing out one temptation to desire after another. Although one of the *Sayings* says that one must not root out passions but resist them,[20] the monks began by trying to root them out. They developed ways of resisting in the same way one develops reflexes. Abba Poemen[21] and Abba Isidore[22] wept when they had to eat. John Cassian advised monks, after periods of effort, to try to practise resisting a mental image of a woman's body so as to measure the progress

---

[13] *PJ*, XIV, 14.
[14] *Coll.*, I, 10.
[15] *Coll.*, X, 3.
[16] *PJ*, IV, 34.
[17] Sisoes, 33.
[18] *Greek Life*, 14.
[19] *Inst.*, IV, 12; *PJ*, XIV, 5.
[20] *Anon.*, 35.
[21] Poemen, 13.
[22] *LH*, 1.

they had made,[23] until they could achieve total indifference. On the basis of the experiences in Egypt, and also those in Syria which were similar, and on this new knowledge of the body and the demands it makes on the mind through the indissoluble tie which unites them, a whole method of teaching was established to teach not only the excellence and the superiority of virginity, but also the means of attaining it. Once the mind had been freed by mastery of the body, the next step was to free the soul by repressing the body.

What might have been simply a short-lived phenomenon in an exploited Egypt came into contact both with male repugnance for marriage in Greek countries and with the aversion of the women of the Roman world to the legal and social conditions of marriage. Some men were able, through obedience, to develop the reflexes they needed to suppress the expression of desire. For the women of Greece and Rome exhortations to frigid but honourable conjugal duty made them into mothers who were quite ready to encourage their sons to adopt a competely new path.

[23] *Coll.*, XIX, 16.

Bibliography

Albinus, *Epitome*, tr. P. Louis, Nouvelle Collection de Textes et Documents, Belles-Lettres, Paris, 1945.

Amélineau, Histoire de S. Packhôme et de ses communautés, *Annales du Musée Guimet*, XVII, Paris, 1889.

—— Histoire des monastères de Basse-Egypte, *Annales du Musée Guimet*, XXV, 1894.

Ammianus Marcellinus, *History*, tr. in 3 vols., John C. Rolfe, Loeb Classical Library, Heinemann, London, 1935–39.

André, J., *L'alimentation et la cuisine à Rome*, Paris, 1961.

Andreev, M., Divorce et adultère dans le droit romain classique, *RHD*, 1957.

Antin, P., La vieillesse chez saint Jérôme, *Revue des Etudes augustiniennes*, XVII, 1971.

Antony, Saint, *Letters: The Letters of St Antony the Great*, tr. D. Chitty, Oxford, 1975.

—— *Life of*, see under Athanasius.

Apophtegmata Patrum: W. Bousset, *Apophtegmata*, Tübingen, 1923, reproduces all the original texts in the languages in which they have survived. The Greek *Apophtegmata* exist in two forms: the first is an alphabetical series listing the sayings attributed to each of the Fathers, to which must be added the anonymous sayings, and the second is a systematic collection.

—— Alphabetical series: *PG* 65, 71–440, tr. Benedicta Ward, *The Sayings of the Desert Fathers*, Mowbray, London, 1975, revised 1981. French trs. J.-C. Guy, *Les Apophtegmes des Pères du désert*, photocopies available from the Abbaye de Bellefontaine; L. Regnault, *Les Sentences des Pères du désert*, with intro., Solesmes, 1981.

—— Anonymous apophthegms: a selection tr. Benedicta Ward, *The Wisdom of the Desert Fathers*, SLG Press, Oxford, 1975. Some ed. F. Nau, *Revue de l'Orient chrétien*, 1907–13.

—— Systematic collection: Latin tr. Pelagius and John, *PL*, 73, 851–1022. French tr. J. Dion et G. Oury, *Les Sentences des Pères du désert*, intro. L. Regnault, Solesmes, 1976 and 1977. Two other collections have been published, Solesmes, 1976 and 1977. J.-C. Guy, *Paroles des Anciens*, Paris, 1976, gives a French tr. of the texts common to both collections, which represent the oldest material.

Aristotle, *Generation of Animals*, tr. A. L. Peck, Loeb Classical Library, Heinemann, London, 1943.

—— *History of Animals*, tr. A. L. Peck, Loeb Classical Library, Heinemann, London, 1970.

Astolfi, R., I beni vacanti e la legislazione caducaria, *Bolletino dell'Istituto di Diritto romano*, vol. LXVIII, 3rd series, 1965.

—— Note per una valutazione storica della lex Julia et Papia, *SDHI*, vol. XXXIX, 1973.

—— *La Lex Julia et Papia*, Padua, 1970.

Athanasius, Saint, *De fuga sua*, PG, XXV; tr. in A Select Library of Nicene and Post-Nicene Fathers of the Christian Church, 2nd series, vol. IV.

—— *Historia Arianorum ad monachos*, PG, XXV; tr. in A Select Library of Nicene and Post-Nicene Fathers of the Christian Church, 2nd series, vol. IV.

—— *Life of Antony*, this work was translated into Latin twice shortly after it had first been written in Greek. One of these translations is given in *Vita di Antonio*, critical text and commentary by G. J. M. Bartelink, Italian tr. P. Citati and S. Lilla, Vite dei Santi, ed. Christine Mohrmann, Mondadori, 1974; the other, by Evagrius of Antioch, is to be found in *PG*, 26, col. 835–976. English trs. Robert T. Meyer, Ancient Christian Writers, 10, 1950; and in A Select Library of Nicene and Post-Nicene Fathers of the Christian Church, 2nd series, vol. IV. French tr. from the Greek, Benoît Lavaud, in *Vies des pères du désert*, Lettres chrétiennes, 4, Paris, 1961.

Audollent, A., *Defixionum Tabellae*, 1904.

Augustine, *De bono conjugali*, and *De adulterinis conjugiis*, tr. in The Fathers of the Church, vol. 27.

—— Letters, tr. in Fathers of the Church, vols. 12, 18, 20, 32.

—— *Select Letters*, tr. J. H. Baxter, Loeb Classical Library, Heinemann, London, 1953.

Baldwin, Barry, The Career of Oribasius, *Acta Classica*, XVIII, 1975.

Bardy, G., Saint Augustin et les médecins, *L'Année théologique augustinienne*, 13, 1953.

Basil of Ancyra, *De Virginitate*, included among the works of Basil of Caesarea, *PG*, XXX, col, 669–809; fragments in old Slavic, A. Vaillant, Institut d'Etudes slaves, III, Paris, 1943.

Basil of Caesarea, *Asceticon*, PG, 31, 889–1306; Latin tr. by Rufinus, in Benedict of Aniane, *Codex Regularum* and *Concordia Regularum*, PL, 103; English tr. *The Ascetic Works of St. Basil*, tr. W. K. Lowther Clarke, SPCK, 1925, and in The Fathers of the Church, vol. 9, tr. Sister H. Monica Wagner, Catholic University of America Press, Washington, 1962. Italian tr. of Greek text E. Leggio, *L'Ascetica di s. Basilio il Grande*, 1934; French tr. Father Léon Lèbe, Maredsous, 1969.

—— Letters, tr. R. J. Deferrari, Loeb Classical Library, Heinemann, London, 1926–39; and in A Select Library of Nicene and Post-Nicene Fathers of the Christian Church, vol. VIII.

Baur, C., *Johannes Chrysostomus*, Munich, 1930.

Belmont, Nicole, Levana ou comment 'élever' les enfants, *Annales (Economies, Sociétés, Civilisations)*, 1973.

Benabou, M., *La résistance africaine à la romanisation*, Paris, 1976.

Bernardi, J., *La prédication des Pères cappadociens*, Paris, 1968.

Besnier, R., L'application des lois caducaires d'Auguste d'après le Gnomon de l'Idiologue, *Mélanges de Visscher*, I, *RIDA*, vol. II, 1949.

—— Pline le Jeune et l'application des lois démographiques, *Mélanges J. Dauvilliers*, Toulouse, 1979.

Bianchi, U., Le 'gnosticisme syrien', carrefour de fois, *Mélanges M. Simon, Paganisme, Judaïsme, Christianisme*, Paris, 1978.

Bidez, J., *Recherches sur la tradition manuscrite des lettres de l'empereur Julien*, Brussels, 1898.

Bidez, J., and Cumont, F., *Les mages hellénisés*, Paris, 1938 (2nd printing 1973).

Bonneau, D., *La crue du Nil, divinité égyptienne à travers mille ans d'histoire* (332 BC–AD 641), Paris, 1964.

Boswell, J., *Christianity, Social Tolerance and Homosexuality*, The University of Chicago Press, 1980.

Bourgey, L., *Observation et expérience chez les médecins de la collection hippocratique*, Paris, 1953.

Brisson, J.-P., *Gloire et misère de l'Afrique chrétienne*, Paris, 1948.

Brown, P. R. L., Aspects of the Christianisation of The Roman Aristocracy, *Journal of Roman Studies*, LI, 1961.

Bucher, Bernadette, *La négresse aux seins pendants*, Paris, 1977.

—— Les fantasmes du conquérant in Lévi-Strauss, 1979, *q.v.*

Caelius Aurelianus, '*Gynaecia*'. *Fragments of a Latin version of Soranus* '*Gynaecia*' *from a thirteenth century manuscript*, ed. Miriam F. Drabkin, Baltimore, 1951.

—— *On Acute Diseases*, ed. and tr. I. E. Drabkin, University of Chicago Press, 1960.

—— *Chronic Diseases*, ed. and tr. I. E. Drabkin, Chicago, 1960.

Camelot, T., Les Traités *de virginitate* au IVe siécle, in *Mystique et continence*, travaux scientifiques du VIIe Congrès international d'Avon, Etudes carmélitaires, Desclée, 1952.

Cantarella, Eva, Adulterio, Omicidio legittimo e causa d'onore in Diritto Romano, *Studi G. Scherillo*, I, Milan, 1972.

Carcopino, J., La table de Velleia et son importance historique, *Revue des Etudes anciennes*, 1921.

—— *Aspects mystiques de la Rome païenne*, Paris, 1941.

—— *Daily Life in Ancient Rome*, tr. E. O. Lorimer, Routledge, London, 1941, Penguin, 1956, reprinted 1978.

Cardascia, G., L'apparition dans le droit des classes d' 'honestiores' et d' 'humiliores', *RHD*, 1950.

Cassian, John, *Collationes*, tr. in A Select Library of Nicene and Post-Nicene Fathers of the Christian Church, 2nd series, vol. XI; intro., Latin text, French tr. and notes E. Pichery, SC, 42, 1955; 54, 1958; 64, 1959 (reprinted 1966 and 1971).

—— *De Institutis coenobiorum*, tr. in A Select Library of Nicene and Post-Nicene Fathers of the Christian Church, 2nd series, vol. XI; revised Latin text, intro., French tr. and notes J.-C. Guy, SC, 109, Paris, 1965.

Chadwick, O., *John Cassian, a Study in primitive Monasticism*, Cambridge, 1950.

Charles-Picard, G., L'épisode de Baubô et les mystères d'Eleusis, *Revue de l'Histoire des Religions*, 1927.

—— Les *sacerdotes Saturni* et les sacrifices humains dans l'Afrique romaine, *RSAC*, 66, 1948.

—— *Les religions de l'Afrique antique*, Paris, 1954.

—— *La civilisation de l'Afrique romaine*, Paris, 1959.

Chastagnol, A., Le sénateur Volusien et la conversion d'une famille de l'aristocratie romaine, *Revue des Etudes Anciennes*, LVIII, 1965.

Chitty, Derwas, *The Desert a city*, Oxford, 1977.

Chrysostom, John, *PG*, vol. 47–64. Complete French tr. J. Bareille, 19 vol., Paris, 1865–73. Twelve vols. of the collection Les Sources chrétiennes are devoted to him.

—— *Les cohabitations suspectes. Comment observer la virginité*, ed. and French tr. Jean Dumortier, Nouvelle Collection de textes et de documents, Les Belles-Lettres, Paris, 1955.

—— *Lettres à Olympias*, ed. and French tr. A.-M. Malingrey, SC, 13, Paris, 1947 and 1968.

—— *De Virginitate*, ed. and French tr. B. Grillet, SC, 125, 1966.

—— *Homilies*, English tr. in Library of the Fathers of the Holy Catholic Church, vol. IV, Oxford, 1839.

Clavreul, J., *L'ordre médical*, Paris, 1978.

Codex Theodosianus, ed. T. Mommsen, Berlin, 1905, reprinted Zurich, 1971; English tr. C. Pharr, *Theodosian Code and Novels, and the Sirmondian Constitutions*, Greenwood Press, London, 1952.

Corpus Juris Civilis, I, *Institutiones*, ed. P. Krueger; tr. R. W. Lee, *The elements of Roman Law*, London, 4th ed. 1956.

—— *Digesta*, ed. T. Mommsen, P. Krueger, Berlin, 1928, reprinted Zurich, 1970.

—— II, *Codex Justinianus*, ed. P. Krueger, Berlin, 1915, reprinted Zurich, 1970.

Courcelle, P., *Les lettres grecques en Occident de Macrobe à Cassiodore*, Paris, 1943, 2nd ed. 1948.

Crouzel, H., *L'Eglise primitive face au divorce*, Collection 'Théologie historique', 13, Paris, 1971.

Cumont, F., *Les religions orientales dans le paganisme romain*, Paris, 4th ed. 1929, reprinted 1963.

—— *Recherches sur le symbolisme funéraire des Romains*, Paris, 1942, reprinted 1966.

Cyprian, Saint, *Letters*, tr. in Library of the Fathers of the Holy Catholic Church, vol. 3, 1839; ed. and French tr. L. Bayard, CUF, 1925.

Daremberg, C., Saglio, E., and Pottier, E. *Dictionnaire des Antiquités grecques et romaines*, Paris, 1877–1919.

de Castro, Josué, *Géopolitique de la faim*, Paris, 2nd ed. 1952.

de Clercq, L'influence de la règle de saint Pachôme en Occident, *Mélanges L. Halphen*, Paris, 1951.

Decret, F. and Fantar, M., *L'Afrique du Nord dans l'Antiquité*, Paris, 1981.

de la Croix, Jean, *La montée du Carmel*, Desclée, 1942.

Delcourt, Marie, Utrumque neutrum, *Mélanges d'Histoire des Religions offerts à H.-Ch. Puech*, Paris, 1976.

Delehaye, H., *Sanctus, Essai sur le culte des saints*, Brussels, 1927.

Demont, P., Remarques sur le sens de τρεφω, *Revue des Etudes grecques*, vol. XCI, 1978.

de Sainte-Croix, G. E. M., Aspects of the 'Great' Persecution, *Harvard Theological Review*, 47, 1954.

Desclaux, P., Ramon, C., Famine et vie sexuelle de l'homme civilisé, in *Nutrition et fonctions de reproduction*, Paris, 1952, Réunions d'études du Centre national de Coordination des études et recherches sur la nutrition et l'alimentation, Paris, 1953.

Desprez, Father Vincent, *Règles monastiques d'Occident d'Augustin à Ferréol*, intro., note and French tr., Bellefontaine, 'Monachisme Occidental' collection, 9.

Détienne, M., *Dionysos mis à mort*, Paris, 1977.

de Villefosse, Héron, *Musée africain du Louvre*.

Diodorus of Sicily, *The Library of History*, tr. C. H. Oldfather, Loeb Classical Library, Heinemann, London.

Dolto, F., *La difficulté de vivre*, Paris, 1981.

Dover, K. J., *Greek Homosexuality*, Cambridge, Mass., 1978.

Duminil, M.-P., La description des vaisseaux dans les chapitres 11–19 du Traité de la Nature des os, *Hippocratica*, Colloques internationaux du Centre national de la Recherche scientifique, no. 583, *Actes* du Colloque hippocratique de Paris (1978), CNRS, Paris, 1980.

Dupont, Clémence, *Le Droit criminel dans les Constitutions de Constantin*, Lille, 1954–5.

Dupont, Florence, *Le plaisir et la loi*, Paris, 1977.

Dupont-Sommer, A., *Le IVe Livre des Maccabées*, intro., French tr. and notes, Bibliothèque de l'Ecole des Hautes Etudes, fasc. 274, Paris, 1939.

Durry, M., *CRAI*, 1955; Le mariage des filles impubères dans la Rome antique, *RIDA*, 3rd series, vol. 2, 1955.

—— Sur le mariage romain, *RIDA*, 3rd series, vol. 3, 1956, reproduced in *Mélanges M. Durry*, *REL*, 47 *bis*, 1970.

Edelstein, L. E., The development of Greek anatomy, *Bull. Hist. Med.*, 1935, vol. 3.

Epiphanius of Salamis, *Panarion, (On Heresies)*, ed. K. Holl, *Epiphanius (Ancoratus und Panarion)*, vol. I, GCS, Leipzig, 1915.

Escoffier-Lambiotte, Dr, La résistance au jeûne, *Le Monde*, 20 May, 1981.

Etheria, *Journal de voyage*, ed. and French tr. H. Pétré, SC, 21, 1964.

Etienne, R., La conscience médicale antique et la vie des enfants, *Annales de démographie historique*, 1973.

Eusebius, *History of the Church from Christ to Constantine*, tr. with intro. G. A. Williamson, Penguin, 1965; ed. and French tr. G. Bardy, SC, 31, 41, 55, 73, Paris, 1958, reprinted 1965–71.

Eyben, Emiel, Antiquity's view of puberty, *Latomus*, vol. 31, 1972.

Eydoux, H.-P., *La France antique*, Plon, Paris, 1962.

Fabre, P., *Saint Paulin de Nole et l'amitié chrétienne*, Paris, 1946.

Festugière, A.-J., *Trois dévots païens*, Paris, 1944.

—— *Antioche païenne et chrétienne, Libanius, Chrysostome et les moines de Syrie*, Paris, 1959.

—— *Les Moines d'Orient, Enquête sur les moines d'Egypte*, Paris, 1964.

Février, P.-A., Guéry, R., Les rites funéraires de la nécropole de Sétif, *Antiquités africaines*, 15, 1980.

Finley, M. I., *Manpower and the Fall of Rome, Aspects of Antiquity, Discoveries and Controversies*, London, 1968.

Fliche, A., and Martin, V., ed., *Histoire de l'Eglise*, vol. III, *De la Paix Constantinienne á la mort de Théodose*, by J. R. Palanque, G. Bardy, P. de Labriolle, Paris, 1950.

Fontanille, M.-Th., *Avortement et contraception dans la médecine gréco-romaine*, Laboratoires Searle, Paris, 1977.

Forbes, R. J., *Studies in ancient technology*, vol. III, Leyden, 1950.

Foucault, Michel, *Histoire de la sexualité*, Paris, 1976.

France, Anatole, *Thaïs*, Paris, 1889.

Frazer, J., *Adonis, Attis, Osiris*, 3rd ed., vol. 1, London, 1914.

Fredouille, J.-C., *Tertullien et la conversion de la culture antique*, Paris, 1972.

Frend, W. H. C., Paulinus of Nola and the last century of the Western Empire, *Journal of Roman Studies*, 59, 1969.

Galen, ed. C. G. Kühn, 20 vols., Leipzig, 1821–30.

—— *Oeuvres anatomiques, physiologiques et médicales de Galien*, French tr. by C. Daremberg, 2 vols., Paris, 1854–6.

—— *On the Affected Parts*, tr. with explanatory notes, Rudolph E. Siegel, Karger, Basel, London, 1976.

—— *On the Natural Faculties*, tr. A.J. Brock, Loeb Classical Library, Heinemann, London, 1916.

—— *On anatomical procedures*, tr. W. L. H. Duckworth, ed. M. C. Lyons and B. Towers, CUP, 1962.

Galley, P., *La vie de Grégoire de Nazianze*, Paris, 1943.

Gaudemet, Jean, 'Justum Matrimonium', *Mélanges de Visscher*, I, *RIDA*, vol. 2, 1949 = *Sociétés et Mariage*, Strasbourg, 1980.

—— La décision de Callixte en matière de mariage, *Studi in onore di Ugo Enrico Paoli*, Florence, 1955 = *Sociétés et Mariage*, Strasbourg, 1980.

—— *L'Eglise dans l'Empire romain, IVe-Ve siècle*, Paris, 1958.

—— *Le droit privé romain*, Paris, 1974.

Germain, Louis R. F., L'exposition des enfants nouveau-nés dans la Grèce ancienne, aspects sociologiques, *Recueils de la Société Jean-Bodin*, XXXV: *L'enfant*, 1st part, Brussels, 1975.

Gori, R., L'hystérie, état limite entre l'impensable et la représentation, in *L'interdit de la représentation*, conference held in Montpellier 30 May, 1981, ed. Adélie and Jean-Jacques Rassial, Paris, 1983.

Goria, Fausto, Ricerche su impedimento da adulterio e obbligo di repudio da Giustiniano a Leone VI, *SDHI*, XXXIX, 1973.

Gourévitch, D., Le dossier philologique du nyctalope, *Hippocratica*, Colloque de Paris, CNRS, Paris, 1980.

Graillot, H., *Le culte de Cybèle, mère des dieux, à Rome et dans l'Empire romain*, Paris, 1912.

Grégoire, H., *Les persécutions dans l'Empire romain*, Brussels, 1951.

Gregory of Nyssa, *De Virginitate*, in A Select Library of Nicene and Post-Nicene Fathers of the Christian Church, 2nd series, vol. V; ed., French tr. and intro. M. Aubineau, SC, 119, Paris, 1966.

Gribomont, J., *Histoire du texte des Ascétiques de saint Basile* (Bibliothèque du Museon, 32), Louvain, 1953.

Grimal, P., *L'amour à Rome*, Paris, 1963.

Grmek, M. D., La légende et la réalité de la nocivité des fèves, *History and Philosophy of the Life Sciences*, vol. 2, 1980.

Grodzynski, Denise, Par la bouche de l'Empereur, in *Divination et rationalité*, intro. J.-P. Vernant, Paris, 1974.

Gsell, S., Les premiers temps de la Carthage romaine, *Revue historique*, 1927.

—— Les statues du temple de Mars Ultor à Rome, *Revue archéologique*, 34.

Guy, J.-C., *Recherches sur la tradition grecque des 'Apophtegmata Patrum'*, Subsidia Hagiographica, 36, Brussels, 1962; see also under *Apophtegmata Patrum*.

Harnack, A., Medicinisches aus der ältesten Kirchengeschichte, *Texte und Untersuchungen zur Geschichteder altchristlichen Literatur*, Heft 4, 1892.

Hartmann, F., *L'Agriculture dans l'ancienne Egypte*, Paris, 1923.

Haussleiter, J., *Der Vegetarismus in der Antike* (Religiongeschichtliche Versuche und Vorarbeiten Bd. XXIV), Berlin, 1935.

Hermas, *Shepherd*, tr. in Early Church Classics, 2 vols., SPCK, 1903; intro., critical text and notes R. Joly, SC, 53, Paris, 1958.

Hippocrates, tr. W. H. S. Jones and E. T. Withington, Loeb Classical Library, Heinemann, London, 1923–43.

—— *Hippocratic Writings*, ed. G. E. R. Lloyd, tr. J. Chadwick and W. N. Mann et al., Penguin, 1978.

—— *On Superfoetation and In the Surgery*, ed. and tr. J. N. Mattock and M. C. Lyons and J. N. Mattock, Cambridge, 1978.

—— *On Superfoetation and In the Surgery*, ed. and tr. J. N. Mattock, and M. C. Lyons, Cambridge, 1968.

—— *Oeuvres complètes*, ed. and French tr. E. Littré, Paris, 1839–61.

—— *Generation* and *Nature of the child*, French tr. R. Joly, *Hippocrate*, vol. XI, CUF, Les Belles-Lettres, Paris, 1970.

Hippolytus of Rome, *Philosophumena or The refutation of all heresies*, tr. F. Legge, 2 vols., SPCK, London, 1921; French tr. A. Siouville, Les Textes du Christianisme, Paris, 1928; ed. of Greek text P. Wendland, GCS, 26, Leipzig, 1919.

—— *Apostolic Tradition*, tr. Burton Scott Easton, Cambridge, 1934; intro., French tr. and notes B. Botte, SC, 11, Paris, 1968.

Historia Monachorum in Aegypto, ed. A. J. Festugière, *Subsidia Hagiographica*, 34, Société des Bollandistes, 1961; tr. Norman Russell, *The Lives of the Desert Fathers*, Mowbray, London, 1980; French tr. Festugière, *Les Moines d'Orient*, IV, I, *Enquête sur les moines d'Egypte*, Paris, 1964; Latin tr. Rufinus, *PL*, 21, 387–462.

Jaccard, R., *L'exil intérieur, schizoïdie et civilisation*, Paris, 1975.

Jerome, *Letters and Select Works*, tr. W. H. Fremantle, in A Select Library of Nicene and Post-Nicene Fathers of the Christian Church, 2nd series, vol. VI; and *Letters* tr. Charles Christopher Mierow, Ancient Christian Writers series, no. 33, 1963; *Correspondence*, ed. and French tr. J. Labourt, 8 vols., CUF, Paris, 1949–63.

Johnson, A. C., *Roman Egypt to the Reign of Diocletian*, in Tenney Frank, *An Economic Survey of Ancient Rome*, vol. V, Baltimore, 1936.

Jonas, H., *The Gnostic Religion*, Boston, 1958, 1963, 1970.

Jones, A. H. M., St. John Chrysostom's Parentage, *Harvard Theological Review*, 46, 1953.

—— *The Later Roman Empire*, Oxford, 1964.

Julian, Emperor, tr. W. C. Wright, Loeb Classical Library, Heinemann, London, 1913–23; *Oeuvres complètes*, ed. and French tr. J. Bidez, CUF, 1960.

Kajanto, Iro. On Divorce Among the Common People of Rome, *Mélanges Marcel Durry, 1970 = REL, 47 bis*.

Ladeuze, P., *Etudes sur le cénobitisme pakhomien*, Paris, 1898, reprinted Frankfurt, 1961.

Laffont, A., *Manuel de gynécologie*, Paris, 1952.

Lassère, J. M., *Ubique Populus*, Paris, 1978.

Leca, A. P., *La médecine égyptienne au temps des Pharaons*, Paris, 1971.

Le Gall, J., La 'nouvelle plèbe' et la sportule quotidienne, *Mélanges d'Archéologie et d'Histoire offerts à A. Piganiol*, Paris, 1966.

Leglay, M., *Saturne africain, Histoire*, Paris, 1966.

Leisegang, H., *La gnose*, Paris, 1951.

Lemossé, Maxime, L'enfant sans famille en droit romain, *Recueils de la Société Jean-Bodin*, XXXV: *L'enfant*, 1st part, Brussels, 1975.

Lepelley, Claude, *L'Empire romain et le christianisme*, Paris, 1969.

—— Iuvenes et circoncellions: les derniers sacrifices humains de l'Afrique antique, *Antiquités africaines*, 15, 1980.

Le Roy Ladurie, E., L'aménorrhée de famine (XVIIe–XXe siècle), *Annales ESC*, 1969, reproduced in *Le territoire de l'historien*, Paris, 1973.

Lévi-Strauss, C., *Textes de et sur Lévi-Strauss*, collected R. Belloun and C. Clément, Paris, 1979.

Libanius, *Selected Orations*, 2 vols., tr. A. F. Norman, Loeb Classical Library, Heinemann, London, 1969, 1977.

—— *Moral Discourses*, intro., text and French tr. B. Schouler, Paris, 1973.

Magne, J., Klasma, Sperma, Poimnion, Le voeu pour le rassemblement de Didaché, IX, 4, *Mélanges d'Histoire des Religions offerts à H.-Ch. Puech*, Paris, 1974.

Maistre, C., *Les déclarations d'innocence, Livre des Morts*, Cairo, 1937.

Mannoni, Maud, *Education impossible*, Le Seuil, collection 'Le Champ freudien', Paris, 1973.

Manson, M., Le temps à Rome d'après les monnaies, in Aiôn, Le temps chez les Romains, *Caesarodunum X bis*, published by R. Chevallier, Paris, 1976.

Manuli, Paola, Fisiologia e patologia del femminile negli scritti ippocratici dell'antica ginecologia greca, *Hippocratica*, Colloque de Paris, CNRS, Paris, 1980.

Marquardt, J., *Das Privatleben der Römer*, 2nd ed. A. Mau, Leipzig, 1886; French tr. Paris, 1982.

Marrou, H.-I., *Histoire de l'éducation dans l'Antiquité*, Seuil, Paris, 1965.

Martin, Annik, L'Eglise et la khôra égyptienne au IVe siècle, *Revue des Etudes augustiniennes*, XXV, 1979.

Melania, *Life of*, Greek text, intro. and notes D. Gorce, SC, 90, Paris, 1962.

Methodius of Olympus, *The Symposium, a treatise on chastity*, (also known as the *Banquet*) tr. and annotated H. Musurillo, Ancient Christian Writers, 27, 1958; *Banquet*, ed. H. Musurillo, French tr. and notes, V.-H. Debidour, SC, 95, 1963.

Minucius Felix, *Octavius*, tr. Gerald H. Rendall, Loeb Classical Library, Heinemann, London, 1931; French tr. Jean Beaujeu, CUF, 1964.

Modrzejewski, J., La règle de Droit dans l'Egypte romaine (Etat des questions et perspectives de recherches), Proceedings of the Twelfth International Congress of Papyrology, ed. Deborah Samuel, *American Studies in Papyrology*, 7, Toronto, 1970.

—— Zum hellenistischen Ehegüterrecht im griechischen und römischen Aegypten, *Zeitschrift der Savigny Stiftung für Rechtgeschichte; romanistische Abteilung*, 87, 1970.

Molè, Marcello, Stuprum, *Novisimo Digesto Italiano*, XVIII, 1971.

Mommsen, T., *Le droit pénal romain*, II, in Mommsen, T., Marquardt, J., and Krüger, P., *Manuel des Antiquités romaines*, French tr., Paris, 1907.

Monceaux, P., *Etude sur la littérature latine d'Afrique. Les païens*, Paris, 1894.

Moreau, J., *La persécution du christianisme*, Paris, 1956.

Musurillo, H., The problem of ascetical fasting in the Greek patristic writers, *Traditio*, XII, 1956.

Naldini, *Il cristianesimo in Egitto. Lettere private nei papiri dei secoli II–IV*, Florence, 1968, no. 93.

Natali, A., Christianisme et cité à la fin du IVe siècle d'après Jean Chrysostome, *Jean Chrysostome et Augustin*, Actes du Colloque de Chantilly, 1975, ed. C. Kannengiesser.

Nehlig, Y., *Le rôle des femmes dans l'Eglise du Ier au IIIe siècle*, master's thesis, Institut protestant de Théologie, Bibliothèque de la Faculté de Théologie de Montpellier, 1981.

Nock, A. D., Eunuchs in Ancient Religion, *Archiv für Religionswissenschaft*, 23, 1925.

Noonan, J.-T., *Contraception. A History of its Treatment by the Catholic theologians and Canonists*, Harvard University Press, Cambridge, Mass., 1966.

Oribasius, *Collection Médicale* (including the *Libri Incerti*), ed. and French tr. U. Bussemaker and C. Daremberg, 6 vols., Paris, 1851; vol. VI by A. Molinier.

—— *Corpus Medicorum Graecorum*, VI, I, 1–2; II, 1–2, ed. J. Raeder, 1928–33.

Orosius, *Historia adversum Paganos*, tr. in Fathers of the Church, vol. 50.

Pachomius, *Life of. First Greek Life*, ed. F. Halkin, *Sancti Pachomii Vitae Graecae*, Société des Bollandistes; English tr. Apostolos N. Athanassakis, Scholars Press, Missoula, Mont., 1975; Festugière, *Les moines d'Orient*, IV^2, *La première vie grecque de saint Pachôme*, Paris, 1965, gives a French tr.

—— *La vie latine de saint Pachôme*, tr. from the Greek by Dionysius Exiguus (6th century), critical ed. J. Van Cranenburgh, Brussels, 1969, which includes the text of the second *Greek Life*.

—— *Life of St. Pachomius and His Disciples*, tr. from Coptic, Greek and Latin, A. Veilleux, Cistercian Publications, 1982.

—— *Pachomiana latina*, critical ed. by A. Boon of Jerome's Latin tr. of Pachomius' *Rule*, his *Letters*, the *Rule* of his successor Theodorus, and the *Teachings* of the third leader of the community, Horsiesios, Bibliothèque de la Revue d'Histoire ecclésiastique, fasc. 7, Louvain, 1932. French tr. of this Latin version P. Deseille, *L'esprit du monachisme pachômien*, 'Spiritualité orientale' collection, no. 2, Abbaye de Bellefontaine, photocopied; *Chronicles and Rules*, tr. A. Veilleux, Cistercian Publications, 1982; *Instructions, Letters and other Writings of St. Pachomius and his disciples*, tr. A. Veilleux, Cistercian Publications, 1983.

Palladius, *Lausiac History*, tr. Robert T. Meyer, Longman, 1965; (*La Storia Lausica*), intro. Christine Mohrmann, critical text and commentary G. J. M. Bartelink, Italian tr. M. Barchiesi, Mondadori, 1974; Greek text ed. Dom C. Butler, Cambridge, I, 1898, II, 1904; French tr. A. Lucot, Paris, 1912; the oldest Latin version attributed to Paschasius, *PL*, 74, 243–342.

Paschoud, F., Entretiens de la Fondation Hardt, XIX, *Le culte des souverains dans l'Empire romain*, Geneva, 1973.

Passio Perpetuae et Felicitatis, ed. and tr. H. Musurillo, The Acts of the Christian Martyrs, Clarendon Press, Oxford, 1972; French tr. France Quéré-Jaulmes, *La femme*, Paris, 1968.

Patlagean, Evelyne, La limitation de la fécondité dans la Haute-Epoque byzantine, *Annales ESC*, 1969.

Paul of Aegina, French tr. of his book on surgery, R. Briau, Paris, 1855.

Paulinus, *The Poems of St. Paulinus of Nola*, P.G. Walsh, Ancient Christian Writers, 40, Newman Press, New York, 1975.

Pauly, A. and Wissowa, G., *Realencyclopädie der classischen Altertumswissenschaft*, Stuttgart, 1893.

Pease, A. S., Medical allusions in the work of St. Jerome, *Harvard Studies in Classical Philology*, 25, 1914.

Piganiol, A., Les *Trinqui* gaulois, gladiateurs consacrés, in *Recherches sur les Jeux romains*, Strasbourg-Paris, 1923.

Plassard, J., *Le concubinat romain sous le Haut Empire*, Paris, 1921.

Pliny, *Letters*, tr. in 2 vols. by Betty Radice, Loeb Classical Library, Heinemann, London, 1969.

Plutarch, *Lives*, tr. in 11 vols. Bernadette Perrin, Loeb Classical Library, Heinemann, London, 1967.

Poinssot, L. and Quoniam, P., Bêtes d'amphitéâtre sur trois mosaïques du Bardo, *Karthago*, III, 1951–2.

Porphyry, *De Abstinencia*, tr. Thomas Taylor, ed. and intro. Esme Wynne-Tyson, Centaur Press, 1965; intro. and ed. J. Bouffartigue and M. Patillon, 2 vols., CUF, Paris, 1977 and 1979.

—— *Life of Pythagoras. Letter to Marcella*, ed. and French tr. E. des Places,

CUF, Paris, 1982; *Letter to Marcella* also given in French tr. in Festugière, *Trois dévots païens*, Paris, 1944.

Préaux, Claire, *L'économie royale des Lagides*, Brussels, 1939.

Prudentius, ed. and tr. H. H. Thomson, Loeb Classical Library, Heinemann, London, 1961; text and French tr. M. Lavarenne, CUF, Paris, 1963.

Puech, H.-C., *Sur le manichéisme et autres essais*, Paris, 1979.

Puschmann, T., *Alexander von Tralles*.

Quispel, G., La conception de l'homme dans la gnose valentinienne, *Eranos-Jahrbuch*, vol. XV, 1947.

Règles monastiques d'Occident d'Augustin à Ferréol (French tr.), intro. and note by Father Vincent Desprez, Bellefontaine, 'Monachisme occidental' collection, 9.

Reinach, S., Le rire rituel, *Revue de l'Université de Bruxelles*, 1911.

—— La naissance d'Eve, *Revue de l'Histoire des Religions*, 78, 1918.

Resch, P., *La doctrine ascétique des premiers maîtres égyptiens du quatrième siècle*, Paris, 1931.

Rey, Abel, *La science dans l'Antiquité*, II: *La jeunesse de la science grecque*, Paris, 1933.

Riché, P., *Education et culture dans l'Occident barbare*, Paris, 1962.

Richet, C. and Delbarre, F., *L'insuffisance alimentaire*, Paris, 1950.

Robin, R., *Histoire et linguistique*, Paris, 1973.

Rousselle, A., La persécution des chrétiens à Alexandrie au IIIe siècle, *RHD*, 1974.

—— Abstinence et continence dans les monastères de Gaule méridionale à la fin de l'Antiquité et au début du Moyen Age; Etude d'un régime alimentaire et de sa fonction, in *Hommages à André Dupont, Etudes médiévales languedociennes*, Montpellier, 1974.

—— Le modèle économique transmis par les règles orientales dans les oeuvres de saint Benoît d'Aniane, *Etudes sur Pézenas et sa région*, IV, 1975.

—— Du sanctuaire au thaumaturge: la guérison en Gaule au IVe siècle, *Annales (Economies, Sociétés, Civilisations)*, 1976.

—— Aspects sociaux du recrutement ecclésiastique, *MEFRA*, 89, 1977.

—— Observation féminine et idéologie masculine; le corps de la femme d'après les médecins grecs, *Annales (Economies, Sociétés, Civilisations)*, 1980.

—— Paulin de Nole et Sulpice Sévère, hagiographes, in *Les Saints et les Stars. Le texte hagiographique dans la culture populaire*, ed. J.-C. Schmitt, Paris, 1983.

Ruesche, F., *Blut, Leben, Seele*, Paderborn, 1930.

Rufus of Ephesus, ed. and French tr. C. Daremberg and E. Ruelle, Paris, 1879.

Sagnard, F.-M., *La gnose valentinienne et le témoignage de saint Irénée*, Paris, 1947.

Sallust, *Bellum Jugurthinum*, tr. J.C. Rolfe, Loeb Classical Library, Heinemann, London, 1980.

Sallustius, *Concerning the Gods and the Universe*, ed. and tr. Arthur Darby Nock, CUP, 1926; *Des dieux et du monde*, text and French tr. G. Rochefort, CUF, 1960. Also given in French tr. in Festugière, *Trois dévôts païens*, 1944.

Sarton, George, *Galen of Pergamon*, University of Kansas Press, Lawrence, 1954.

Saumagne, C., La persécution de Dèce en Afrique d'après la correspondance de saint Cyprien, *Byzantion*, XXXII, 1962.

Sauneron, S., Le germe dans les os, *BIFAO*, 1960, vol. 60.

Scriptores Historiae Augustae, ed. and tr. D. Magie, vol. 1, London, 1921.

Soranus of Ephesus, ed. and Latin tr. C. G. Kühn, Leipzig, 1827, vol. III; and by J. Ilberg, Teubner, Leipzig-Berlin, 1927 (*Corpus medicorum graecorum*, IV). English tr. and notes by Owsei Temkin, *Soranus' Gynecology*, Johns Hopkins Press, Baltimore, 1956.

Sozomen, *Ecclesiastica Historia*, VI, 29, 16, ed. J. Bidez, GCS, Berlin, 1960.

Spanneut, M., *Le stoïcisme des Pères de l'Eglise de Clément de Rome à Clément d'Alexandrie*, Le Seuil, Paris, 1957.

Sulpicius Severus, *Vita Martini* and *Dialogi*, tr. B. M. Peebles, Fathers of the Church, 7, New York, 1949.

—— *The Works of S. S.*, tr. A. Roberts in A Select Library of Nicene and Post-Nicene Fathers of the Christian Church, 2nd series, 11, Cushing, Ann Arbor, Michigan, 1964.

Taubenschlag, R., *The law of Greco-roman Egypt in the Light of the Papyri*, 332 B.C.–640 A.D., 2nd ed., Warsaw, 1955.

Tertullian, *Ad Nationes*, tr. in Ante-Nicene Christian Library, XI, 1869; French tr. André Schneider, Bibliotheca helvetica romana, IX, *Le premier livre 'Ad Nationes' de Tertullien*, Institut suisse de Rome, 1968.

—— *Apology*, tr. T. R. Glover, Loeb Classical Library, Heinemann, London, 1931; French tr. J. P. Waltzing with Albert Severyns, CUF, 1971.

—— *On the Veiling of Virgins*, in Ante-Nicene Christian Library, XVIII.

Texte, Politique, Idéologie: Cicéron, Histoire ancienne, 20, *Annales littéraires de l'Université de Besançon*, vol. 187.

Thomas, Yan, Parenté et stratégies endogamiques à Rome. Etude d'une mutation, in *Production, pouvoir et parenté dans le monde méditerranéen de Sumer à nos jours*, Actes du Colloque du CNRS et de l'EHESS, Paris, 1976.

Tomulescu, C. St., Justinien et le concubinat, *Studi in onore di Gaetano Scherillo*, I, Milan, 1972.

Turcan, R., Le culte impérial au IIIe siècle, *Aufstieg und Niedergang der römischen Welt*, II, 16^2, Berlin, 1978.

—— Le sacrifice mithriaque: innovations de sens et de modalités, in *Le sacrifice dans l'Antiquité, Entretiens sur l'Antiquité classique*, 27, Geneva, 1981.

Valabrega, J.-P., *Théories psychosomatiques*, Paris, 1954; *Phantasme, mythe, corps et sens*, Paris, 1980.

Vandier, J., *La famine dans l'Egypte ancienne*, Recherches d'Archéologie, de Philologie et d'Histoire, VII, Publications de l'IFAO, Cairo, 1936.

Vatin, C., *Recherches sur le mariage et la condition de la femme mariée à l'époque hellénistique*, de Boccard, Paris, 1970.

Veith, Ilza, *History of Hysteria*, Chicago, 1965.

Verbeke, G., *L'évolution de la doctrine du pneuma du stoïcisme à saint Augustin, Etude philosophique*, Paris-Louvain, 1945.

Veyne, P., La famille et l'amour à Rome, *Annales (Economies, Sociétés, Civilisations)*, 1978.

—— Suicide, fisc, esclavage, capital et droit romain, *Latomus*, XL, 1981.

Vidal-Naquet, Pierre, *Les Juifs, la mémoire et le présent*, Paris, 1981.

Villers, R., Le statut de la femme à Rome jusqu'à la fin de la République, Recueils de la Société Jean-Bodin, vol. XI¹: *La Femme*, Brussels, 1959.

—— *Rome et le droit privé*, Albin Michel, Paris, 1977.

Visky, K., Le divorce dans la législation de Justinien, *RIDA*, XXIII, 1976.

Vogel, Cyrille, Facere cum virgia(-o) sua(-o) annos . . . L'âge des époux au moment de contracter mariage d'après les inscriptions paléochrétiennes, *Revue de Droit canonique*, 16, 1966.

Volterra, E., *Istituzioni di diritto privato romano*, Rome, 1961.

—— Sulla *D*, 23, 2, 45, 6, *Bulletino dell'Istituto di Diritto Romano*, 75, 1972.

Wissa-Wassef, Cérès, *Pratiques rituelles alimentaires des Coptes*, Cairo, 1979.

Witkowski, G. J., *Histoire des accouchements chez tous les peuples*, Paris, 1887.

Young, V. R., Scrimshaw, N. S., The physiology of starvation, *Scientific American*, Oct. 1971, vol. 225, no. 4, pp. 14–21.

Yoyotte, J., Les os et la semence masculine, à propos d'une théorie physiologique, *BIFAO*, 1962, vol. 61.

Index